Played in Glasgow

Charting the heritage of a city at play

Played in Glasgow
© Malavan Media 2010

Malavan Media is a creative
consultancy responsible
for the Played in Britain series

www.playedinbritain.co.uk

Printed by Zrinski, Croatia
ISBN: 978 0 954744 557

Series designer Doug Cheeseman

Series editor Simon Inglis

Production and additional research
Jackie Spreckley

For image credits see page 226

Maps by Mark Fenton of
English Heritage

This publication has been grant
aided by Historic Scotland, an
executive agency of the Scottish
Government charged with
safeguarding the nation's historic
environment and promoting its
understanding and enjoyment.

Historic Scotland
Longmore House, Salisbury Place
Edinburgh EH9 1SH

Played in Glasgow
Charting the heritage of a city at play

Ged O'Brien

Editor Simon Inglis

With photographs by Stuart Wallace

Glasgow was one of the first British cities to embrace the exciting new sport of speedway, brought over from Australia in 1927 and making its Glasgow debut at an East End venue known grandly as the Olympic Sports Ground, in March 1928. Since then five other venues have staged speedway, Hampden and Celtic Parks included, and there have been teams called the Giants and the Lions. But only the Tigers have stayed on track, having been based at the Ashfield Stadium (*above*) since 1999.

Page Two Roller skating on a new rink laid out in Kelvingrove Park in 1951. Changing trends saw this converted to a skateboard park in 1978, with a cycle track and children's play area added in 2004.

Title page A fine July day in 2009 at the Wellcroft Bowling Club in Queen's Park. One of three clubs that lays claim to being the oldest in the city, Wellcroft were founded in 1835 and moved to Queen's Park in 1876. The ornate ironwork seen on their pavilion may be older still, resembling as it does that of their previous clubhouse, built on Eglinton Street in the 1850s.

Contents

Held in safe keeping at Glasgow Academicals' New Anniesland ground, JW Arthur's faded velvet cap – awarded for his appearances in the world's first ever rugby internationals, against England in March 1871 (played in Edinburgh) and February 1872 (in London) – is one of many rare and yet little known sporting treasures dotted around Glasgow. Described as 'well known in Glasgow for his benevolence and Christian worth' Arthur was one of five signatories who issued the initial challenge to their English counterparts, via *The Scotsman* and *Bell's Life*, in December 1870. Only one other cap of this vintage is known to exist, awarded to one of the England players, and now held by the RFU Museum at Twickenham.

Foreword

by Councillor Steven Purcell, Leader of Glasgow City Council

Known the world over as the 'Friendly City', Glasgow is a modern, vibrant and dynamic metropolis that loves to compete and thrives on competition.

It is the perfect host for the thousands of athletes and visitors from around the world who in 2014 will come to enjoy the Commonwealth Games.

In the past decade alone, Glasgow has staged numerous international events, among them the UEFA Champions League Final in 2002, the Special Olympics in 2005, the UEFA Cup Final in 2007, the World Acrobatic Gymnastic Championships in 2008, and the Commonwealth Table Tennis Championships in 2009.

But Glasgow has long been at the forefront of sport.

On more than one occasion I have reminded my far-flung friends that the modern form of Association football can be traced back to Glasgow, where the 'beautiful game' was first honed by the amateurs of Queen's Park FC during the 1870s.

Such was the popularity of football that by the early 20th century Glasgow's three leading football clubs had the largest purpose-built stadiums in Britain.

Beyond football there exists in Glasgow an equally rich tradition in sports such as swimming, curling and gymnastics, and, making full use of the wealth of green space in Glasgow, athletics, bowling and golf.

The city boasts no fewer than 90 public parks, more per head of population than any other European city.

The largest of these is Glasgow Green, the finishing point for the Great Scottish Run, which in 2009 enjoyed a record entry of nearly 21,000, while Kelvingrove Park is home to one of the city's most popular public bowling greens, first laid out by the Corporation in 1905, and where the 2014 Commonwealth Games bowls tournament will be staged.

Fittingly so, for as I learn from these pages, Glasgow was the birthplace of the modern laws of bowling in 1848, and even today enjoys a higher concentration of bowling greens than any other city in Britain.

Sport is fundamental to the resurgence of Glasgow's fortunes, particularly in the East End, where we have started building the new Sir Chris Hoy Velodrome and National Indoor Sports Arena, and will follow by adding a second 50m pool at Tollcross. These inspirational venues will form a lasting legacy for the city well beyond 2014.

Sports development is another key target for Glasgow over the coming five years.

Channelling the excitement surrounding 2014 we seek to inspire our young people to become ever more active, to make sport an intrinsic part of their lives, and to support those who strive for sporting excellence.

As you will discover, *Played in Glasgow*, which we and Historic Scotland are happy to have supported, is wonderfully written and full of stunning photography.

I am confident it will be treasured by Glasgow's residents and provide those new to the city with yet further reason to visit, and enjoy, one of the friendliest welcomes in the world.

Scottish middle distance runner Yvonne Murray, a gold medallist at the 1994 Commonwealth Games, takes up the Queen's Baton outside the Kelvingrove Museum and Art Gallery in November 2009. The baton, which began its journey at Buckingham Palace a month earlier, will have been relayed across 70 countries and over 124,000 miles before reaching New Delhi for the start of the Games in October 2010. Glasgow's Commonwealth Games, another chapter in the city's rich sporting history, commence on July 23 2014.

On a quiet street in the West End of Glasgow stands the beautifully preserved Arlington Baths Club, designed originally by the noted Scottish architect John Burnet, and opened for swimming in August 1871. One of many historic treasures in the city, it is the oldest private baths club in Britain, and perhaps even the world.

Introduction

by Malcolm Cooper, Chief Inspector of Historic Scotland

For many people heritage has typically been about country houses and their collections, castles both still in use or ruined, and the remains of prehistoric settlements or stone circles.

Heritage is about education and tourism.

However, over recent decades there has been a broadening of our understanding of heritage, to include a range of sites from simple cottages to Second World War airfields and Cold War bunkers.

Hand in hand with this has been a recognition that our historic environment can and does make a far broader contribution to society. Whether contributing to our sense of identity, helping to strengthen social cohesion, offering opportunities for inward investment or employment, heritage has a key role to play.

Sports heritage is one of those key areas of growth, and one that has huge potential for Scotland.

Of course some sports are very long-lived, frequently developing out of military activities or hunting. The remains of Roman amphitheatres at Newstead

and Inveresk, and tiltyards (for jousting) at Edinburgh and Stirling Castles illustrate this relationship, as do the remains of the deer park at Falkland and specific deer traps at Rum. Falkland also contains an extraordinary surviving 16th century real tennis court.

A wide range of sports buildings and facilities has been recognised as important in Scotland and given statutory protection of one form or another. The links at St Andrews, the earliest of which is thought to date from the 15th century, is on our Inventory of Gardens and Designed Landscapes.

The Edwardian country estate at Manderston in the Scottish Borders includes a cricket field laid out for the benefit of estate staff and the local community, recalling the vivid description of the match played between the house and village in LP Hartley's *The Go Between*.

Another protected landscape is the lawn at Balmoral, where the Highland Gathering and Games took place in the 19th century.

Indeed there are few parts of Scotland which cannot boast their

own historic sporting facilities in one form or another.

More broadly sports grounds, buildings and other facilities associated more generally with sports in Scotland have been given protection, ranging from sailing through to bowling.

The picturesque Art Deco lido, boating pool, tea pavilion and changing rooms at Tarlair on the east coast contrast with the Victorian Drumsheugh Baths and the 1970 Royal Commonwealth Pool in Edinburgh. Similarly the 1960s grandstand at Gala Fairydean FC in Galashiels has been protected, as has the 1920s stand of Archibald Leitch at Ibrox.

But while some parts of Scotland's sporting heritage, such as the golf courses at St Andrews, have iconic status worldwide, it is important to remember that alongside these sits a broader sporting heritage that is valued by players and by the communities within which they sit.

Played in Glasgow helps us understand and appreciate both the diversity and the importance of Scotland's sporting heritage.

From humble sheds, like this scoreboard at New Anniesland, to sumptuous pavilions and towering stadiums, Glasgow's stock of historic sports-related buildings is surprisingly extensive. As of 2009, 27 such buildings were listed by Historic Scotland in various categories, the majority of them featured in *Played in Glasgow*. But might there be others worthy of similar consideration? Read on to find out...

Chapter One

Played in Glasgow by Simon Inglis, Played in Britain series editor

Taken from the sixth century preachings of St Mungo, the words 'Let Glasgow Flourish' were enscribed on the city's first coat of arms in 1866 and subsequently repeated on countless badges and pins produced by Glaswegian sports clubs. St Mungo actually prayed that the city would flourish 'by the preaching of the word...' But the sober sportsmen who founded the Glasgow Bowling Association in 1888 would have seen no contradiction. After all, did not a healthy body lead to a healthy mind?

One of the attributes of a great city is that no matter how much is written about its history, there is always more to discover.

Played in Glasgow is the fourth city study in the *Played in Britain* series, a series that emerged from the cultural programme accompanying the Commonwealth Games in 2002.

Since then, city studies focusing on Manchester, Birmingham and Liverpool have been published, joined by a further five nationwide thematic studies, in which the sporting heritage of Scotland has featured strongly, from Shrove Tuesday ba' games in the Borders to the 'uppies and doonies' of Kirkwall, from skittles in Duddingston to swimming and quoits in Stonehaven (*see Links*).

Although originating south of the border, *Played in Britain* has always recognised that modern British sport, and indeed the wider international sporting scene, owes a debt to Scotland that is quite disproportionate to the country's size or the scale of its population.

Glasgow in particular has been a regular port of call for

Played in Britain researchers; most recently for our 2009 study of indoor swimming pools, and for our biography of the Glasgow born football ground architect, Archibald Leitch, whose South Stand at Ibrox Stadium (*page 102*) is one of only two listed structures in senior British football.

As Scotland's largest and most industrialised city, it is of course to be expected that Glasgow has played such a key role in the evolution of British sport.

As a port and trading city, it is equally the case that Glaswegians have contributed significantly to the export of British sport to the far corners of the globe, taking footballs to Latin America, golf clubs to the United States, curling stones to Canada and bowls to New Zealand.

There are, however, a number of other factors pertaining to Glasgow that have led to its sporting heritage taking on a character that is quite distinct from, say Edinburgh or Aberdeen, Manchester or Liverpool.

Played in Glasgow is an attempt to identify what those distinctive

characteristics are, and, in the spirit of Joseph Strutt (*see below*), to assess what they tell us about the city and people of Glasgow today.

Sporting heritage is generally manifest in five different forms.

Historic sports buildings

First, and most easily identifiable, are sports-related buildings of historic and/or architectural significance, such as pavilions, grandstands and swimming pools.

Such is the pace of modernisation in sport – driven by the changing requirements of spectators, players and the media, and by ever more stringent building regulations and safety legislation – that Britain's stock of historic buildings diminishes with every year that goes by.

In this respect, Glasgow is no better nor worse off than most major cities.

But to set against some regrettable losses (for example both the tennis and bowling clubs in Pollokshields), there are some notable survivals.

Among them, apart from the previously mentioned South Stand

Joseph Strutt sums up the *Played in Britain* ethos in his seminal study of 1801, *The Sports and Pastimes of the People of England*.

IN order to form a just estimation of the character of any particular people, it is absolutely necessary to investigate the Sports and Pastimes most generally prevalent among them.

at Ibrox, are the Arlington Baths Club of 1871 (*page 204*), almost certainly the oldest of its type in the world, and the 1900 pavilion of the Partick Curling Club (*page 163*).

Glasgow City Council (and its predecessor as District Council) also has a comparatively good record when it comes to restoring historic sports facilities, even if, such as at Ruchill Park golf course (*page 126*), and Maryhill Baths (*page 212*), the impetus has often emanated from pressure groups.

North Woodside Baths (*page 209*), built in 1882 and revamped in 1991, is Britain's oldest public baths remaining in use, and in the coming years further restoration is expected of the 1905 West Boathouse (*page 32*) and of the 1917 Govanhill Baths (*page 214*).

Another category includes those historic buildings that, although built for other purposes, have gained new life through sport.

Among them are four listed houses now used by golf clubs (*Chapter Eight*), Kelvin Hall (*page 23*), the Palace of Art (*page 98*) and Ibrox Church (*page 221*).

Grounds and sportscapes

The second category considered in any assessment of sporting heritage are 'sportscapes', that is sports grounds or open spaces on which sport has taken place at one time or another.

In a city whose original name of *Glasgu*, or in Gaelic, *Glaschu*, is said to have meant 'dear green place', several much cherished sportscapes fall into this category.

The oldest of these, used for organised sport since at least the 1670s, is Glasgow Green, part of which, Fleshers' Haugh, is still in use as a football centre.

That an area of public space should have enjoyed more than »

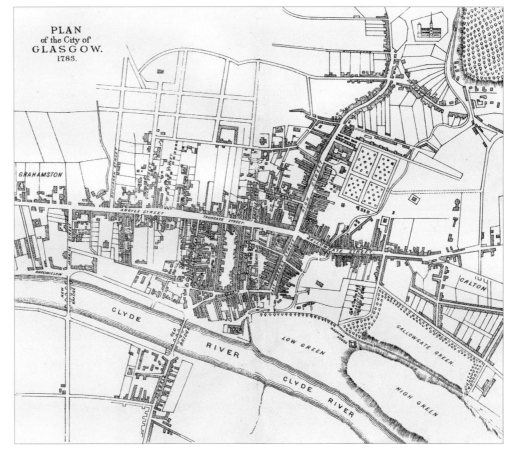

▲ The location and distribution of Glasgow's modern day sportscapes is a direct consequence of the city's spread since the early 19th century.

This map shows the full extent of **Glasgow in 1783**; a town which over the course of the 18th century grew from 12,000 to 84,000 inhabitants. Most lived and worked in tight proximity on either side of Saltmarket and High Street, which ran north from the Clyde up to the Cathedral (*top right*).

East of Calton there was little settlement. Further west from Jamaica Street (laid out in 1763), Grahamstown was still considered a separate village, while the first signs of expansion south of the Clyde can be seen in the Gorbals.

Sporting activity at the time was concentrated on **Glasgow Green**, seen here before it was tamed in the early 19th century. Note that the **Washing House** (in the top right hand corner of Low Green) was where Glasgow's first public baths were sited in 1878 (*page 208*).

Between Gallowgate and the Cathdedral lay **College Green**.

Before the University moved west in 1870, this area was used for sport by students and for a number of public sporting events.

Not marked here are the town's only enclosed sports grounds before the 19th century, that is, two **bowling greens**. These were on Candleriggs (dating from c.1695) and between Gallowgate Green and the Gallowgate (c.1750), both detailed in Chapter Nine.

From various banning orders issued by the Kirk we also know that games such as football and shinty were played in the streets and in churchyards.

Today, only one major sports-related building falls within this area, the Gorbals Leisure Centre on Ballater Street.

▲ From *The London Illustrated News* of August 1867, this etching shows **College Green** during the Celtic Society's **Highland Games**.

On the right is the original building that housed the Hunterian Museum, with the College tower to its left and Blackfriars Church in the background. The grandstand in front of the church – described in David Murray's memoirs of the College (*see Links*) as a 'shed' – was still there three years later when photographer Thomas Annan (*right*) paid a visit, just as demolition of the College buildings was starting, in order to make way for High Street railway station.

(The University's move to a new campus at Gilmorehill in 1870 was a major factor in Glasgow's shift to the west thereafter.)

Over the centuries College Green had been well used for football.

According to Murray, games would continue all day, with students dropping in and out as their lessons allowed. In the tradition of Scottish ba' games the ball was 'hailed' (rather than scored) by it being touched against a particular spot at either side of the green. Only in later years were goalposts introduced. Cricket, wrote Murray, was less popular because only medical students were in residence during the summer.

Today the site is covered by Parsonage Square, between High Street Station and Bell Street.

>> three centuries of recreational use is remarkable by any standard (though not unique, the golf links at St Andrews go back further).

But Glasgow Green is not the only historic sportscape in the city.

In Partick, the West of Scotland cricket ground (*page 176*) may not have within its boundaries any buildings or structures of special historic interest, but the ground itself is of immense significance as the venue for the world's first ever football international in 1872.

Golfers show similar reverence towards their own 'dear greens', such as the course at Pollok (*page 84*), revered as the work of the respected golf course architect, Dr Alister MacKenzie.

Sportscapes can also be waterscapes, of which both the Clyde, once a favourite spot for swimming and still popular for rowing, and Bingham's Pond (*page 159*), are prime examples.

But whether on dry land, water, or even ice, it is the longevity and continuity of use that evokes that sense of 'the power of place' which is so central to our understanding of the value of heritage.

When Celtic fans refer to their stadium as 'Paradise' or when fans generally refer to 'sacred turf', they are not being maudlin, but merely expressing that deep-seated connection with a place from which they derive a sense of identity and belonging.

Whatever one feels about sport, such attachments form an important part of the glue that binds together otherwise diverse and geographically spread urban communities.

Archaeology, art and artefacts
There are three other areas in which sporting heritage can generally be found.

These are archaeology (of which, as yet, there is none in Glasgow, apart from the crumbling terraces of Cathkin Park), art (in the form of paintings, posters, sculptures and so on), and artefacts (which may range from valuable silverware to mass produced enamel badges).

Glasgow is especially rich in sporting artefacts.

For example the earliest featured in this book is the Silver Club of the Glasgow Golf Club (*page 28*), first awarded in 1787.

Other significant treasures are the 1857 Eglinton Jug (*page 149*), the Scottish Cup (*page 220*), first awarded in 1873, and the Glasgow Celtic Society Cup from 1879. Each is the oldest trophy in the world in its own sport, respectively bowls, Association football and shinty.

At the more ephemeral end of the spectrum, Glasgow is also well blessed with collectors, >>

▲ Like a scene from Louisa Alcott's 1869 novel *Little Women*, the sombrely attired ladies of **Ibroxhill House** enjoy the newly fashionable game of **croquet** in c.1861.

Ibroxhill was one of many properties photographed by Thomas Annan in his book *The Old Country Houses of the Old Glasgow Gentry*.

This was published in 1870 at a time when the whole townscape of Glasgow was, as Annan put it, being flooded by 'present prosperity', putting at risk so many historic buildings.

Croquet was itself a symbol of that prosperity. Partly this was thanks to the recent invention of the lawn mower, which allowed those with fewer staff to maintain good quality, flat lawns. Partly it was the manufacture of boxed croquet sets by rival games manufacturers (a rivalry that ended up in an 1864 court case to determine who had copied whom).

Above all, croquet was a game considered suitable for women.

As Annan predicted, like so many of its ilk Ibroxhill was ultimately doomed, though not because of the 'march of villas and coal-pits' but because Glasgow Corporation absorbed it within Bellahouston Park in 1903. For a few years it served as a tea room, before being demolished in 1914.

Some of its masonry was turned into a rockery, but otherwise only its porch survives today, as the entry to a sculpture garden attached to the House for An Art Lover (*see page 99*), which more or less occupies the site of Ibroxhill.

Croquet too was about to be eclipsed, by the arrival of lawn tennis, a game needing only half the area and appealing more to men. Croquet has not disappeared totally however. A Glasgow Croquet Club formed in 1960 and plays at Kelvingrove Park (*see page 143*).

▲ While the Ibroxhill ladies played croquet, in working class circles one of the most popular games in Victorian and Edwardian Britain, now all but forgotten, was **quoiting** (pronounced 'kite-ing' in Scotland).

This is the **Cross Arthurlie Quoiting Club** in 1914, outside their clubhouse behind the Gillies Hotel on Main Street, Barrhead (now the Arthurlie Inns), a favourite watering hole for local mill workers.

First mentioned in Britain in 1361 (in a royal ban issued by Edward III), quoits caught on amongst agricultural workers in the 1820s, but later found favour with coal miners, dockers and other workers in heavy industry whose muscles proved well suited to throwing iron quoits, some as heavy as 10–16lbs, across a distance of 18 or 21 yards.

Today, although still moderately popular in the north and north east of England and in Suffolk, only three quoiting clubs survive in Scotland, none in Glasgow.

And yet in the late 19th and early 20th century quoits was almost as widespread as curling and bowls, games with which it shares several characteristics. For example it too is played on a rink, with players aiming to get as close as possible to a target. In the case of quoits the aim is to land one's quoit on or near a pin, or 'hob', set in the centre of a clay bed.

Despite the formation of a Scottish Quoiting Association in 1880, few records exist from the 19th century, leaving us to hunt for quoiting grounds on maps (see page 62) or in newspapers for match reports.

From these sources we know of clubs in Pollokshaws, Bridgeton, Dalmarnock, Barrhead and one venue whose location is unknown, the Melaugh Quoiting Ground, where, in 1870, as historian Neil Tranter has discovered, a reported 5,000 crowd saw the leading Scot, Robert Walkinshaw, face the London champion, George Graham.

On other occasions crowds of 500–1,000 were routine.

For most spectators the main attraction of such gatherings was, inevitably, gambling and drinking, which is one reason quoits failed to gain the respectability of bowls.

But since the 1950s its near total demise has more likely been owing to the parallel decline in heavy industry.

More on quoits can be found in *Played at the Pub* (see *Links*).

>> whose postcards, posters, programmes and badges adorn many of the pages that follow.

These individuals, backed up by numerous club historians and the efforts of the Mitchell Library and various local museums, have ensured that, collectively, Glasgow has already made great strides towards preserving the tangible assets of its sporting heritage.

Intangible heritage

There is one further aspect of sporting heritage that has no physical presence, and which is often referred to as 'intangible heritage'. This is the heritage that is bound up, for example, in long running competitions and rivalries; the fact that Wellcroft Bowling Club have been playing their counterparts at Whitevale since 1839, and that the West of Scotland v. Academicals rugby fixture dates back to 1867.

Similarly intangible is the fact that although they may not all play on their original grounds, Glasgow is unusually, uniquely even, endowed with sports clubs of a venerable age.

As of 2009, 16 of the clubs featured in *Played in Glasgow* were at least 150 years old. By 2020 that list will have grown by a further twelve. Dozens more, meanwhile, have reached, or are about to reach their centenaries.

Not all aspects of Glasgow's intangible sporting heritage are so positive, however.

Played in Glasgow is not the appropriate forum in which to tackle such complex social and cultural issues as the sectarian rivalry between Rangers and Celtic, the so-called 'Old Firm'.

Or the fact that so many sports clubs have, over the years, denied membership to individuals on the grounds of their religious or ethnic identities, or their gender.

Or the invidious effect that drinking and gambling have had upon certain aspects of the sporting scene.

Many other histories and sociological studies have already examined all these difficult areas.

Nevertheless, it cannot be denied that such aspects of Glasgow's sporting life form an omnipresent 'elephant in the room' within the overall narrative.

Glasgow's sporting mix

That said, no assessment of Glasgow's sporting heritage can be made without reference to the contribution of migrants who have made Glasgow their home over the past two centuries and more.

Following the Union in 1707, English soldiers brought with them to Glasgow the game of cricket, while during the mid 19th century, former pupils of English public schools helped introduce the new code of rugby football.

The influx of Highlanders, west coast islanders and Argyll folk, many of them Gaelic-speaking, also had a profound impact on sporting life in the city.

In the Kirk Session Records of Glasgow, October 16 1589, we read of a ban on games being played within the church yard, namely 'futeball, goff, carrick or schynnie', meaning the Gaelic game of shinty.

Shinty is an example of a sport which is barely touched upon in *Played in Glasgow*, simply because the physical manifestation of its heritage is comparatively limited.

That is, it has always been played in football stadiums, on the grounds of other sporting clubs, or in public parks. (The same may be said of hockey.) »

▲ For readers still pondering how the sports ground shown on the front cover – built for the **1901 International Exhibition** in **Kelvingrove Park** – related to its surroundings, this view should make its location much clearer.

Looking west from the top of the University Tower in 1905, the photograph was taken by the firm of T & R Annan. (Thomas died in 1887, but his sons carried on the business.) Behind the north end of the cycle track (*on the right*) is University Avenue, with the tall chimney of the Western Infirmary in the centre, on Byres Road.

This was a landscape that had been utterly transformed over the previous half century, a period during which Glasgow's population more than doubled from 330,000 to nearer 760,000. In 1850 Byres Road had been hardly more than a quiet drovers' road.

But while a large proportion of the new Glaswegians lived in squalor in the old town and the East End, the new West End was predominantly middle class, many of its residents having been drawn there by the opportunities created as a result of the University's move from the High Street.

Amid this building frenzy, there did remain a few gaps, where bowling and tennis clubs took root. But for the University, which built over the sports ground soon after this photograph was taken, and for the schools and colleges of the West End, the nearest area where they could find open space for sport would be out towards Hyndland, Kelvinside, Anniesland and Jordanhill (*see Chapter Seven*).

Note that on the 1901 Exhibition plan (*right*) the Machinery Hall on the left would, in 1927, be replaced by **Kelvin Hall** (*page 23*), while the Industrial Hall on the lower right was cleared to make way for **public bowling greens** in 1905 (*page 142*).

▷ Posing here in 1910, **Govan Clarion Club** were members of the **National Clarion Cycling Club**, set up in 1894 and named after *The Clarion*, a socialist newspaper launched by Robert Blatchford in Manchester. By 1900 the NCCC had over 8,000 members.

Clarion clubs went on cycling runs for fun rather than in a spirit of competition, handing out leaflets *en route*, or, in the case of the Glasgow Socialist Cycle Club, canvassing for their local Labour candidate. (A display of Clarion artefacts may be seen at the Scottish Transport Museum at Kelvin Hall.)

As their attire confirms, Govan Clarion's cyclists were no manual labourers. To afford a bicycle, even then, was confined only to skilled workers – 'the labour aristocracy' as sometimes described.

Just visible on their banner are the words 'boots' and 'spurs'. Members of Scotland's two remaining Clarion clubs, in West Lothian and the West of Scotland, still call out these words when greeting one another.

In contrast, many workers were content to join their company sports clubs, of which one of the largest was that of the sewing machine manufacturer, **Singer** (*right*). At its peak in 1913, Singer employed over 14,000 people at its works in Kilbowie, Clydebank.

Sports days such as this one in 1916 were taken very seriously. In the 1950s the film star Dorothy Lamour was the guest of honour.

Most of Glasgow's works' clubs operated between the 1920s and the 1970s. But a handful of their grounds survive. For example Albert Park in Langside was originally the ground of Weir Engineering, whose cricket team is still based there, and there remain several bowling greens once owned by companies.

>> Nevertheless, as historian Hugh Dan MacLennan has shown (*see Links*), it was largely in Glasgow that shinty would become organised as a national sport in the 1870s, by which time Glasgow's Gaelic community numbered around 45,000.

Highlanders may not have persuaded their Lowland counterparts of the benefits of shinty, or of the so-called 'heavy' games, such as tossing the caber.

But the four youths who formed Rangers Football Club in 1873 were all from Argyll, while for many years the large numbers of Highlanders who joined the Glasgow police force gathered at Rangers' Ibrox Park for their annual sports days, which featured several elements of a typical Victorian Highland Games.

Meanwhile most of the founders of Queen's Park Football Club hailed from around Inverness and Aberdeen. (To which we must add in passing that it was a Thurso man, William Alexander Smith, who founded the Boys' Brigade in Glasgow, in 1883, a movement that now extends to sixty countries worldwide.)

Nor should we overlook the contribution of those who arrived in Glasgow from areas such as Ayrshire, Fife and Lanarkshire, bringing with them their love of bowls, curling, handball and quoits, or, lest we forget, the influence of those in Edinburgh who provided models for several of Glasgow's earliest sporting societies, such as in golf and archery.

Then there were the Irish, both Protestant and Catholic.

The traditional Irish sports of hurling and Gaelic football did not take hold in Glasgow. But of course Irish Catholics made a

huge impact by setting up Celtic Football Club in 1887 (*page 66*), thereby initiating one of the great local rivalries in world football.

Celtic's first secretary-manager, the Newry born Willie Maley, combined his playing and managerial career with chartered accountancy, running a shop and a restaurant, and still found time to serve as president of the Scottish Amateur Athletic Association.

He was also largely responsible for bringing to Glasgow its first major international sporting event, the World Cycling Championships, held at Celtic Park in 1897 (*page 68*).

Other Irish entrepreneurs such as James Grant and John McMahon also did much to back sports such as athletics and greyhound racing.

This extraordinary cultural mix of displaced people from Ireland, the Lowlands of Scotland, the Highlands and Islands, >>

▲ Several billiard halls opened in Glasgow during the late 19th and early 20th centuries, but none were as distinctive as the billiard room at **Miss Cranston's Tea Rooms** on **Buchanan Street**, a joint effort between designer **George Walton** and **Charles Rennie Mackintosh**.

Opened in 1897, in common with the billiard rooms at Miss Cranston's other premises (on Argyle Street, Sauchiehall Street, and Ingram Street), plus one at her family home in Nitshill, Mackintosh designed all the fittings, including the marker-boards and cue-racks, and even the tables (in conjunction with the London billiards firm of Burroughes and Watts).

How frustrating therefore that not a single one of these items is known to have survived after the rooms were decommissioned between the wars.

Mackintosh, incidentally, was the son of an Irish born policeman who helped set up the Glasgow Police Athletic and Rowing Club in 1882, captained its Tug o' War team, and was also a keen bowler.

▲ Pupils at the **Whitehill Public School for Girls** keep their chins up in the gymnasium in 1916.

That the school even had a gymnasium says much about changing attitudes at this time.

In the private sector, Glasgow Academy became the first school in the city to include team sports in its curriculum in 1866.

For children at Board schools however – set up in the wake of the 1872 Education (Scotland) Act – military drill would be the mainstay for boys (based on German models of education), with girls allowed a gymnastic programme based more on movement and dance (a regime associated with Swedish methods).

Teachers at Whitehill were to play a key role in loosening these restrictions in the public sector by adopting some of the methods of the private schools. As historian Peter Bilsborough has noted (*see Links*), this led to Whitehill forming its own cricket team in 1899,

followed by football, hockey and even golf in 1901.

Thus inter-school competition quickly sprouted in the public sector, a process that would have a profound impact on the map of Glasgow by forcing the Glasgow School Board to start subsidising the rental of playing fields in 1909. The citywide network of ball courts (*as above in the 1930s*)

and red blaes or shale pitches we see today (*page 194*) is a direct consequence of this early 20th century movement.

Another advance during this period was the construction of school swimming pools between 1885–1904, prompted by Socialist members of the Govan School Board. Two of these pools remain in use today (*page 211*).

>> and Argyll, together with an infusion of Italians, Jews and yes, even the English, created a potent, and almost certainly unique blend of sporting culture that places Glasgow quite apart from any other major city in the English speaking world.

To which has been added in the latter decades of the 20th century a thriving Asian community, which has helped breathe new life into the local cricket scene.

Rules and regulations

Glasgow was no different from the rest of Britain in its staging of horse racing and cock fighting at fairs and on special occasions.

From the outlying village of Pollokshaw in 1754 came a typical account of proceedings.

'A horse race, three to start at least. The first gets twenty shillings, the next five shillings.

'A goose race. He that pulls off the head gets the goose.

'A cock race. He that catches the cock in his teeth and walks three paces with him gets the cock and half a crown. Their hands must be tied behind their backs that try the race.

'A sack race, the first five shillings, the second three, the third two, the fourth one, and the fifth sixpence.'

All very clear, if not quite to everyone's taste. But it does provide a hint of a trend that was to characterise Glasgow's politer sporting circles in the 19th century, which was a penchant for drawing up precise rules.

Three main factors contributed to this trend.

Firstly, the advent of the railways in the 1830s and improved communications via the Clyde and the local canal network allowed a greater degree of inter-club >>

▲ Photographed around the time of its opening in 1924, this was the pavilion of the **Western Lawn Tennis Club**, on Hyndland Road, a building that might easily have been built at any time during the preceding 30 years.

Yet rather than bemoan the club's conservativism, in hindsight its timeless elegance appears apt for both its purpose and setting; as if, for the young professionals who settled in the West End, part of the Western's attraction was that it offered a retreat from modernity.

This was a garden club; a world of lush turf, of weekend parties and romantic possibilities.

The trouble is that, as we report throughout *Played in Glasgow*, most clubs soon outgrew pavilions of this type. Often the issue was a lack of provision for women. But in the post war years it was also a lack of space to provide the kind of facilities – lounges, gyms and so on – that were becoming increasingly *de rigueur*.

Western's salvation came in the 1960s when it amalgamated with Kelvinside TC. From the £15,000 raised by the sale of that club's Beaconsfield Road site, Western was able to knock down the old pavilion and start afresh.

That its replacement was, and remains, a building of no great character compared with the old one is, for the club at least, not an issue. Survival is, which has been secured by incorporating into the pavilion three squash courts and facilities clearly to the liking of the club's near 1,000 members.

Meanwhile other clubs in desirable areas have faced different pressures. At **Partickhill Lawn Tennis and Bowling Club** (*right*), formed in 1905, the courts seen above, on North Gardner Street, have lain disused for years and in theory, if sold for housing, could offer the bowls club a secure future.

There have been precedents. In the 1970s Hillhead Tennis and Bowls Club sold out to the BBC, as did Pollokshields TC to a residential developer. In the 1990s Glasgow University sold its Garscadden sports ground for housing, followed by the West of Scotland Cricket Club selling off a portion of its land for flats, a measure that saved the club (*page 177*). In 2009 Hillhead Sports Club (*page 116*) were planning a similar partial sale for the same reason.

Faced with such pressures, all too often, unfortunately, the aesthetics of pavilion architecture is a club's last concern.

▲ Although not directly linked with sport, the story of **Fyfe & Fyfe's Palais de Danse** on **Dumbarton Road, Partick,** tells us much about the often ephemeral nature of 20th century popular culture in Britain.

Opened in 1910 as the Star Palace, it was the first of many cinemas designed by architect Charles James McNair. But like many early cinemas it soon needed a revamp, carried out in 1920 by William Reid (who had also worked on Partick Thistle's ground at Meadowside, *see page 181*).

This refit also failed, so in 1925 the building was again updated, as seen above in 1940, by two impresarios, Fyfe & Fyfe. Three nights a week it was a *palais*

de danse, capitalising on the dance craze that swept 1920s Britain. The other three nights it hosted **roller skating**, another fad, originally known as 'rincomania' that had already come and gone twice before, in the 1870s and in the early 1900s.

'The F&F' stayed in business until the 1960s, when, perhaps inevitably, it entered a new phase as a bingo hall. Indeed it remains one today, run by Carlton, even though, regrettably, its Art Deco entrance was replaced by flats and shops in 2009.

Other shortlived roller rinks were on Argyle Street and Cathcart Road (*below left*), and from 1951–78, in the open air at Kelvingrove Park.

A similar tale emerges on James Street, Bridgeton, where a Victorian drill hall was converted into a rink, then in 1910 turned into the King's Picture Theatre. Its 1930s façade does survive, but since the cinema closed in 1959 the building has served as a furniture warehouse.

All over Britain are buildings with similar stories; changing their use every few decades to cash in on the next 'big thing'.

》 competition, meaning that an agreed set of rules became imperative.

Secondly, for sport to be freed from its association with the tavern or with corruption (then rife in such sports as horse racing and boxing), there had to be respectability, and in Victorian middle class circles respectability was borne from patronage, which had to be earned. In short, orderly games were the mark of orderly gentlemen.

The patronage that resulted is best seen in Chapter Five, emanating from Sir John Stirling Maxwell of Pollok House, and in Chapter Nine, from the Earl of Eglinton's support for bowls.

But thirdly, and perhaps most tellingly in the context of Glasgow's industrial revolution, for men whose everyday lives were bound up in facts and figures, weights and measures, contracts and ledgers, it was natural that the same principles of management and governance should be applied to their sports and games.

Thus it was in Glasgow that the first rules of bowling were drawn up by a solicitor in 1849 (*page 137*), while the first standardised bowls were manufactured by a Glasgow firm, Thomas Taylor, the oldest bowls making company in the world (*page 151*).

In the world of football, Scottish historians argue that it was the scientific approach of Queen's Park's pioneers in the 1870s that effectively elevated the Association game from its embryonic form to the passing game we know today.

Similarly, it was the aforementioned Archibald Leitch, who was the first engineer to apply modern techniques to stadium design in the early 1900s.

Certainly with the opening of Hampden Park in 1903, to add to Celtic Park (1892) and Ibrox Park (1899), Glasgow led the world as far as stadium provision and attendance figures were concerned.

It was also in Glasgow that the first rules of water polo were devised (*page 204*), by a local bathsmaster who also wrote the first comprehensive manuals on swimming, diving and life saving.

Another Glaswegian, the president of the Glasgow Skating Club, George Anderson, wrote a similar guide for figure skaters in 1852, under the pen name Cyclos.

This apparent passion for marrying art with science, combined with a plethora of organisations and associations formed during the second half of the 19th century, gave Glasgow, the 'Second City of the Empire', at least equal prominence with London, if not actual superiority in terms of sporting governance. 》

◄ Unlike London, Liverpool and Newcastle, Glasgow never had an arena specifically designed for boxing. Instead, Gorbals born flyweight **Benny Lynch** fought some of his top bouts at Glasgow stadiums, such as Celtic Park, Cathkin Park and, in October 1937, **Shawfield Stadium**, where he was watched in training by a large crowd (*far left*), before an even larger record crowd of 40,000 packed the stadium a few days later on a wet and wild evening to see him retain his World title against Peter Kane from Liverpool.

Nine months earlier it is said that at least 100,000 turned out to welcome Lynch home after he won the World title by beating Filipino Small Montana at Wembley.

Like so many boxers Lynch did not meet a happy end. Having succumbed to a lifetime's addiction to alcohol, and finally to malnutrition, he died in 1946 at the age of just 33.

There is a Benny Lynch Court, close to his birthplace in Florence Street. But the real place of pilgrimage for his admirers is his restored grave at St Kentigern's Cemetery, recently 'erected by boxing fans'.

Another Glasgow champion, less heralded but certainly more clean living, was **Jimmy Flockhart**, arguably one of Scotland's best ever cross country runners, seen in 1937 (*on the far left*) promoting fitness with fellow members of the **Shettleston Harriers**.

Formed in 1904 the Harriers were among many athletic and sporting clubs to support a national fitness campaign launched in response to German militarisation.

The Harriers are still going strong today, from their base at the East End Healthy Living centre on Crownpoint Road (*page 60*).

Population and land pressures

In 1707 Daniel Defoe famously said of Glasgow, 'in a word, 'tis the cleanest and beautifullest, and best built city in Britain, London excepted.'

And yet by 1839 the government inspector JC Symons reported, 'I did not believe, until I visited the wynds of Glasgow, that so large an amount of filth, crime, misery and disease existed in one spot in any civilised country.'

Glasgow's fluctuating fortunes, from tobacco to cotton to shipbuilding, from wynds to tenements to high rises, from wealth to depression to post-industrial re-invention, inform every aspect of this book.

But as significant, if not more so, has been shifts in Glasgow's population.

Comparisons are not always accurate owing to boundary changes, but in essence, here is a city that shot up from 330,000 in 1851 to a peak of just under 1.1 million in 1931, but since the 1960s has dropped to its present level of around 580,000.

Reflecting this, there has been an inevitable decline in the number of sports clubs. Yet as a measure of how strong the city's sporting sector remains, the wonder of Glasgow is not how many clubs have disbanded, but how many have survived.

But there are other concerns.

Today, in terms of land use for sport, Glasgow appears to be a city of two halves.

While in the East End, in the north and in outlying areas there is space aplenty, in the West End and in certain areas on the South Side, rising land values (at least before the credit crunch) have placed tremendous pressure on private sports clubs.

▲ Two rare example of 1930s sports pavilions in the Glasgow area have suffered different fates in recent years. Glasgow University's pavilion on **Kingfisher Drive, Garscadden** (*top*) – designed by TH Hughes, opened in 1936 and listed Category C(S) in 1989 – found itself stranded when the sports ground it served was sold for housing in 1999.

It has since been converted into town houses itself, gaining an extra storey in the process.

In marked contrast, the Category A listed **Penilee Pavilion**, on **Penilee Road** (*above*) designed for Paisley Grammar School by Harry Cook in 1937, lay unused for several years before, in 2008, Renfrewshire Council embarked upon a superb £3.59 million revamp.

Now renamed the **Ralston Community Sports Centre** this truly inspiring Modernist pavilion reopened in early 2010 with dance and aerobics studios, and changing rooms serving one synthetic and two natural turf football pitches.

The only other 1930s building of quality to be in sporting use in the Glasgow area is the Palace of Art at Bellahouston Park (*see page 98*).

Some, with declining fortunes, have indeed sold their sites and disappeared. Others have been forced out when their landlords have sold up to developers.

But a recent saga surrounding Dowanhill Tennis Club in the West End appears to have created a watershed in Glasgow sport.

Briefly, although a thriving club in the 1990s, thereafter Dowanhill's membership started to fall as few, if any, applicants wanting to join were successful in gaining admittance.

Then in 2004 it emerged that the fifty or so remaining members had allegedly been offered a sum of around £5 million to sell the site for flats; a site, moreover, that the club had reportedly bought for a token £250 in 1950.

Even after paying off its dues to sportscotland (which had grant aided various improvements), plus sundry fees and capital gains taxes, the club's remaining members calculated that they could move over and refurbish the disused courts at nearby Partickhill and still have enough left for each member to receive a substantial payout.

Whatever the moral issues raised by this proposal, or the planning objections raised by local residents anxious to retain the site as an open space, the danger arose that if the Dowanhill deal went through, this might lead to a string of clubs selling up, thereby radically reducing access for local people to sporting facilities.

For Dowanhill the saga remained unresolved at the time of writing.

But as far as other would-be selling clubs were concerned, a preventative measure since adopted by the Council has had a major effect.

Now, in order for any club to qualify for relief on its annual rates – which can amount to a major

◀ Come 2014 and **Kelvin Hall** will host the boxing tournament of the Commonwealth Games, just as it has staged boxing many times in the past, such as in 1959 (*above*).

Since opening as an exhibition centre in 1927 it has also housed an ice rink (in the late 1930s), and since 1987 has been Scotland's leading indoor athletics venue, with another section housing the popular Museum of Transport.

But when the **National Indoor Sports Arena** opens in the East End as the main indoor venue for 2014, alongside the **Sir Chris Hoy Velodrome** (*left*), and the transport museum moves to a new location by the Clyde, Kelvin Hall's future will once again be at stake.

In sport as in life, the only constant is change...

burden – the Council requires it to insert into its constitution a clause forbidding the sale of its site for the personal gain of members. The same clause is also now required by various funding bodies, to protect the public interest.

This one simple measure, it can only be hoped, will help greatly to preserve the sporting map of Glasgow for future generations.

What it cannot help with is that other great problem faced by many Glasgow clubs, and that is the need to recruit younger members and get them interested and involved in the running of the club.

This is a particular issue in the one sport that has traditionally been so strong in Glasgow, and that is bowls. But it affects many other sports too. 〉〉

The public sector

Whether incentivising private clubs to stay in business by offering rate relief, or by furthering the cause of sport in the public sector, Glasgow's civic leadership can itself be said to have played a lead role in shaping the sporting heritage of the city.

In the late 19th century the Council's predecessors were relatively slow to invest in sport, before catching up quickly in the early 1900s by providing a network of public golf courses, football pitches, bowling greens, tennis courts and swimming baths.

As demand for certain sports has ebbed and flowed, this provision has taken on a quite different form. For example, Glasgow now leads the way in providing artificial football pitches for public rental (*see Chapter 12*), and offers free access to under 18s and over 60s wishing to play such sports as golf and tennis.

In tennis this has led to a fourfold increase in participation.

Thus the Council now actively promotes sport, rather than simply providing for it, as was largely the case before the late 20th century.

To manage this process better, in 2007 the Council adopted the approach of several other local authorities by handing over the management of its facilities to a company limited by guarantee and with charitable status, Culture and Sport Glasgow.

As may be seen from plans now underway for the East End, sport in the 21st century has also become a driver of urban regeneration. Whole swathes of land that once housed factories and workshops are now being cleared to make way for a new indoor arena, a velodrome and the athletes' village for the Commonwealth Games.

For those who have argued for sport to be taken more seriously, these developments represent an unprecedented breakthrough.

At the same time, it should also be noted that Glasgow City Council is one of few local authorities in Britain to maintain its own in-house design team.

Once this was common. City and borough architects and engineers were responsible for most, if not all swimming pools, pavilions and municipal grounds.

Today, the norm is for these to be designed by outside consultants.

But not in Glasgow. All 23 of the city's leisure centres built or refurbished since the 1960s are 'home-made'; yet another intriguing element of how the city's sporting heritage may be viewed in the civic context.

Played in Glasgow

Finally, this book is divided into two sections. The next six chapters focus upon what we call 'sporting clusters'. The areas selected for this approach have been chosen not only because they are home to a cluster of venues, but because a study of them *en bloc* can help in understanding how sport has evolved in the city.

The later chapters detail individual sports, but across the whole city. Inevitably some readers will be disappointed that their favourite sport has not featured as much as others, or even not at all.

But above all what we hope is that *Played in Glasgow* prompts readers to go out and visit some of the venues and sports featured, and in doing so, see for themselves just what an extraordinary and diverse sporting city Glasgow is, and, it would seem, looks certain to remain as it prepares to welcome the world in 2014.

This map shows the area covered by *Played in Glasgow* and the main sports related sites of architectural or historic interest (with the pages on which the sites are featured or illustrated in brackets).

1. former **Garscadden Pavilion** Kingfisher Drive (*22*)
2. **Old Anniesland** and **New Anniesland** (*118-119*)
3. **Hillhead Sports Club** Hughenden (*115-117*)
4. **Scotstoun Stadium** Danes Drive (*122-123*)
5. **Partick Curling Club** Victoria Park (*162-165*)
6. **West of Scotland Cricket Ground** Hamilton Crescent (*176-177*)
7. **Willowbank Bowling Club** Downside Road (*136*)
8. **Western Baths Club** Cranworth Street (*206-207*)
9. **Kelvin Hall** Kelvingrove (*23*)
10. **St Vincent Bowling Club** St Vincent Crescent (*157*)
11. **Arlington Baths Club** Arlington Street (*204-205*)
12. **North Woodside Swimming Pool** Braid Square (*209*)
13. **Partick Thistle Football Club, Firhill** (*186-189*)
14. **Maryhill Sports Centre** Burnhouse Street (*212*)
15. **Glasgow Golf Club** Killermont, Bearsden (*128*)
16. **Cawder Golf Club** Bishopbriggs (*129*)
17. **Saracen Park/Ashfield Stadium** Hawthorn Street (*201*)
18. **Balornock Bowling Club** Wallacewell Road (*156*)
19. **Alexandra Park Golf Course** (*125*)
20. former **Dennistoun Baths Club** Craigpark (*207*)
21. **Whitevale Bowling Club** Whitehill Street (*141/148*)
22. **West Boathouse, Glasgow Green** (*31-32*)
23. **Shawfield Stadium** (*199*)
24. **Thomas Taylor Bowls Manufacturer** (*151-153*)
25. **Celtic Football Club, Celtic Park** (*66-77*)
26. **Tollcross Leisure Centre** (*215*)
27. **Cambuslang Bowling Club** West Coats Road (*145*)
28. **Cathkin Braes Golf Club** Cathkin Road (*133*)
29. **Clarkston Bowling and Tennis Club** Eastwoodmains Road (*144-145*)
30. **Newlands Bowling Club** Langside Drive (*146*)
31. **Hampden Park** and **Scottish Football Museum** (*48-57/184-185*)
32. **Cathkin Park** former Third Lanark FC (*45-47*)
33. **Queen's Park Bowling and Tennis Club** (*38-39*)
34. **Govanhill Baths** Calder Street (*214*)
35. **Wellcroft Bowling Club** Queen's Drive (*138-139*)
36. **Titwood Bowling and Tennis Club** Glencairn Drive (*88-89*)
37. **Clydesdale Cricket Club** Titwood (*174*)
38. former **Pollokshaws Baths** Christian Street (*213*)
39. **Poloc Cricket Club** Shawholm (*80/178*)
40. **Pollok Golf Club** Pollok Park (*84-85*)
41. **Cowglen Golf Club** Barrhead Road (*86*)
42. **Cartha Queen's Park Rugby Football Club** Pollok Park (*83*)
43. **Palace of Art Sports Centre** Bellahouston Park (*98*)
44. **Rangers Football Club, Ibrox Stadium** (*100-111*)
45. **Govan Bowling Club** Vicarfield Road (*90*)
46. **Ralston Community Sports Centre** Penilee Road (*22*)
47. **Ralston Golf Club** Paisley (*127*)

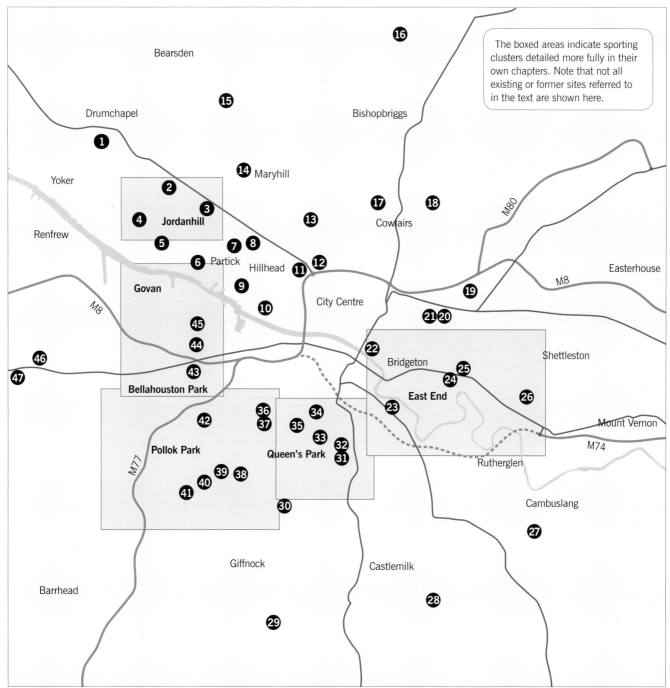

The boxed areas indicate sporting clusters detailed more fully in their own chapters. Note that not all existing or former sites referred to in the text are shown here.

Bearsden

Bishopbriggs

Drumchapel

1

Yoker

15

14 Maryhill

2

3

4 Jordanhill

17

18

Renfrew

5

Cowlairs

7 **8**

13

6 Partick

Hillhead

11 **12**

Govan

9

City Centre

10

19

45

21 **20**

44

22

Bridgeton

Shettleston

46

43

25

47

Bellahouston Park

24

East End

42

36

34

26

37

Mount Vernon

35

23

Pollok Park

33

32

39 **38**

Queen's Park

31

Rutherglen

40

41

Cambuslang

30

27

Giffnock

Castlemilk

Barrhead

28

29

Easterhouse

M80

M8

M8

M77

M74

Chapter Two

Glasgow Green

'Cricket, rounders, football, shinty and golf. Numerous groups of youthful operatives, after the toils of the week, all earnestly engaged in these healthful and exciting games.' Written in the *Glasgow Citizen* in 1850 and now adorning this memorial stone on Glasgow Green, these are the words of Hugh MacDonald. A cradle of sport since at least the 17th century, the Green was the birthplace of five of Glasgow's oldest and most illustrious sporting clubs.

Nowhere is more appropriate to start our survey of sporting heritage in Glasgow than Glasgow Green; 55 hectares of open space in the heart of the city, stretching along the banks of the Clyde from Saltmarket to Bridgeton.

Although its existence as an open space was first identified in 1178, Glasgow Green's status as common land was enshrined in 1450, following its grant to Bishop William Turnbull and 'for ever the City of Glasgow' by James II.

At that time its rough and mainly boggy expanse was split by the Camlachie and Molendinar burns into four areas, later known as the High and Low Greens, the Calton and the Gallowgate Greens.

Mostly these areas were used for grazing, the washing and bleaching of linen, for drying fishing nets and for bathers to access the Clyde.

As now, the Green was also the focus for public gatherings, such as the annual Glasgow Fair, an event that was often accompanied by sporting activities. In the Burgh records of April 3 1675, for example, is a proclamation announcing the 'rouping' (or roping) of the green so that a 'foot raice' three times around the Green could be staged, for a prize of 20s sterling.

There is also evidence of casual sporting use, with Highlanders playing shinty and Irish youths handball. Indeed complaints of rowdy behaviour and damage to the Green led to both these games being banned from the Glasgow Fair after 1790.

Golf was however tolerated, with the Town Council issuing its first official permits for the game in 1780. As will be detailed later, this led to the formation on the Green of the town's first formally constituted sports club, the Glasgow Golf Club, in 1787.

No doubt its members were delighted that in 1792 the Green was extended from 59 to 136 acres by the purchase from Patrick Bell of Cowcaddens of land to the east, known as Fleshers' Haugh.

But while the Green has barely altered in size since, the form we know it in today dates largely from the early 19th century.

Britain's first monument to Lord Nelson was erected in 1806. Then from 1813–26 the town's first Superintendent of Public Works, James Cleland, oversaw a programme of landscaping, planting and drainage, employing weavers who had lost their work during the depression that followed the Napoleonic Wars.

Clearly the Council was anxious to protect their new pride and joy.

In 1814 a ranger was appointed to stop youths playing ball games, followed in 1819 by an outright ban on 'golf, cricket, shinty, foot ball or another game' subject to prosecution 'with the utmost vigour of the law'.

Yet there was no stopping a women's boxing match taking place, as reported in the *Glasgow Herald* in October 1828.

Nor could the Council prevent a whole range of sports taking place as the town's population more than tripled within four decades, topping 200,000 by the time of the census in 1831.

According to the reminiscences of David Drummond Bone, at least a dozen cricket teams were playing on the Green by 1848.　　　》

▲ Looking east in 2009, the importance of **Glasgow Green** as a green lung for the city need hardly be emphasised.

From a sporting perspective, the key point is the fourth bridge from the camera. This is the Clyde Pipe Bridge, dating from 1949, which also marks the location of a weir. It is from this weir eastwards that rowing on the river is concentrated.

Hence, beyond the weir can be seen the red tiled roof of the **West Boathouse**, home to both the Clyde ARC and Clydesdale ARC.

Along the same bank, in front of the blue St Andrew's Suspension Bridge – the most beautiful of all the Clyde's bridges, completed in 1856 – is the boathouse of the **Glasgow Humane Society**, set up in 1790, partly to rescue the many swimmers who fell into difficulties along this stretch of the river.

Beyond the suspension bridge is the red brick **East Boathouse** (just visible, left of the tower block), while beyond that, hidden behind the trees, lies Fleshers' Haugh and the Glasgow Green Football Centre.

Rather more prominent in the top left stands Celtic Park (featured in the next chapter), while on the Green itself are marquees being set up for yet another event. On the right of these is the Nelson Monument, and beyond, the glass conservatory of the People's Palace in front of the former Templeton Carpet Factory in the centre.

As will be revealed, the turfed area between the Palace and the Monument hides a sporting secret all of its own.

▶ Not only is **Glasgow Golf Club** Glasgow's oldest surviving sports club but it also has two of the oldest sporting artefacts in the city, both now on display at Killermont, home of the club since 1904 (*see page 128*). This is the **Silver Club**, purchased at the time of the club's foundation on Glasgow Green in 1787, and copied from similar trophies introduced in Edinburgh in 1744 and St Andrews in 1754.

Each of the silver balls bears the name of the winner of the annual Silver Club tournament, who would as a result serve as club captain for the next year. The addition of each ball was marked by a procession.

The first ball, bearing the name James Clark, dates from 1787. There are then gaps between 1794 and 1809, owing to the Napoleonic Wars. The 24th and last ball, awarded to James McInroy, is dated 1835, after which the club appears to have gone into abeyance, as explained right, until reforming in 1870.

By then, no-one knew what had happened to the Silver Club, until in 1901 the mystery was solved when members visiting the International Exhibition at Kelvingrove saw it on display, described as the property of William McInroy, the son of the last named captain.

Convinced it was a family heirloom, McInroy only finally returned it to the club in 1913, after stumbling across a letter in which it was clear that his father had, after all, been appointed only as a custodian.

A Also on display at Killermont is this list of the 22 founders of the **Glasgow Golf Club**, in 1787, enscribed on a piece of vellum.

Nowadays it seems extraordinary that a potentially hazardous game such as golf should have been played in public areas. And yet this had been the case in Glasgow, and in the streets furthermore, since at least 1589 (*see page 124*).

When golf first appeared on Glasgow Green is unclear, but we know from James Arbuckle's famous eulogy to the Clyde (*page 125*) that it was established by 1721.

A further reference from 1765 is the tale of how, on one of his regular Sunday walks on the Green, the inventor James Watt had been pondering how to make steam engines more efficient. In his own words, by the time he reached the 'golf course' he had hit upon the answer (a Eureka moment now commemorated on the Green by the James Watt Boulder).

That golf was sanctioned at all by the Council is a reflection of the status of its players. As the club's history shows (*see Links*), from the list above, John Hamilton was a Minister of the Church of Scotland, William Clark was a customs officer, John Struthers was

a maltman and brewer, and James Muir a surgeon. Amongst the others were ten merchants (mainly dealing in tobacco or other West Indies trade) and four army officers.

A further indication of the members' influence was that in 1792 the Council was persuaded to build a two roomed structure on Glasgow Green, one of which was rented to the club as their headquarters, for £10 per annum.

By 1800 membership had grown to 48, including five manufacturers, three solicitors (known then as 'writers'), two brewers, two tailors and the City Chamberlain.

But for all their connections, they could do nothing to halt the Council's programme of works on the Green, starting in 1813 with the culverting of Camlachie Burn, and the levelling of large tracts.

This, and no doubt other factors – Hugh MacDonald in the 1850s mentions creeping pollution from neighbouring factories – led to the club lapsing some time after 1835 (or so the lack of records would suggest), not to resurface until a club of the same name started afresh at Queen's Park, in 1870. It then moved to Alexandra Park in 1874, before establishing its first settled home at Blackhill in 1895.

» As we have noted, Hugh MacDonald also recorded rounders, football and shinty, as well as golf, during the 1850s.

'Youthful operatives' many of the participants may have been. But in the absence, yet, of formal sportsgrounds elsewhere (bowling greens apart), many of them were from the middle classes too.

In 1857 the Town Council amended Glasgow Green's status from that of common land to that of a public park, one of their first acts being to refuse permission for the Garrison Cricket Club to play there. But in common with other local authorities of the time, it proved impossible to stem the demand for sport. As we shall relate, the Clydesdale Gentlemen Amateur Rowing Club formed on the riverbank in 1857 followed by the Clyde ARC by at least 1865.

The popularity of football on Fleshers' Haugh then led to the formation of Rangers FC in 1873.

Bowling was the last arrival, two greens being laid out in 1903, with four more added in 1907 and 1911.

None of these greens remain, whereas football continues to thrive, still on Fleshers' Haugh but contained now within the Glasgow Green Football Centre, opened in 2000, with 18 turf and artificial pitches of varying sizes.

In 2014 this area will also be the venue for the hockey tournament in the Commonwealth Games.

But there is one other form of recreation that Glasgow Green might still have been able to offer had it not been for World War Two.

In the 1990s excavations carried out by Glasgow University's Archaeological Research Division into the labyrinth of underground air raid shelters built during the war, discovered the foundations of an Olympic-sized open air

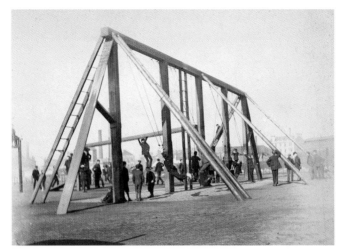

swimming pool, north east of the Nelson Monument.

Apparently started in 1938, once war broke out the pool was filled in, to remain forgotten and almost entirely unrecorded until the University's extraordinary find.

A lido on Glasgow Green? Now there is a prospect for the 'youthful operatives' of today after their toils of the week.

◄ Three years after **Glasgow Green** was re-constituted as a public park in 1857, this 'outdoor gymnasium' was erected on an area south of what is now Templeton Street. Mainly timber, the equipment was donated by a Glasgow merchant, MG Fleming, who had seen similar apparatus in use in Manchester.

Amazingly, the exposed iron frame of a later, but similar 'adult gymnasium', dating from the Edwardian period, can still be seen 50m south east of the University Boathouse, albeit stripped of the rings and chains that made it so beloved by Glasgow's bolder youths.

This 1920s view shows that despite measures to raise ground levels and add drainage, the cinder pitches at Fleshers' Haugh were still prone to flooding. At this time there were ten pitches, served by just one 'dressing shelter'. Today's footballers on Fleshers' Haugh, by contrast, have their own pavilion and rather better turf and artificial surfaces on which to play.

THE ANNUAL REGATTA OF THE CLYDESDALE AMATEUR ROWING CLUB, RECENTLY HELD AT GLASGOW.

▲ Another gentleman's club whose activities were based on Glasgow Green was the **Clydesdale Amateur Rowing Club**, whose 1862 regatta, 'the Scottish Henley', was featured in the *Illustrated London News* in September of that year (the artist having positioned himself on the Suspension Bridge).

Formed in 1857 at Steele's Coffee Room – their first chairman being Arethusa Albert Small Esq. – Clydesdale ARC were at this time based on the Gorbals riverbank (*left*), opposite the current base of the Humane Society. The club's founder was wine merchant James Henry Roger, whose other great legacy was the Rogano Restaurant.

From at least 1830 onwards regattas drew substantial crowds to both banks of the river, some sources, the *Glasgow Herald* included, putting the figure as high as 50,000. But although the ethos of the organisers was strictly amateur – professional boatmen were barred – for the crowds much of the attraction lay in betting.

Note that in front of the Nelson Monument lie what appear to be linen sheets, drying on the grass slopes, an age-old practice that finally died out with the opening of the Greenhead Baths and Wash House on the north side of the Green in 1878 (*see Chapter 14*).

Clydesdale ARC are one of only two Glasgow rowing clubs from this era to have survived. The other is Clyde ARC, which may have existed at the time of this image, but was not formally constituted until 1865.

◀ In professional sport, clubs rarely share facilities. But in amateur sport this has long been common, as at **The Boathouse**, on Glasgow Green, home of both **Clydesdale ARC** and **Clyde ARC**.

Built in 1905 to the designs of AB McDonald in the Office of Public Works, and now listed Category B, The Boathouse was partly funded by wine merchant John Henry Roger, but only on condition that Clyde occupied the west side, while his club, Clydesdale, grabbed the favoured eastern half (east being the direction in which rowing takes place, away from the weir).

And thus domiciled the two clubs have remained ever since.

▶ Despite the allure of modern rowing facilities at Strathclyde Park, twelve miles south east of Glasgow, rowing on the Clyde by Glasgow Green is said to be more popular now than at any other time in living memory. The fact that the river itself is cleaner than ever since the mid 19th century is no doubt a major factor in this.

Photographed here in 2009 is one of three coxed four boats owned by **Clydesdale ARC**. Each is named after a Scottish island, while the eights are named after Scottish mountains, the pairs after glens, and the singles after rivers, although curiously, not the Clyde.

Clydesdale ARC, it will be recalled, occupy the east side of the 1905 boathouse. But the boathouse itself is now better known as the **West Boathouse**.

This is because further along the riverbank lies what is known as the **East Boathouse**, seen here shortly after its opening in 1933 (*right*). This is home to, amongst others, the **Glasgow University Boat Club**, formed in 1867.

Alas both East and West Boathouses are now in the same boat, each having suffered from severe subsidence problems.

In 2007 a **Glasgow Green Boathouse Trust** was therefore set up to consider how best to proceed, its conclusion being that, funds willing, the East Boathouse will make way for a £4.5m replacement, to be designed by the Civic Design team of Glasgow City Council (which owns both boathouses), and to house all the rowing clubs based along this stretch of the river.

Meanwhile, in consultation with Historic Scotland, it is hoped that the listed 1905 West Boathouse will be restored for use as a restaurant and café.

▷ Another major Glasgow sporting institution to have emerged from Glasgow Green was **Rangers Football Club**, as depicted in this 1998 mural by Senga Murray, displayed in the Blue Room at Ibrox Stadium (*see page 108*).

The story goes that among the many youths who rowed on the Clyde during the early 1870s was a group of friends, mostly hailing from Gareloch in Argyll. Seeing a game of football taking place one day on Fleshers' Haugh they decided to try it for themselves, with the result that four of them, the brothers Moses and Peter McNeil, William McBeath and Peter Campbell, all teenagers, decided to form their own team.

It was Moses McNeil who suggested the name Rangers.

Whilst not contradicting this version of events – recounted in the most reliable early history of the club by John Allan (*see Links*) – one subsequent theory suggested that various founding members of Rangers might also have been members of the **Clydesdale Amateur Rowing Club**. This is because the rowing club's minutes from this period include a complaint that members were devoting too much time to football.

But while there is no reason to doubt that this was the case, there is no evidence that either of the McNeils, or McBeath or Campbell, were ever members of Clydesdale ARC, or indeed any rowing club, at least not in a formal sense.

Instead, more recent research by Gary Ralston (*see Links*) has identified connections between Rangers and not Clydesdale ARC but its neighbour in The Boathouse, Clyde ARC.

The first link is a photograph of the Rangers team that played in the Scottish Cup Final of 1877. This,

the earliest known photograph of any Rangers eleven, shows the players wearing white shirts with a six pointed star on the breast, a form of star that appears to match exactly the badge of Clyde ARC.

A second connection is that one prominent member of that 1877 team was Tom Vallance.

Vallance, Ralston discovered, was also a member of Clyde ARC.

How significant these two connections may be remains open to further interpretation. But they do reinforce the impression that many of the individuals seen on Glasgow Green in those years did not confine themselves to one sport.

Indeed Vallance was a prime example of an all-round talent. In addition to rowing for Clyde ARC and playing for Rangers (and for Scotland too), in 1881 he broke the Scottish long jump record at the Queen's Park FC annual sports.

Not only that but he had two paintings accepted for exhibition by the Royal Scottish Academy, and also ran a restaurant and smoking club on Paisley Road that became a favourite haunt of many a sportsman in Glasgow.

There is one other reason why the name of Clydesdale ARC might have been mistakenly linked with Rangers during its formative period.

In 1885 both Moses and Peter McNeil, and Tom Vallance, helped found yet another new club, called Clydesdale *Harriers*.

Could someone in later years have confused this athletic club with the Clydesdale *ARC*? If so, it was easily done, not least because even more confusingly there was also a Clydesdale Cricket and Football Club (the cricket section of which still exists, *see page 174*).

Incidentally, another curio to have arisen from research into

Clydesdale Harriers is that two of its other early members were Tom and Willie Maley, both of whom played a key role in the early years of Celtic FC, formed in 1888.

In short, whatever their other allegiances, here amongst the pioneers of Glasgow sport was a band of genuine all-rounders.

It is in that context that Glasgow Green should be judged as the fertile ground from which so many healthy shoots would emerge.

Chapter Three

Queen's Park

A laced-up football takes top billing on this adaptation of the Glasgow city crest, stamped upon a silver medal awarded by Queen's Park Football Club on the occasion of its annual sports day in 1883. Ironically, the medal may well have been awarded not for football but for athletics or cycling, or any one of the other events that characterised the summer sports days run by Glasgow's leading football clubs until well into the 20th century. But then there has always been more to Queen's Park than just football. Golf, bowls and tennis have also been played in what is still a much prized green lung on the city's south side.

Stroll across the turfed slopes and through the woods of Queen's Park today and you may take in three private bowling clubs and two public greens, five tennis courts, an 18 hole pitch and putt course, a commercial five a side football centre, a recreation ground and a former boating pond.

But for the city fathers who purchased this area for the benefit of the South Side's growing population in 1857, the allocation of space for these activities would have been quite an anathema.

As in other towns and cities of the period – the likes of Preston, Birkenhead, Manchester and Derby – Britain's early public parks were intended for polite perambulation and horticultural display; for relaxation and moral improvement rather than for common games.

But the public had other ideas, and between 1870 and 1914 not only did Queen's Park evolve into a stronghold of Glasgow sport, but the spread of sports facilities to the park's immediate environs turned the area into a hub of national, and even international significance.

Football fans around the world have heard of Queen's Park, even if they have no idea of where it is based or how it relates to Victorian Glasgow.

The park itself, named not after Victoria but after Mary Queen of Scots – whose armies had been defeated at the Battle of Langside in 1568, on a site on the southern edge of the present day park – was the third open space tamed by Glasgow Town Council, after Glasgow Green (*see Chapter Two*) and Kelvingrove Park (in 1854).

But whereas Glasgow Green lay within the town boundaries, the land for Kelvingrove and Queen's Park lay beyond, in the latter case in a part of Renfrewshire beyond Govan Colliery and known to those on the southern edge of Glasgow, in the newly established districts of Pollokshields and Govanhill, as 'No Man's Land'.

Places such as Crossmyloof and Strathbungo, now totally absorbed within the city, were then small villages. Pathhead Farm, whose buildings survive next to the pitch and putt course, stood almost alone on the country road linking

Cathcart with the Gorbals, while Crosshill, which lay between the new park and Govanhill to the north, lasted only 20 years as an independent burgh before being swallowed up by Glasgow in 1891 (along with Mount Florida, Langside and Shawlands).

Thus it could be said that the acquisition of the Queen's Park site was not merely for the benefit of the spreading middle classes. It also represented the flexing of Glasgow's gubernatorial muscle; a bridgehead from which further expansion could be launched.

In total the Council purchased 143 acres for Queen's Park, bought *en bloc* from Neale Thomson of Camphill House. Something of a local hero – having started up a bakery in Crossmyloof to give working people access to affordable, unadulterated bread – Thomson charged only £30,000 for the land, less than it had cost him. But he was by then an ailing man and would die in June 1857.

To design the park Glasgow called in the top landscape architect of the day. Famed for his work at the Crystal Palace six years earlier, Joseph Paxton had contributed plans to Glasgow's Botanical Gardens, opened in 1841, and to Kelvingrove Park.

But as in several schemes to which Paxton's celebrity was attached, elements of his plans, such as a Winter Garden, proved too costly, and so it required a local professional, in Queen's Park's case John Carrick, City Architect from 1862–90, to take control. The groundworks, meanwhile, were carried out by unemployed men.

As at Kelvingrove, and indeed most of Britain's early park schemes, the intention at Queen's Park was to subsidise the costs by feuing a third of the acreage for residential development.

This resulted in the eventual construction of several handsome sandstone villas and tenements lining Langside Avenue to the south west, and Queen's Drive to the north east. The completion in 1873 of Crosshill Queen's Park Church, with its prominent octagonal spire – Carrick insisted that spires add a 'picturesque' touch to the skyline – also provided a landmark that still dominates (*see right*).

As stated earlier, neither Paxton nor Carrick took sport into consideration. There were formal drives, winding paths, ornamental fountains, flower beds and shrubberies. But in any case, although certain parks elsewhere did set aside token space for archery, the only field sports then being played at an organised level were cricket and an early form of rugby, both mainly middle and upper class pursuits whose adherents had secured grounds elsewhere in Glasgow, such as at Burnbank and Hamilton Crescent.

Queen's Park was officially opened in September 1862. »

▲ One of the snowiest winters on record was clearly not enough to deter South Siders from enjoying the slopes of the **Queen's Park Recreation Ground** in late 1947.

Once the fields of Pathhead Farm and forming part of the original land purchase from Neale Thomson in 1857, this stretch of open ground originally extended south west to Grange Road, and formed the only reasonably level patch of Queen's Park on which largescale sport could take place. (Another flat area, on the west side of Camphill, facing Pollokshields Road, had been formally landscaped).

Indeed it was on this southwest corner of the Recreation Ground where, it is thought, members of the Queen's Park Football Club played their first tentative games under Association rules in 1867.

Between games they stored their equipment in the lodge of the recently opened Deaf and Dumb Institute on Prospecthill Road.

That lodge is gone, as is the patch on which Queen's Park supposedly played – built over by the New Victoria Hospital in 2006. But the distinctive Deaf and Dumb Institute itself still exists, converted into flats next to Langside College.

Otherwise the above scene, viewed from the rise next to which the Glasgow Indoor Bowling Club now stands, is little changed today. The changing huts on the far side, backing onto the Queen's Park Bowling Club, opened also in 1867, have been removed. Less evident these days are the hordes of footballers and spectators. Unlike in 1947, numerous other pitches are now available in close proximity.

Least changed of all, outwardly, and still standing sentinel across the road, is the Category A listed Crosshill Queen's Park Church. However it too, like the Deaf and Dumb Institute, has recently been converted to flats.

As it happens, the footballers of Queen's Park FC barely ever played in the church's shadow. Within months of its completion in 1873 they were on the move, to their first enclosed ground, a few hundred yards to the east.

» In the park's early years the Town Council showed a stern resolve to limit sporting activity (as it did also on Glasgow Green). Indeed an edict of the sort that would become all too familiar to generations of children to come was issued, stating that 'No Games of any kind shall be played in or upon any part of the Park, except upon such portions thereof as are specifically set apart for that purpose' (by which was meant the Recreation Ground).

As such, in 1864 an application by Crosshill residents to lay out a bowling green was rejected, and in 1870 a park ranger was appointed to keep sport in its place.

But by then the tide had turned. As the surrounding population grew, and with it the demands for recreational space, the Council's position softened.

First to gain a foothold was the newly formed, and clearly well-connected Queen's Park Bowling Club, who in 1866, in return for a ten year lease at £10 rental per annum, were permitted to lay out a green on a corner of the Recreation Ground and build a modest clubhouse. The Council did however insist that Parks Superintendent Duncan McLellan should oversee the work.

The bowling club opened the following June.

Four weeks later, in July 1867, another set of sportsmen gathered on the other side of the Recreation Ground. These were the founding members of the Queen's Park Football Club. In common with their counterparts at the bowls club, these were respectable citizens, with elected officials, a rule book and, most importantly, sufficient leisure time in the evening and on Saturday afternoons to enjoy their sport.

Then in 1870 another group of sportsmen staked a claim.

Since the disbanding of the Glasgow Golf Club at Glasgow Green in the 1830s, local golfers had had to travel over 30 miles to Prestwick for a game. Tired of this, and perhaps encouraged by what they saw of other sports at Queen's Park, a new Glasgow Golf Club emerged and was allowed to lay out a course, provided that it maintained the greens and gave free access to non-members. Tellingly, one of the founders was Bailie James Salmon, architect of the Deaf and Dumb Institute and Convener of the Parks Committee.

After complaints about the course, however, its threadbare greens and overcrowding, in 1874 the club moved to the city's newest creation, Alexandra Park, four miles northwards (*see page 125*).

But if golf proved unsuited to Queen's Park, other sports flourished. The Wellcroft Bowling Club arrived in 1876 (*see page 139*), followed by Camphill in 1888. In fact such a magnet for bowling did Queen's Park become that by 1929 there were 33 private and 11 public greens within a 1¼ mile radius, an extraordinary concentration.

Meanwhile the final piece of the Queen's Park jigsaw came in 1893, when a further 58 acres around Camphill was added to the park, including Camphill House, Neale Thomson's former residence.

That fine Neo-Classical pile, like the Crosshill church and the Deaf and Dumb Institute, has since been converted to flats, a sign at least that Queen's Park remains a desirable place to live. But what of the possibilities for play, and what of the local clubs that, in the 20th century, would transform this corner of Glasgow into a place of international renown?

This map shows sports-related sites in and around Queen's Park, not all of which can be identified. Note: BC (Bowling Club), FG (Football Ground)

1. **Goals Soccer Centre** (2000-)
2. **Camphill BC** (1888-)
3. **Wellcroft BC** (1876-)
4. **Queen's Park public bowls and tennis centre** (1905-)
5. **Queen's Park BC** (1867-)
6a. former **Queen's Park Recreation Ground** now site of new Victoria Infirmary, and **6b** remaining **Recreation Ground**
7. **Glasgow Indoor BC** (1961-)
8. **Hampden BC** (1905-)
9. **1st Hampden Park** (1873-83) *estimated location*
10. **Old Cathkin Park, Third Lanark FC** (1875-1903) and adjoining drill ground
11. **2nd Hampden Park** (1884-1903), **New Cathkin Park** (1903-67)
12. **3rd Hampden Park** (1903-)
13. **Lesser Hampden** (1925-)
14. **G & J Weir Ltd Sports Ground** (1919), now **Albert Park**
15. **Holmlea Park** (1929-70s)
16. **King's Park BC** (1909-2005)
17. **Mount Florida BC** (1909-)
18. **Kingswood BC** (1928-)
19. **Curling pond** (c.1890s), now Curling Crescent
20. **Toryglen Regional Football Centre** (2009-)
21. **Holyrood Sports Centre** (2000-)
22. **Toryglen Golf Course** (1930s)
23. **Polmadie FG** (1890s)
24. **Polmadie BC** (c.1870s-1905)
25. **Govanhill FG** (1880s)
26. **Govanhill Baths** (1917-2001)
27. **Victoria Road drill ground, 3rd Lanark RV FC** (1872-75)
28. **3rd Lanark Drill Hall** (b.1884)
29. **Victoria Baths Club** (1878-c.1939)
30. **First Lanark Rifle Volunteers Drill Hall** (1870s), now garage

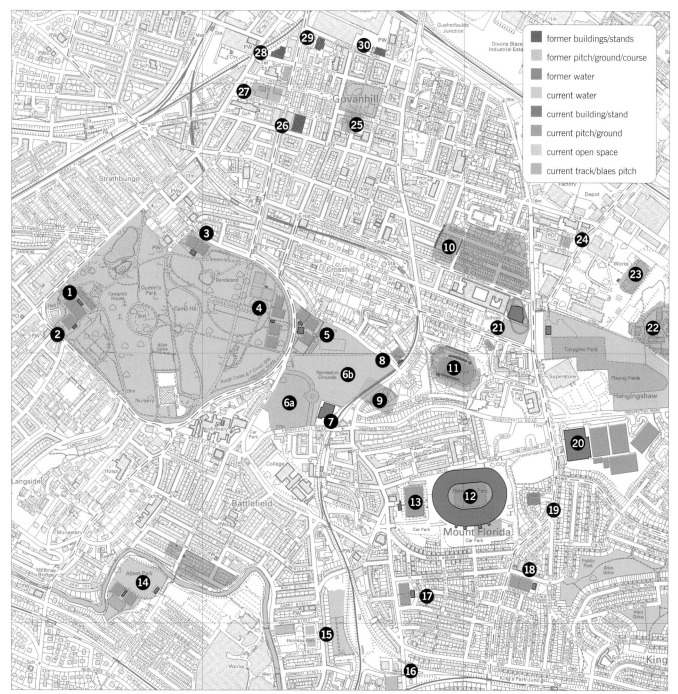

former buildings/stands
former pitch/ground/course
former water
current water
current building/stand
current pitch/ground
current open space
current track/blaes pitch

▲ The **Queen's Park Bowling and Tennis Club** may not be Glasgow's oldest club. As we learn in Chapter Nine, 18 clubs predate it, including Wellcroft, formed in 1835 and since 1876 based nearby on the northern corner of the park.

But there can be no doubt that with its 200 or so members, three greens and two distinctive pavilions, Queen's Park is as revered in bowling circles as its namesake is in the world of football. For example until 1989, the club was the venue for the annual Scottish National Championships.

Having persuaded the Town Council to lease the site in 1866, the club showed its strength from the off by raising £604 in shares, then spending over £1,200 on establishing two greens, using turf from Kilwinning in Ayr, and a small clubhouse. These facilities were inaugurated in June 1867, and were joined in 1889 by the laying out of six lawn tennis courts and a conservatory, in which a Mrs Scott, wife of the greenkeeper, would serve 'hame-baked bannocks, scones and farles' every Saturday.

When the tennis courts proved less popular than anticipated, a

third green was created in 1894, this time with turf brought in from the Isle of Bute. (In fact tennis has not been played on the remaining courts since 1998, but the club are reluctant to change their name.)

Most bowling club pavilions, as will become apparent, are an agglomeration of extensions built around an original core, seldom in harmony or matching styles.

Queen's Park, in contrast, has two wonderfully unspoilt buildings.

Designed by John Ballantine, the larger of the two cost £5,000 and was opened by the Lord Provost, David Mason, in 1929. Its top-lit vaulted hall (*above*) serves as a social and dining area, and in winter as an indoor rink, using rolled out mats. The honours board (on the far wall) is particularly fine.

For most clubs this clubhouse would have been enough. But in 1938 the conservatory was replaced by an annexe, echoing the form of its larger neighbour, and offering views over the east and west greens.

Queen's Park have now been leasing their site from the Council for over 140 years. Model tenants, obviously, and a model club too.

Hampden Terrace — Mount Florida
W. & P. Craig, Mount Florida

▲ When, for their first enclosed ground, Queen's Park FC secured a site south east of Queen's Park, in 1873, they named it after the nearest buildings in view, a new terrace above Prospecthill Road.

Apparently its builder, George Eadie, often named his terraces after historical figures, and in this case chose Oliver Cromwell's cousin, John Hampden.

Thus, by such random choices, Scotland's national football stadium came to bear the name of an English Parliamentarian, an irony not lost on both sides of the border.

Today's **Hampden Park** is of course not the same as in 1873.

But **Hampden Terrace** is still easily recognisable from this Edwardian postcard.

▶ Posing in front of their new pavilion – bought in February 1878 for £65 from the Caledonian Cricket Club at Burnbank, plus a further £84 for its re-erection – the players and officials of **Queen's Park FC** soon found that despite their strictly amateur ethos, as the club historian Richard Robinson wrote in 1920, 'with the ground came greater prosperity'.

Laid out on fields that once belonged to Pathhead Farm, the **first Hampden Park** was rented from the Town Council for £20 in the first year, on condition that the club would 'maintain the fences' and not sublet it.

Queen's Park had already supplied the entire eleven that represented Scotland in football's first ever international at Hamilton Crescent in 1872 (*see page 176*).

Now, with the ability to collect gate money, they were able to add a grandstand, and in 1876 stage the first of what would become annual sports days. For an amateur outfit they quickly evolved into a well run business.

But it was on the pitch that Queen's Park most excelled. At a time when most other teams played an ill-defined game of kicking and dribbling, Queen's Park perfected the art of passing and running – the so-called Combination game – and in so doing helped create the game we know today.

This fascimile from 1905 (*right*) reproduced the match card of the day the football world changed.

The Wanderers were the greatest English team of their day, five times winners of the FA Cup between 1872–78. But at the first Hampden Park in October 1875 they were crushed 5-0.

Note how instead of numbers, players were distinguished by the colours of their caps or stockings.

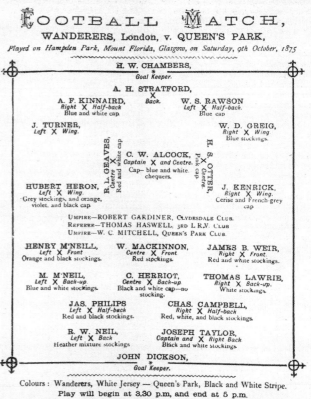

FOOTBALL MATCH,
WANDERERS, London, v. QUEEN'S PARK.
Played on Hampden Park, Mount Florida, Glasgow, on Saturday, 9th October, 1875

H. W. CHAMBERS,
Goal keeper.

A. H. STRATFORD,
Back.

A. F. KINNAIRD,
Right X Half-back.
Blue and white cap

W. S. RAWSON
Left X Half-back.
Blue cap

J. TURNER,
Left X Wing.

W. D. GREIG,
Right X Wing.
Blue stockings.

R. L. GEAVES, *Centre X Wing.* Red and white cap

C. W. ALCOCK,
Captain X and Centre.
Cap– blue and white.
chequers.

H. S. OTTER, *Centre X* Pink cap

HUBERT HERON,
Left X Wing.
Grey stockings, and orange, violet, and black cap

J. KENRICK,
Right X Wing.
Cerise and French-grey cap

UMPIRE—ROBERT GARDINER, Clydesdale Club.
REFEREE—THOMAS HASWELL, 3RD L.R.V. Club.
UMPIRE—W. C. MITCHELL, Queen's Park Club.

HENRY M'NEILL,
Left X Front.
Orange and black stockings.

W. MACKINNON,
Centre X Front.
Red stockings.

JAMES B. WEIR,
Right X Front.
Red and white stockings.

M. M'NEIL,
Left X Back-up.
Blue and white stockings.

C. HERRIOT,
Centre X Back-up.
Black and white cap—no stocking.

THOMAS LAWRIE,
Right X Back-up.
White stockings.

JAS. PHILIPS
Left X Half-back
Red and black stockings.

CHAS. CAMPBELL,
Right X Half-back
Red, white, and black stockings.

R. W. NEIL,
Left X Back
Heather mixture stockings.

JOSEPH TAYLOR,
Captain and X Right Back
Black and white stockings.

JOHN DICKSON,
Goal Keeper.

Colours : Wanderers, White Jersey — Queen's Park, Black and White Stripe.
Play will begin at 3.30 p.m. and end at 5 p.m.

PLEASE DO NOT STRAIN THE ROPES.

DAVID WILSON, the Queen's Park forward, learned most of his football in Langside Athletic, whence he graduated to the Hampden club. He has represented the Scottish League in their English and Irish Inter-League encounters, and also played for Scotland against Wales in 1900.

▲ This is the pavilion at the **second Hampden Park**, built by Queen's Park originally as a single storey building in 1884, but with a second storey added in 1889.

The first brick pavilion to have been built in Scottish football, its initial phase had been overseen by a club member, the architect John Hamilton, who was listed at the time as living in Hampden Terrace.

As may be seen, among several elements rescued from the pavilion at the first Hampden (*opposite*) were the ornate bargeboads.

Queen's Park had been forced to vacate the first Hampden in 1883 when the site was required for the development of the Cathcart Circle Railway. But in truth the railway company did the club a favour.

By way of compensation for the disruption, the railway contractors shifted much of the earth that they had dug for a cutting across the old pitch, and used it to level the new one, 2-300 yards to the north east,

and in the process create a much larger arena. Another advantage of the railway's arrival was that the new Crosshill Station opened up Queen's Park to a wider audience.

For almost a year while these groundworks were in progress Queen's Park played at Clydesdale's ground at Titwood (*see page 174*), until the second Hampden was finally ready for its inaugural match, v. Dumbarton, watched by 7,000 spectators in October 1884.

But however encouraging this attendance must have been – by this time gates in Glasgow were already higher than in England – the second Hampden was still on rented land, on a five year lease only. (Their new landlord was Dixon & Co., whose ironworks north of Crosshill burned so brightly they were known as Dixon's Blazes.)

Moreover, no-one knew quite how long football mania would last.

Queen's Park therefore built steadily, and prudently.

In total the new ground cost just over £1,000, including £95 on the pavilion, £40 for an uncovered stand, and £300 to lay a cinder athletics track. But this outlay was soon recouped. In its first season the takings topped £2,300.

A second stand was then added, the builder taking on the work in return for half the admission fees for the first three years.

For the extension of the pavilion to two storeys in 1889 the club was able to call in more favours, using the services of a former player, architect Ninian McWhannell.

So it was that Hampden clung on to its status as Scotland's prime venue for Cup Finals and internationals. But already there was stiff competition. A few hundred yards to the north lay the fine ground of Third Lanark FC. Ibrox Park opened in 1887. Celtic Park followed the year after.

Queen's Park, the amateurs, could not afford to relax.

▲ Club colours and shirt design form part of every football club's heritage. But there are only so many combinations, and it is therefore all the more remarkable that no other senior clubs share Queen's Park's strip of narrow black and white hoops. It is because of this design that the team is nicknamed 'The Spiders'.

Apparently the strip was first aired on the day the first Hampden Park was inaugurated, in October 1873, on the occasion also of the first ever match in the Scottish Cup.

Seen here is **David Wilson**, a Spiders player from 1897–1906, and the man who gained the distinction of scoring the first ever goal at the third Hampden Park, in October 1903.

◀ Another sports club to bear the name of that distant English Parliamentarian is the **Hampden Bowling Club**, on Kingsley Avenue.

Formed in 1905 by members of the Polmadie BC, whose green (*see page 37*) had been requistioned for housing, legend has it that the Hampden green sits on a comer of what had once been the first Hampden Park football ground, and that a section of the clubhouse we see today – albeit enlarged in 1924 – formed part of Queen's Park original pavilion from 1878–83 (*see page 40*).

Club members go further by adding that the current women's dressing room sits on the exact spot where England's team would have changed before their victorious internationals at the first Hampden in 1878, 1880 and 1882.

These are of course tantalising claims, offering tangible connections with one of the most important early sites in international football.

But alas no proof can be found.

Firstly, although the precise location of the first Hampden is not marked on any surviving maps, from descriptions in various Queen's Park histories, and from close study of the changes effected by the arrival of the Cathcart Railway in 1883 – which included, *inter alia*, Queen's Park being forced to move – it appears that the first Hampden almost certainly lay further to the south of the green, as indicated on page 37.

After all, had it been on the site of the green, why name it after a terrace some way in the distance, and not after any one of the other much nearer buildings, roads or landmarks?

But the matter is hardly clear cut, and is complicated by the fact that the old Cathcart Road, on which the first Hampden was said to have been situated, had to be realigned eastwards by the coming of the railway. Its original path followed more closely the line now taken by Queen's Park Avenue.

Secondly, concerning the origins of the bowling club's pavilion, given that Queen's Park had vacated the first Hampden 23 years prior to 1905, and had in any case taken sections of the pavilion with them, it does seem unlikely that elements of the original would have survived, unused, in situ, for so long, in an area where so much building work was taking place and where the railway line had so markedly altered the landscape.

But again we cannot be certain, for many clubs at this time bought and re-erected wooden pavilions, or elements of them, from other clubs.

Indeed Queen's Park had themselves purchased their pavilion from Caledonian Cricket Club at Burnbank in 1878.

At best therefore, there may just be some timber sections of Hampden BC's pavilion which did originate from the first Hampden, and which were incorporated into the new pavilion erected in 1905.

Equally, it is possible that these elements came not from the first Hampden, but from the nearby second Hampden, whose pavilion (*as seen on the previous page*) Queen's Park dismantled in 1903, only two years before the bowling club was formed.

One thing is for sure. There is no friendlier place in Glasgow to debate such arcane matters than the Hampden Bowling Club.

That it survives at all is something of a miracle, given how often the pavilion and green were showered in sparks from passing locomotives, before, to the club's immense relief, the line was electrified in 1962.

The narrow confines of the site have also meant that despite various extensions, the function room has never been large enough for the club to earn the sort of income from room hire that other clubs in the area have come to depend upon.

Yet it is perhaps because of this intimacy (*see also Chapter Nine*), that Hampden is known for the warmth of its welcome, as anyone who is vaguely familiar with the green as they trundle past on the train would discover should they care to alight at Crosshill and find their way to its doors.

From its surrounding banks and benches Hampden not only offers excellent vantage points, but there are always members on hand to explain the game, to share their love for this characterful club and, no doubt, to engage in a lively debate as to the true pedigree of this historic enclave.

▲ As Hampden BC were settling in, Glasgow's Parks Department finally bowed to demand by laying out two public greens on the Queen's Drive side of **Queen's Park**, served by a 'bowl-house' (*below*) designed by the Office of Public Works under AB McDonald, and opened in 1905.

So popular were these greens that a third was added closer to the road in 1907, to create the setting captured above in 1950.

Meanwhile, in 1911 another pair of public greens was added close

by, facing Langside Road, followed by two more on the Camphill side of the park, next to Pollokshields Road.

The former pair remain in use, whereas the Camphill pair has been built over by the Goals Soccer Centre, and the greens seen above currently lie disused. The pavilion has also been demolished.

However McDonald designed an almost identical pavilion for Kelvingrove Park, also in 1905 and this still stands (*see page 142*).

▶ That the name of **Third Lanark Football Club** still retains the power to provoke nostalgia and outrage in equal measure, over 40 years after the club's controversial demise in 1967, says much about sport's place in the collective urban psyche.

Known variously as the Warriors, the Redcoats or the Hi Hi's (after a popular terrace chant), the 3rd Lanark Rifle Volunteers FC, as they were officially named, were one of at least 20 Glasgow teams to emerge from the numerous volunteer companies that had formed in Britain during the 1850s, in response to the threat of a French invasion.

They started out on a pitch off Victoria Road, Govanhill. Close by, their regimental headquarters, as rebuilt in 1884, can still be seen on Coplaw Street (*above right*), now converted into flats. Seen to the right of this are modern flats, built on the site of the drill hall.

As they had to pay for their own uniforms, rifle volunteers tended to be middle class or skilled workers. They joined for social reasons as much as patriotism. But the 3rds proved to be adept footballers and, crucially, managed to secure their own ground in 1875 (*right*).

They then proceeded to beat near neighbours, Queen's Park, in the Scottish Cup Final of 1876.

In short, competition on the South Side was building rapidly.

▲ Since historians have tended to focus on the early years of Queen's Park, **Cathkin Park**, home of 3rd Lanark from 1875–1903, is often overlooked, despite the fact that at its peak it held at least 16,000 spectators, staged three Cup Finals during the 1880s, two internationals in 1884, v. England and Wales, and was said to have had the finest pitch in Scotland.

Named, it is thought, because the volunteers held summer camps at Cathkin Braes, it was rented from Dixon's ironworks (as was Hampden), and formed the western end of a drill ground on Dixon Road.

Shown here is action from the 1895 Glasgow Charity Cup Final, Celtic v. Rangers. On the left can be seen the tower of Dixon Halls, formerly the shared burgh hall

of Crosshill and Govanhill, both annexed by Glasgow in 1891, and now listed Category B.

When Cathkin Park was feued for housing, the 3rds found a handy replacement only 300 yards to the south. Thus, confusingly, the Cathkin Park we see here would thereafter be known as first Cathkin Park, while the second Hampden was retitled New Cathkin Park.

▲ For football fans on the South Side unimpressed by the somewhat aloof stance of the amateur Queen's Park (whose third Hampden Park we will come to shortly), but also uneasy with the high octane rivalry of Rangers and Celtic, **New Cathkin Park** – seen here after the terracing had been concreted in 1947, and looking towards the spire of Crosshill Queen's Park church – offered the perfect balance.

The ground was also, incidentally, ideally placed for the area's Jewish fans, many of whom, for religious reasons, would not drive or take public transport on Saturdays.

Although occupying the site of the second Hampden, New Cathkin was, as its name suggested, a new ground, with the pitch shifted 20 yards or so south eastwards (*see page 37*), and a stand and corner pavilion built from scratch.

To finance this work the Hi Hi's formed a limited liability company, cut off their links with the military, and changed their name to Third Lanark Athletic Club.

The move proved an immediate success. The club won the League in 1904 and the Cup in 1905. Attendances of over 10,000 also showed that they could command a decent share of Glasgow's crowded football market. In 1954 a record 45,455 crammed in for a Cup tie v. Rangers. A cover was then built over the popular side, and in 1963 a new main stand built.

Yet two years later the Hi Hi's were relegated, and two years after that the club suddenly folded, leaving New Cathkin Park (*below*) to gather weeds, and the stunned supporters to cry foul.

A cry that can still be heard today.

▲ For all the vagaries of the professional game, only rarely do senior football clubs go to the wall, and when they do, it is usually owing to lack of support or insurmountable financial problems.

Third Lanark, on the other hand, were brutally despatched by an asset stripping chairman.

In the Board of Trade enquiry that followed their demise in 1967, a litany of unethical business practices and morale-sapping measures was revealed. Players, it transpired, had been denied hot water after games. They were paid in shillings and sixpences, and told to find their own way home from away games. Most bizarre was an instruction to players to boot the ball into touch from kick off so that it could be replaced with a whitewashed old ball and the 'new' ball saved for another day.

It was of course no way to run a club, until it quickly emerged that New Cathkin Park had already been sold to a developer for housing.

No doubt sensing the anger felt all around the football community, Glasgow City Council opted not to grant planning permission.

But the ongoing legal row left it too late for the Hi Hi's to recover, and in the late 1970s the decision was taken to honour Third Lanark's memory in a unique way...

▲ The spire of Crosshill Queen's Park church peeks out behind the trees. A few twisted old barriers remain on sections of terracing.

The place: **New Cathkin Park**. The date: May 19 2007, when to mark the 40th anniversary of the Hi Hi's last outing, the recently revived amateur Third Lanark took on a youth XI from the ground's original tenants, Queen's Park.

All over Britain there are sites where evidence of former grounds can be found; a wall here, a mound there. Highbury Stadium in London has been turned into flats and gardens. Middlesbrough's Ayresome Park, now a housing estate, is dotted with artwork marking the former pitch and penalty spots.

But nowhere is there a site quite like Cathkin Park, where football,

albeit now in the lower reaches of a local Glasgow league, can still be watched. True, the barriers are not the originals. Sections of the terraces have been reconcreted, others planted with trees, and there is no trace of any former stands.

Here then, is Glasgow's Olympia, an historic stadium, hidden in the woods. Here is heritage, literally, at grass roots level.

LIFE IS SHORT
ART LONG
OPPORTUNITY
FLEETING
EXPERIENCE
TREACHEROUS
JUDGEMENT
DIFFICULT

Crudely carved but reverentially placed by an anonymous hand, the words of Hippocrates carry a surreal resonance on a bank at the not-so-New Cathkin Park, while behind the north west corner, studs in a pathway depict the old Third Lanark badge (*left*), with its number three in the centre. For Glasgow nostalgics and visitors from around the world, this modest arena is a place of pilgrimage. Haunted, but magical also.

▶ The **third Hampden Park**, located on Mount Florida, 500 yards south of its predecessor and opened in 1903, never quite matched the lustre of this tinted postcard. But its conception was no less fanciful, arising as it did from a rivalry so intense that, in the early years of the 20th century, in terms of stadium construction Glasgow emerged as the most advanced footballing city in the world.

This is of importance not only to historians, however, for the train of events that led to the third Hampden's construction, and the legacy that this would create, have continued to shape the football map of the city, and the much wider politics of Scottish football, until the present day.

The basic background was this.

The Scottish Football League formed in 1890. There were ten clubs, six of which were based in or around Glasgow. However, Queen's Park, the amateurs whose motto was, and remains, *Ludere Causa Ludendi* (to play for the sake of playing), chose not to join.

Then in 1893 the Scottish Football Association finally sanctioned professionalism (eight years after its English counterpart).

Football was now big business, and the biggest money-spinner of all was the biennial Scotland v. England international. The second Hampden had staged this showpiece match in 1886, 1888 and 1890, but in 1892 Ibrox Park was chosen, followed two years later by the new Celtic Park. In desperation Queen's Park offered Hampden free of charge, but Celtic's capacity of 57,000 was more than twice that of Hampden and the offer was refused.

Rangers then upped the ante by agreeing, in March 1899, to build a new Ibrox holding 80,000.

Yet instead of standing aside and accepting that their moment had passed, Queen's Park joined the League in 1900 and started considering their ground options, not least because their lease from Dixon's expired in 1899 and their future tenure was in serious doubt.

After failing to buy enough surrounding land to expand what they already had, the club made a deal with Henry Erskine Gordon of Aikenhead to purchase 12½ acres of farmland at Mount Florida for £10,240. Preparing the ground would add a further £4,000.

It says much of Queen's Park's status as an establishment club, representing a class of society instinctively wary of professionalism in sport, yet not averse to business, that at the time they were hatching this colossal scheme they had barely £5,000 in the bank. And that they were able to call on the free services of Gordon's surveyor, Alexander Blair, a former champion cyclist who later rose to high government office in Edinburgh.

Utilising the natural bowl formed by the land dropping down from Somerville Terrace, Blair designed terracing around an athletics track, with, somewhat oddly given the sightline issues, two stands on the south side, linked by a central pavilion. Designs for this pavilion, by leading architect James Miller (as depicted on the tinted postcard), were however never realised.

There was also to have been a cycle track, as at Celtic (*see page 68*), but this too was dropped when it was agreed that the sport no longer drew sufficient crowds. Blair was thus able to increase the banking from 40,000 to 57,000.

After three years work, the new Hampden Park was opened with great ceremony by the Lord Provost Sir John Ure Primrose (a Rangers

Queen's Park Football Club, New Ground.

supporter) on October 31 1903, Celtic being the opponents.

Seeing this vast enclosure (*shown above centre c.1905*), both they and the visitors from Rangers (whose own stadium had been the scene of an appalling disaster the year before, *see page 101*) must have despaired, not least because with acres of spare land, Hampden had plenty of room to expand.

As indeed it did. By the time a temporary pavilion was added in 1906 (*above*), the capacity had reached 80,000. By 1910 it had grown further to 120,000.

The amateurs of Queen's Park could now therefore boast the largest purpose-built football stadium in the world. Not only that, but they had reached this point with barely a debt to their name.

As pioneers of modern stadium design it was inevitable that Queen's Park's consultant engineers should make mistakes (as did their counterparts at both Rangers and Celtic during the same period).

At **Hampden Park** the misguided plan to position a pavilion between two stands was finally ironed out in 1914 by the construction of a linking stand, designed by engineers Baptie, Shaw & Morton.

Topped by a 100 seater rooftop press box, as seen here in 1920, this offered players a gymnasium, a reading room and sunken baths (referred to proudly by Queen's Park as 'swimming ponds').

Another design issue, attributed to Alexander Blair, was the use of wire ropes slung between concrete uprights to act as crush barriers; a reasonable idea in theory but uncomfortable in practice.

Blair had also used steel ropes to divide each section of terrace into pens. But this system became discredited too, and was replaced in 1927 (*as shown overleaf*).

Baptie, Shaw & Morton also designed the castellated turnstile block in the stadium's north west corner (*left*), in 1909. Clearly intended to look robust, it replaced the corrugated iron originals (*see opposite*), destroyed when Rangers and Celtic fans rioted in protest that extra time had not been played after the replay of that year's Cup Final.

▶ With both Ibrox and Celtic Park consigned to hosting only the lesser internationals (against Wales and Ireland), and losing out altogether for the right to stage Cup Finals after 1924, Hampden's *de facto* status as the **national stadium** gave Queen's Park the confidence, and the funds to continue their expansion plans between the wars.

In 1923 **Lesser Hampden** was laid out (just visible in this c.1925 image, behind the west terrace), for the use of the club's junior teams. The site now covered 33 acres.

Note, incidentally, **New Cathkin Park** at the top.

Then from 1927–37, under the auspices of the now veteran Glaswegian stadium designer, Archibald Leitch, Hampden itself received a further makeover (*below right*). Leitch's own patented crush barriers replaced those of Blair. The South Stand was extended, and a new North Stand completed.

All told these works cost over £63,000 and required Queen's Park to borrow from the Scottish FA against future earnings, thereby irrevocably changing the delicate balance between the club and the governing body. On the other hand, the SFA agreed to commit all England games and Cup Finals to Hampden for 21 years, paying Queen's Park a third of all takings.

But again, the expenditure paid off because on completion of this phase a staggering 149,515 attended for England's visit in April 1937 (although it was said some 10–20,000 more had snuck in).

So Hampden maintained its status as the world's largest stadium, a claim it held until the 200,000 capacity Maracana Stadium opened in Rio de Janeiro in 1950. By then Hampden's limit had been cut for safety reasons, to a more modest 134,000.

◀ April 1954 and on this occasion there were just under 130,000 in attendance to see Celtic beat Aberdeen 2-1 in the Cup Final.

By comparison, the largest crowd ever to have attended a Queen's Park match was 95,772, for a Cup tie v. Rangers in January 1930.

In this image New Cathkin Park is again visible, as is the former running track, on Aikenhead Road (*top right*), and a corner of the Queen's Park Recreation Ground (*top left*). Also apparent is that as car ownership increased during the post war period, every space that could be used for parking on match days offered local residents and businesses (Third Lanark included) a useful boost in income.

Three features of Hampden Park during this phase became especially noteworthy. First was the **Hampden Roar**, the sound which rose up from the terraces and seemed to echo around the bowl in an ethereal manner. This, combined with swirling wind patterns made life particularly discomfiting for visiting English players.

Second was the unnerving sight of the perilously leaning **press box** (rebuilt after a fire in 1945), as seen left during the epic European Cup Final between Real Madrid and Eintracht Frankfurt in May 1960.

A third feature often commented upon were the **square goalposts**, especially by players aggrieved at the way the ball had bounced off them, rather than into the net.

Most square posts had long since been replaced by elliptical posts, as introduced in England in 1922. But at Hampden they were part of the furniture. Indeed, a set has been preserved by the Scottish Football Museum, at Hampden, having been bought at a charity auction for £6,000 by a Scot exiled in England, Bill Campbell.

Scottish boxer **Jackie Paterson** fought six times at Hampden (*left*), his World title fight v. Peter Kane in 1943 lasting just 61 seconds, much to the chagrin of the 60,000 crowd (although Mike Tyson needed only 38 seconds to despatch Lou Savarese at the stadium in June 2000.)

As chronicled in the stadium's centenary history (*see Links*) other sports to be staged at Hampden include rugby union (in 1906 and 1999), ladies hockey (1959), American football (2001–04) and tennis, with an exhibition match by Suzanne Lenglen in 1925.

Also between the wars Hampden staged several of the annual Scottish Amateur Athletics Association's championships, including Eric Liddell's final track appearance in 1925 before he set off to work as a missionary in China.

But Hampden's largest crowd for a non-footballing event came in 1933, when 130,000 inside the stadium, augmented by an estimated 100,000 outside, attended a service to celebrate the 50th anniversary of that great institution, the Boys Brigade, founded at the Free Church Mission Hall on North Woodside Road, Glasgow, in October 1883.

▼ The potency of individual events to enrich a city's sporting heritage is amply demonstrated by the iconic status of one Hampden match. The stadium's capacity alone was enough to commend it to the organisers of the new **European Cup**, and the Glasgow public did not disappoint, a tournament record of 127,621 turning up to see the greatest team of the age, Real Madrid (victors over Rangers in the semi-finals) beat Eintracht Frankfurt 7-3 in the final, on a memorable evening in May 1960.

But it was not just the dazzling goal feast that made this such a seminal moment. In the same year,

plans were announced for a new Glasgow airport at Abbotsinch. This opened in 1966, and a year later Celtic returned to it from Lisbon as the first British club to win the European Cup.

Nor could it be forgotten that while the English football authorities had been reluctant to embrace the new era, Scotland did not hesitate, with Hibernian being the sole British club to enter the first European Cup in 1955-56.

Hampden has since staged the final twice, in 1976 and 2002, plus the European Cup Winners Cup Finals in 1962 and 1966, and the UEFA Cup Final in 2007.

▲ Like any other stadium owners, over the years Queen's Park have had to hire out Hampden whenever possible. As seen below, in 1969, Hampden became home to the **Glasgow Tigers** speedway team, after the White City Stadium had been demolished to make way for the M8 motorway (*see page 198*).

But even crowds of 10,000 – huge for post war British League speedway – seemed lost. Nor did it help that the Council banned the broadcast of music between races, thereby deflating the atmosphere further, or that one rider was killed in 1972. The following year the Tigers moved to the more compact Cliftonhill Stadium in Coatbridge.

OFFICIAL PROGRAMME

EUROPEAN CUP

1/-

EUROPEAN CUP FINAL
EINTRACHT, Frankfurt v. REAL MADRID
HAMPDEN PARK, GLASGOW, MAY 18th, 1960
Kick-off at 7.30 p.m.

▶ Despite its capacity for massive crowds – culminating in another European Cup record of 136,505 for Celtic's semi-final v. Leeds in 1970 (a figure unlikely ever to be exceeded) – there could be no denying that Hampden's facilities appeared increasingly outdated.

There were some developments. In 1961 floodlights were finally erected, on four 230 foot high pylons whose leaning gantries identifed themselves as those of Miller & Stables, an Edinburgh firm who supplied many a Scottish and English football ground.

In 1968 a basic cover was built over the West Terrace (*above right*).

This, however, left Queen's Park heavily in debt which, combined with a spate of arson attacks on the South Stand, sparked off a heated debate as to whether Hampden should be transferred to public ownership, or even dispensed with altogether, allowing Rangers and Celtic to share the showcase matches between them.

As one Scottish fanzine noted, 'Other nations have a parliament. We have Hampden Park'.

Meanwhile, as a result of tighter safety regulations following a second major disaster at Ibrox Park, in 1971, the capacity was reduced to 81,000, meaning that the 1973 Cup Final, Rangers v. Celtic, watched by 122,714, was the last match to draw a six figure gate.

Planning for a major revamp, with financial backing from the government in Westminster, began in 1978. But it was a painful business. After the newly elected Conservative government reneged on its predecessor's promises in 1980, Queen's Park and the SFA were forced to lower their sights.

Matters were not helped by a serious outbreak of hooliganism during the 1980 Cup Final.

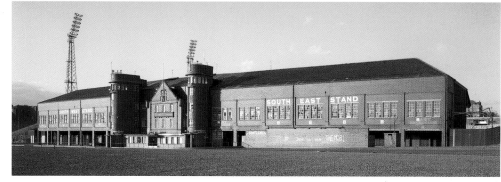

In an ideal world Hampden's huge banks of terracing would have been cleared (as at Ibrox), and the fans brought closer to the action in a more compact stadium, tailor-made for football. Instead, between 1981–86 the existing terracing was simply reconcreted, the now crumbling North Stand demolished, and the capacity cut to 74,000.

But before a second phase to cover the remaining terraces and rebuild the South Stand could be started, the Hillsborough disaster of 1989 changed the agenda entirely.

Stadiums would now have to be seated only, while the English FA abruptly decided to end the annual England v. Scotland fixture.

Reeling from the consequences of this break with tradition, Queen's Park's desperate attempts to raise funds were further stymied when plans to sell Lesser Hampden for development were turned down by the City Council in 1990.

The football map of Glasgow, and the delicate balance of power between Queen's Park, Rangers and Celtic, had in effect been shaped in the 1890s.

Now, in the 1990s, it was decision time again.

▼ The eastern half of the **Queen's Park sporting cluster,** viewed from the north in 2009.

On the left is the reconstructed Hampden Park and the revamped Lesser Hampden; lower left is the old New Cathkin Park, with, to the right of this, the Hampden Bowling Club, the Queen's Park Recreation Ground, the Queen's Park Bowling and Tennis Club, and on the far right, in Queen's Park itself, the two remaining public bowling greens and the pitch and putt course. The modern white buildings in the centre right make up the New Victoria Hospital, built on that part of the Recreation Ground where Queen's Park first played in 1867.

It required a prodigious effort in fund raising, and a good deal of bargaining and diplomacy to ensure that Hampden Park not only survived as part of this cluster, but also was able to meet the ever more stringent stadium criteria set down by the government and by the international football bodies.

Of the original Hampden, nothing remains, save for its elliptical, bowl shaped plan; preserved, for good or ill, for reasons of expediency and economy during the course of two phased redevelopments.

Architects Thomson McCrea, who had overseen the design of the original West Terrace roof in 1967–68, worked with contractors Sir Robert McAlpine and engineers Thorburn Colquhoun on the first phase, starting in 1992. This saw a completely new, seamless and single tier stand spanning from the south east corner to the north west corner, covered by a steel framed, cantilevered roof, spanning 42.5m at its widest point, and a revamp of the outer pedestrian concourse.

Funded jointly by the government, the Football Trust and the SFA, this phase cost £12 million, and was completed in 1994.

The next phase began in 1996 with the demolition of the old South Stand, and its replacement by a two tier, 17,500 seat stand, designed by Percy Johnson-Marshall architects, linking up the east and west ends to form a complete bowl. As well as the usual facilities for players, officials and guests were executive boxes at mid level, and at the rear, offices for the SFA and the Scottish League, plus space for a world first, a national football museum for Scotland (*see pages 184–185*).

The West Stand, in addition, was re-roofed (the terraces having been converted to seats earlier, in 1991).

The all new Hampden Park was finally ready in May 1999.

But for Queen's Park the struggle was not yet over.

Of the second phase's costs of £59 million, £24.2 million came from the National Lottery's Millennium Commission, grants from various bodies, a debenture issue and sponsorship.

But Queen's Park still faced enormous debts, and in 2000 was rescued only at the eleventh hour by a deal in which an SFA subsidiary took over the running of Hampden for 20 years, while Queen's Park remained as overall owners of the site, but in temporary offices at Lesser Hampden.

Like a laird forced to live in the gate lodge whilst his tenants took over the main house, this was no easy transition. And yet it saved both the stadium and the club after three decades of uncertainty as to whether either would be possible.

▲ October 2009, and a fairly typical attendance of 598 gathers in Hampden's South Stand to watch **Queen's Park** play Stranraer in the Third Division of the Irn Bru Scottish Football League, leaving the remaining 51,505 seats unoccupied.

It is a scene that has been captured many times over the course of the stadium's last half century or so, and one that never fails to intrigue outsiders.

In their early years as a League club Queen's Park enjoyed rather larger support, and also special treatment, being granted immunity from relegation until a rule change sent them down in 1922. But they fought back in a season, finished 5th in 1929, often did better than their full-time neighbours Third Lanark, and only finally slipped out of the top division in 1958.

And if it is of any consolation to fans who complain of the distance between the pitch and the seats in the back rows, the retention of the bowl has at least provided Glasgow with an arena that will be relatively simple to convert to athletics when it comes to staging the 2014 Commonwealth Games.

▲ With good reason we return to Mount Florida as it appeared shortly after Hampden Park opened in 1903.

Thought to have been originally called Mount Floridale, or even Floridon, this was an area first built up in the 1860s, but which really developed after the opening of the station on the Cathcart District Railway in 1886.

Viewed from Cathcart Road, looking east, one of the area's newly built tenements – apparently especially popular amongst skilled workers and young professionals – can be seen on Somerville Drive (*left*). Hampden's terracing can just be made out in the distance.

But the real interest lies in the foreground. On the left is the Mount Florida United Presbyterian Church, designed in 1884 by John Hamilton, whom it will be recalled from page 41 was a member of Queen's Park FC and helped with the pavilion at the second Hampden, also in 1884.

The other buildings form Clincart Farm, thought to date from the early to mid 19th century, and clearly still a working farm with a haystack in the yard on the right.

▲ Once again Mount Florida looking eastwards, but in 2009.

When laid out for Queen's Park's reserve team, The Strollers, and their other junior elevens, in 1923, **Lesser Hampden** was said to have had a better pitch than the main stadium. Today it is certainly different, having been replaced in 2008 by an artificial surface, as part of a £500,000 revamp.

But note the buildings looking down on this pitch (*left*). On the right is Mount Florida Church, now listed Category B. As to the white buildings, these, remarkably, are what survives of **Clincart Farm**.

Since 1923 the main building has served as changing rooms. To the left, the old barn houses the groundsman's equipment.

Given that the pair probably predate 1850, it is entirely possible that they are oldest structures in the world in use for football.

And as Lesser Hampden will be used as a warm up facility for the 2014 Commonwealth Games, they will offer a unique link with this part of the South Side's rural past.

Yet one more reason why the Queen's Park cluster is one of the most fascinating, and historic sporting enclaves in Britain.

Chapter Four

East End

Dominating the East End in so many different ways, Celtic FC started as a charitable institution in 1888 and now constitutes one of Glasgow's best known brands. Their 'Bould Bhoys' nickname on this Edwardian postcard is thought to have derived from Gaelic spelling. Note also that although their colours of green and white remain the same, they adopted their famous hoops only in 1903.

While the sporting cluster of Queen's Park evolved as a direct result of the layout of a public park, our next cluster owes its sporting character to the development of industry and to the activities of its predominantly working class inhabitants.

Owing to the prevailing winds, many of Britain's Victorian cities located their more noxious and polluting industries eastwards, allowing those with sufficient wealth to enjoy cleaner air in the west. However, as we learned in previous chapters, it was not so much industry, as the coming of the railways, over-population and poverty that caused the focus of Glasgow to shift westwards in the mid 19th century, so that what we now consider to be the oldest parts of the East End, around the Cathedral, Bridgeton Cross and the Gallowgate, were originally part of the city centre.

The onset of industry in the east effectively began in the 1720s, with the exploitation by potteries of the Mount Blue clay bed, which stretched from Glasgow Cross to Parkhead.

By the mid 19th century cotton was king, hence the likes of Muslin Street and Poplin Street in Bridgeton and Dalmarnock.

After the American Civil War cotton made way for engineering and steel works, using blackband ironstone and Lanarkshire hard splint coal to forge the steel that shipbuilders over in Govan would fashion into maritime behemoths.

Leading the way was William Beardmore's iron and steel works at Parkhead, which by 1896 covered 25 acres, and during the First World War employed 20,000 workers. Meanwhile Sir William Arrol's ironworks, founded in 1873 at Dalmarnock, employed 4–5,000 men at its height and was responsible for engineering, among others, the Forth Railway Bridge and London's Tower Bridge.

In the midst of these industrial giants a web of smaller enterprises sprang up; printers, chemical works, leather works, furniture makers and warehouses. And as the air grew ever fouler, the Clyde ever more polluted, and uncaring landlords crammed more and more families into single rooms,

ironically the city's booming economy increasingly granted to its workers the one commodity that would lead to sport taking off in the East End.

Time. Or rather, time off from their labours.

By 1880 most skilled workers in Glasgow finished work on Saturdays by 2.00pm at the latest, followed over the next decade by unskilled workers.

In the 1890s this resulted in a variety of East End outlets; quoits pitches and recreation grounds, billiard halls, and, feeding the gambling habits of thousands of working men, trotting tracks and later greyhound stadiums, located close to factories in order to attract custom during lunch hours and on half day holidays.

But without question the most popular sport in the East End was football. Among dozens of clubs formed within a few square miles – some of whom, even at junior level, developed relatively large, enclosed grounds – two came to dominate; Clyde FC, whom we note opposite, and Celtic, whose headquarters lay close to the »

▲ In what is considered to be the earliest known action photograph of a Scottish football match, taken at **Barrowfield Park** in the East End in 1894, **Clyde** (in the vertical stripes) are on the attack against St Mirren.

The visiting goalkeeper, it will be noted, sports a cap, but otherwise wears the same shirt as the outfield players. Not until 1909 would goalkeepers be required to wear a differently-coloured jersey.

Note also the absence of goal nets. These had been patented in 1890 and made compulsory in England a year later. Celtic were the first Glasgow club to fit nets, in January 1892, but it would take several years before they became standard in the Scottish League.

For their part, Clyde (whose first secretary was, perhaps significantly,

a keen rower) had been formed in 1877, possibly by members of another club with the equally apt name of Eastern Athletic.

In common with Queen's Park Clyde resolved to remain amateur, refusing an invitation to join the Scottish League in 1890. But in 1891 they changed their mind and in one of their first League matches, the 'Bully Wee', as they became known, drew an estimated 10,000 for the visit of their near neighbours Celtic.

Barrowfield Park was typical for its day, with a pavilion in one corner and a single stand backing onto Carstairs Street. A map of 1894 (see right) shows also a cycle track and, behind the southern goal (from where the photograph above was taken), a tennis court.

To the east and west the ground was sandwiched between a cotton mill, an engine works, an iron foundry and a leather works, while to the north, seen in the distance, are two buildings, both of which still stand today on Poplin Street. On the left is the Category B listed Barrowfield Weaving Factory, designed by Miles Gibson and opened in 1889. On the right are the barrel roof sheds of Glasgow Corporation's No. 1 Gasworks, now a soil treatment centre.

Barrowfield's problem was not its neighbours, but its poor facilities, often complained about by visiting teams. In 1898 therefore Clyde built a new ground across the river at Shawfield (*see page 199*), leaving Celtic as the sole professional club in the East End.

» Parkhead Forge, and whose constituency lay among the area's large Irish Catholic community.

Such is the depth of sporting heritage rooted in the East End that this chapter forms only a brief introduction, leaving it to later chapters to look in more detail at junior football, swimming and greyhound racing. The East End's unique network of home-made doocots (for pigeons) also merits its own study, in Chapter 15.

Today's East End is of course a much altered environment. With the late 20th century decline in industry came a significant drop in the population. The site of the Parkhead Forge is now a shopping centre, 'The Forge'.

Yet poverty, poor health and high unemployment levels still blight the area, and it is no accident that, starting with the Glasgow Eastern Area Renewal project in 1976, various agencies, including the City Council and the Scottish Development Agency, have used sport as a driver of regeneration. Most recently, the city's showpiece 50m swimming pool, opened in 1997, is at Tollcross, while using the 2014 Commonwealth Games as a spur, as seen right, the area south of Celtic Park is set to be transformed by the construction of the new National Indoor Sports Arena and the Sir Chris Hoy Velodrome.

This map shows the known sports grounds and sports-related sites in the East End and its environs, not all of which can be identified or dated accurately. Note: BC = Bowling Club; FC = Football Club; RC = Rowing Club

1. **Clydesdale Amateur RC** and **Clyde Amateur RC** (1905-)
2. **Glasgow Green** (see Chapter 2)
3. **Greenhead Swimming Baths** (1878-1960)
4. **Glasgow University Boat Club** (c.1922-)
5. **James St Roller Rink**
6. **Fleshers' Haugh, Glasgow Green Football Centre,** (2000-) and **2014 hockey centre** site
7. **Glasgow RC** (1997-)
8. **Hutchesontown BC** (1866-) and former **curling pond**
9. **Braehead Park, Thistle FC** (1892-94)
10. **Richmond Park** (1899-)
11. **Shawfield Stadium** Clyde FC (1898-1986), greyhound racing (1932-) (see page 199)
12. **West of Scotland Indoor BC** (1964-) (see page 155)
13. **Rosebery Park** (c.1920s-80s) (see page 63)
14. **Toryglen Golf Course** (1930s)
15. **Southcroft Park, Rutherglen Glencairn FC** (1896-2008)
16. **New Southcroft Park, Rutherglen Glencairn FC** (2008-)
17. **Shawfield Works BC** (1923-68)
18. **Farme BC** (1925-2006)
19. **Ballochmill Riding Track** (1930s)
20. **Tollcross BC** (1877-)
21. **Fullarton Park, Vale of Clyde FC** (1932-)
22. **Victoria Biscuit Works,** sportsground (opened 1925)
23. **Tollcross Leisure Centre** (1997-) (see page 215)
24. **Tollcross Park** (1897-)

25. **Shettleston Baths / Sports Centre** (1924-2005)
26. **Shettleston BC** (1907-)
27. **Greenfield Park, Shettleston FC** (1933-)
28. **Greenfield Football Centre** (2008-)
29. **Wester Carntyne trotting track** (c.1913) and **greyhounds** (1927-72) (see page 197)
30. **Helenvale Sports Ground** (1924-c.1990s) and **Parkhead BC** (1983-)
31. **Helenslea Park, Parkhead Juniors FC** (1880-1963)
32. **New Barrowfield, Bridgeton Waverley FC** (1923-62), now Celtic FC youth ground
33. **Westthorn Recreation Ground** (1933-c.2000)
34. **Belvidere BC** (1861-)
35. **Springfield Park, Strathclyde FC** (1888-1965)
36. **2014 Games Village** site
37. **Dalmarnock Recreation Ground** (early 1900s-c.1970)
38. **Barrowfield Park, Clyde FC** (1877-98)
39. **Baltic Lane curling pond** (c.1857)
40. **Victoria Racecourse** and **trotting track** (c.1900-14)
41. **Queen's Recreation Ground** (1890s)
42. **Thomas Taylor bowls manufacturer** (see page 151ff)
43. **National Indoor Sports Arena/ Sir Chris Hoy Velodrome** (2014)
44. **Celtic Park** (1888-92) (estimated orientation)
45. **Celtic Park** (1892-)
46. **Olympic trotting track** (1920s) **Nelson Athletic Ground** (1928-39) greyhounds/speedway
47. **East End Healthy Living Centre/Crownpoint Sports Complex** (1984-)
48. **Whitevale Swimming Baths** (1902-86), now disused
49. **Whitevale BC** (c.1835-65)

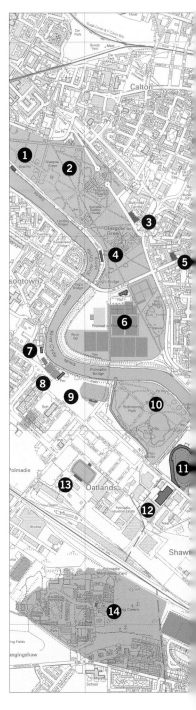

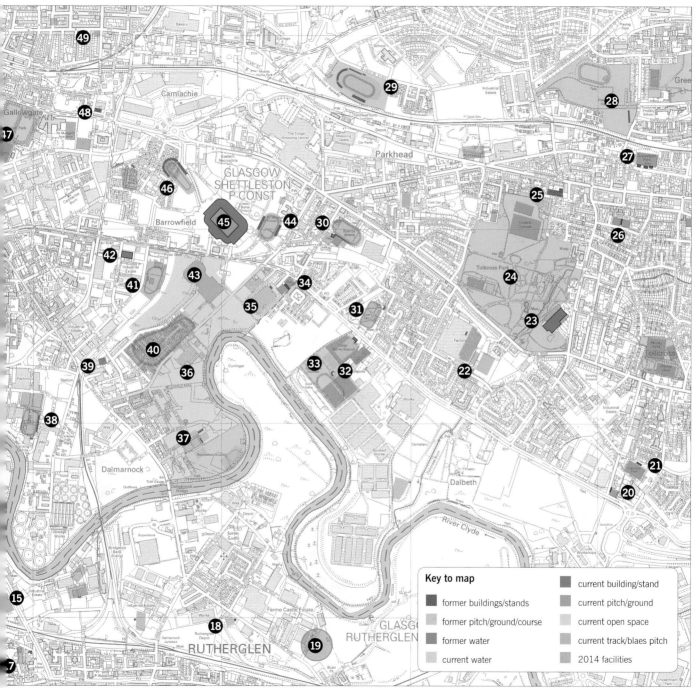

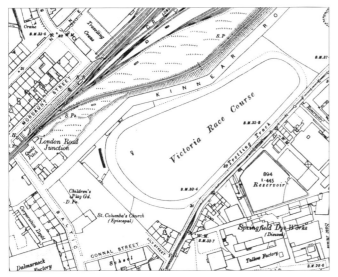

▲ Some 500 yards north east of Barrowfield Park, another shortlived sports ground in the East End was the **Victoria Racecourse**, seen here on a map of 1912, between Springfield Road and Kinnear Road.

Built in c.1904 on one of Glasgow's ubiquitous brickfields, the course was almost certainly designed for what was known at the time as **trotting**, but is today called harness racing.

In essence this is a modern version of chariot racing, in which a horse pulls a two wheeled cart (or 'sulky') on which sits a 'driver'.

The compact nature of the track made this kind of racing ideal for urban areas, and for spectators. But most of all trotting was a sport which thrived on gambling.

Intriguingly the track at the Victoria Racecourse was kidney shaped, a form that was echoed at another shortlived East End venue, known as the Queen's Recreation Ground, on the west side of the London Road Goods Depot in the 1890s, and also at a recreation ground in Govan (*see page 91*).

Two other trotting tracks in the East End, at Wester Carntyne, later a greyhound track (*page 197*), and on Janefield Street – the grandly titled Olympic Sports Stadium – had tracks that tapered at one end.

Whether these irregular shapes were deliberate is not known, but certainly harness racing tracks today – such as at Corbiewood, near Bannockburn – are uniformly oval or elliptical, as was the trotting track at Shawfield, which Clyde FC took over in 1898.

No trace survives of any of the East End's trotting tracks, although the boundaries of the Victoria Racecourse, now covered in housing, can still be discerned, bordered by the site of the athletes' village being constructed for the 2014 Commonwealth Games.

Nor is trotting the only East End sport to have been lost in Glasgow. Shown on the map above, on the corner of Baltic Street and Mordaunt Street, was a pitch for quoits, a sport once hugely popular among dockers, miners, forge hands and blacksmiths (*page 14*).

One of the great sporting crazes of the late 19th and early 20th century, all over Britain, was billiards (and its later offshoot snooker), made affordable to working men by the opening of commercial billiard halls equipped by competing manufacturers. This one is Mair's, on Shettleston Road, in c.1925, since converted into the Drum public house.

▲ Although not in the East End, being just across the River Clyde, this 1964 view of **Rosebery Park** in **Oatlands** is instructive because its form and setting were typical of community football grounds dotted around the East End throughout the 20th century (see page 61).

That is, it was fully enclosed, with a single terrace cover on one side and a modest pavilion on the other, surrounded by earth banks with cinder terracing and railway sleepers used as footings.

From 1918–60 Rosebery Park was the home of **Shawfield FC**, a junior club (that is, not a youth team but one step below League level), best known for winning the Junior Cup in 1947. One of their most illustrious players was the Arsenal and Scotland half back, Frank McLintock, a Gorbals boy, who first came to prominence in the 1950s on this ground, as did hundreds of Glasgow schoolboys for whom Rosebery Park was a regular venue for schools finals.

The ground was named after the Liberal Prime Minister, Archibald Primrose, 5th Earl of Rosebery and patron of the Scottish FA. Uniquely, the Scotland team played several times in shirts using his primrose and pink racing colours rather than the more traditional dark blue.

In the late 1990s, in common with Rutherglen Glencairn's ground at Southcroft Park (see page 193), Rosebery Park was found to be contaminated with chrome waste. The site has since been cleared and absorbed within an Oatlands regeneration scheme.

▲ The realisation during the First World War that so many working men lacked basic physical fitness prompted companies and public bodies all over Britain to build sports facilities for their employees during the 1920s.

Two such works grounds were in the East End; at the Victoria Biscuit Works (opened 1925) and this, the **Helenvale Recreation Ground**, laid out by **Glasgow Corporation Transport** next to their recently opened Parkhead tram and bus depot on Tollcross Road.

Opened in September 1924 with a friendly between Rangers and Partick Thistle – the Duke of York (later George VI) performed the opening ceremony – Helenvale was, by any standards, a remarkably substantial ground with a large

stand (seen here behind the bowls pavilion) and terracing for at least 10,000 spectators.

GCT ran a busy programme of sports, including in-house competitions for bowls, football, athletics, golf and swimming, and in common with the likes of Rangers and Celtic, staged well attended annual sports days.

At this one (*right*), thought to be from the late 1920s or early 1930s, GCT's General Manager, Lachlan Mackinnon, is on hand to see a silver platter awarded to one of the victors, sporting a shirt bearing the crest of St Mungo.

In the background can be seen the gable ends of the GCT sheds on Tollcross Road, which remain in use today for buses operated by the First Group.

▲ Viewed in 2009, the abandoned terraces of **Helenvale Park** (as the GCT's Recreation Ground was later renamed) make for a sorry sight.

In post war years the ground was a hub of both cycling and athletics. In 1949 it made the headlines when Irish runner John Joe Barry, 'The Ballincurry Hare', unsuccessfully tried to break the four minute mile on its track.

In the 1980s the laying of an artificial pitch gave it a new lease of life, allowing for hockey to be staged. But the pitch eventually fell into disrepair and the site has lain abandoned since, leaving only the **Parkhead Bowling Club** to stay on in the original pavilion and maintain one of the greens.

In the distance lies Parkhead's other historic arena, Celtic Park.

▲ So impressed were Celtic fans when their new stadium opened in 1892 that some called it 'Paradise'.

And by the time this iconic image was taken eight years later **Celtic Park** had improved even further.

April 7 1900 was one of the occasions on which Scotland's national team donned the primrose and pink colours of Lord Rosebery.

In front of 65,000 paying fans (plus no doubt thousands more who gained entry), they then beat the 'Auld Enemy' England 4-1.

As this match was taking place, work was already advanced on Rangers' new Ibrox Park, and was just starting on the new Hampden.

Truly, a turning point in football history, and the East End too.

At a time when one in eight Glaswegians were Irish born – two thirds or more of whom were Catholic – Celtic had been founded in 1887 by Brother Walfrid, a member of the Marist Brothers Catholic order.

Born in County Sligo, Walfrid had seen how Hibernian FC in Edinburgh and its counterpart Dundee Harp had rallied other Irish Catholic communities, and concluded that a similar club in Glasgow would offer the ideal means of raising money for the poor and starving of the East End.

At a packed meeting in St Mary's Church Hall on East Rose Street (now Forbes Street) – a building only recently demolished, although the church itself still stands on Abercromby Street and is Category A listed – it was Walfrid who chose the name Celtic. Normally in Britain this is pronounced 'Keltik', but apparently speakers of Irish Gaelic pronounced it 'Seltik' and it was their version that prevailed.

Celtic's first ground opened the following May and was located on the north side of Janefield Street (*see page 61*), at a time when little else lay between this area and Parkhead Forge to the north,

other than brickfields, the Eastern Necropolis and the Belvidere Hospital for Infectious Diseases.

But so popular did the new team become that in 1891 their annual rent was raised from £50 to £450.

As the club secretary John McLaughlin railed, 'Being an Irish club it was natural that they should have a greedy landlord...'

It needed an army of volunteers and 100,000 cartloads of earth to level their next site, another brickfield, just across Janefield Street. The Irish nationalist Michael Davitt laid the first sod of turf, containing Irish shamrocks. (This was later stolen, either by

a souvenir hunter or a nationalist opponent, famously causing a poet to write 'blast the hand that stole the sod that Michael cut; may all his praties turn to sand – the crawling, thieving scut'.

But with or without shamrocks, Celtic had clearly made the right move, for the stadium, opened with the club's annual sports day in August 1892, outstripped both Ibrox and Hampden, and was rewarded with its first international v. England, in 1894, watched by a record Glasgow crowd of 46,000.

By then Brother Walfrid had moved to London, leaving Celtic in the hands of hard-headed businessmen. Indeed it was their decision to invest in a concrete track in order to stage the 1897 World Cycling Championships – no small matter given that previous hosts had been Chicago, Antwerp, Cologne and Copenhagen.

Over 40,000 attended this, one of Glasgow's first major international sporting events, but staging it had been a huge risk all the same, especially as cycle racing was then starting to lose its appeal.

A further sign of ambition was the decision to turn the club into a limited liability company and, in 1898, to purchase the site from Lord Newlands for £10,000.

With the site now secured, that same year one of the new directors, a publican called James Grant, offered to build a stand in return for a share of the takings.

Once completed in late 1899, the **Grant Stand** (*above right*) was unlike any structure ever seen before. Raised on stilts (which made it a steep climb to the upper deck), it had padded, tip-up seats and, most unusual of all, sliding glazed screens at the front, which promised 'freedom from atmospheric inconveniences'.

Tickets cost 2s 6d and were sold from Paterson Sons & Co on Buchanan Street.

Nowadays executive boxes are standard at stadiums. But in 1899 Grant's unnamed designers had embarrassingly failed to cater for the effects of condensation, and the screens were soon removed.

▶ When cyclists gather at the Sir Chris Hoy Velodrome in 2014 they will be only a few laps from where this scene took place, 117 years earlier. A rare image from the **World Cycling Championships** in August 1897, it shows the starting line in front of the Janefield Street Stand on what, judging by the boaters, was clearly a sunny day.

Celtic were not the only football club to install a concrete track, banked for racing. So too did Bolton (in 1895) and Aston Villa (1897). Others laid down flat tracks. But banked or not, none survived, partly because cycling lost its pulling power, but mainly because tracks took up space. By removing theirs in 1914, Celtic's capacity rose by 25,000 to 70,000.

As at Ibrox, Hampden and Firhill (home of Partick Thistle), however, they kept their running tracks in order to maintain the popular, if hardly profitable Glasgow tradition of annual sports.

Willie Maley, Celtic's legendary secretary-manager from 1897–1940, a former sprinter himself, was particularly supportive of athletics, and was no doubt there, along with 40,000 others to see **Eric Liddell** (*right*) breast the tape in the 120 yard sprint at Celtic's annual sports in August 1922.

In 1928 the club also flirted briefly with the new track sport of speedway (*see Chapter 13*).

NEW STAND CELTIC PARK   Nº 80.

▲ The late 19th century practice of building a free-standing corner pavilion alongside a main stand arose almost certainly from the fact that early football ground designers looked to cricket for their inspiration. But while there was a handful of examples of later English grounds following this pattern – most notably Fulham's Craven Cottage, whose 1905 pavilion is the only one of its kind still serving in first class football, and that designed by a Scotsman, Archibald Leitch – in Scotland it was the norm until the First World War.

But whatever their layout, all grounds, with their preponderance of timber, were susceptible to fire, from fans smoking, from faulty electrics, from gas-fired boilers, from airborne sparks from nearby chimneys or passing locomotives and, inevitably, from arson attacks.

This postcard shows **Celtic Park** in 1905, after a fire the year before – its cause never revealed – forced a complete rebuild.

Before the fire the stand had contained 3,500 seats (*see opposite*). But as the club now had full control over the seats in the Grant Stand (now without its glazed screens), the older stand's replacement, as seen above, was designed for standing only.

It was this covered terrace that in later years would famously be dubbed 'The Jungle'.

Behind the terrace lay the Eastern Necropolis, with the chimneys of Parkhead Forge peeping above the roof. To the left of the pavilion, on Gallowgate, can be seen Parkhead Church (no longer extant), built within an existing parish in order to cope with the area's booming population.

Note that Celtic are playing in their new hooped shirts, and that two flags are flying. Another Scottish tradition – this one not emulated in England – was for winners of the Scottish League and Scottish Cup to fly a flag celebrating their achievement throughout the following season.

By the time this photograph was taken Celtic had already won five championships over the course of the previous 15 seasons (compared to Rangers' four).

But over the following years 'The Bhoys' were rampant, winning five championships in succession.

To gain a further idea of what Celtic Park looked like during this period, brief footage of the 1921 Scottish Cup Final, between Partick Thistle and Rangers, may be viewed on the website of the British Pathé newsreel archive (*see Links*).

▶ Although Glasgow was hit hard by the Depression, both Celtic and Rangers embarked on major stand construction programmes during the late 1920s.

At Celtic the plans, drawn up in February 1929, were to replace the now dilapidated Grant Stand. A month later, coincidentally or not, a fire destroyed the old pavilion.

The result was this, the new **South Stand**, opened in August 1929 and designed by engineers Duncan and Kerr.

David Mills Duncan had earlier worked on Firhill's new stand (*see page 187*), and before that had been a draughtsman in the Glasgow office of the ground specialist Archibald Leitch. This may explain why some sources have credited Leitch with the Celtic stand, when in truth Archie, a Rangers man through and through, never worked at Parkhead.

Nor, it would appear from the stand's lower terrace (*right*) were Celtic wont to install Leitch's patented steel crush barriers, preferring simpler post and beam designs instead.

But otherwise the South Stand did resemble a typical Leitch stand.

While clearly less sumptuous than the one Leitch was designing for Rangers at the same time (*see page 101*), and costing £35,000 compared with £95,000, it had a central gable on its roof (a favourite Leitch detail), housing a press box, and a red brick street frontage.

Concentrating the main club facilities in the South Stand meant that the ground's focus switched from Janefield Street to a new main entrance off London Road, where, as seen above, there was clearly plenty of room for a director, or member of staff to park his saloon.

Not Willie Maley though. He always went to work on the tram.

▷ Viewed from the south east in 1965, looking through the haze towards Gallowgate, the sheer scale of **Celtic Park** within the East End cityscape becomes readily apparent.

That presence had increased in 1959 with the addition of four classic Miller & Stables 'Drenchliting' floodlight pylons. Costing £40,000 and towering 208 feet above pitch level, they were described at the time as the tallest in Britain.

The only other addition to the ground since 1929 was a cover erected in 1957 over the rear of the West, or 'Celtic End' (because on derby days Rangers fans stood on the opposite east terrace).

Celtic Park's capacity at this time was stated as 83,500; a figure that had been established as the ground record for the traditional New Year's Day match v. Rangers in 1938 (although the attendance has been frequently cited as 92,000).

The photograph depicts a Parkhead quite different from today, the Eastern Necropolis apart.

The factory to the west of the ground (*centre left*), marked as a chocolate factory in the 1930s, is long gone, its site now serving as a match day coach park. Adjoining the factory, the post war tenements forming a triangle – built on the site of the 1930s Olympic trotting track (*see page 61*) – have also gone, replaced with low rise housing.

Gone too are the factory and post war tenements beyond the northern corner of Celtic Park (abutting the cemetery), the inter war tenements immediately behind the East Terrace and the railway cutting seen in the bottom right, plus all trace of the railway once known as the Switchback, seen snaking behind the south west corner of the ground.

Indeed just about the only recognisable building that does still stand, Celtic Park having itself been almost completely rebuilt, is London Road School, just behind the South Stand. Opened in 1907 and listed Category B, Celtic hope to turn this into a club museum with bars and restaurants, in time for 2014. Meanwhile the tenements facing the school have been cleared to make way for the National Indoor Sports Arena and velodrome that will occupy the site in the lower left corner.

How durable Celtic have proved in the midst of all this change. And yet, as this image was taken, a fresh chapter was about to unfold with the appointment in March 1965 of a new manager.

His name, Jock Stein...

▲ **John 'Jock' Stein** (1922–85), from the mining village of Burnbank, South Lanarkshire, had only a moderate playing career with Celtic, but achieved unprecedented success as their manager.

During his thirteen years at the helm Celtic won nine successive Championships between 1966 and 1974, the Scottish Cup on eight occasions, and most famously of all, the European Cup in 1967, making Celtic not only the first British club to win that illustrious trophy, but the first club north of the Alps.

This bust of him, donated by the Celtic Supporters Association, is on display in the foyer of the South Stand.

▲ By modern day standards the improvements made to **Celtic Park** during the Jock Stein years appear conservative and piecemeal, as was true of most ground developments in Britain in the period 1960–90.

Above all, to save costs the club retained the ground's bowl shape, even though the track was now little used and fans standing at the back of the end terraces were an eye-straining 140 yards from the centre circle (some 40 per cent further than the recommended ideal).

In 1966 the terracing on the north side, or 'Jungle' (backing onto the cemetery), was fully concreted and re-covered by a new double-pitched roof. Hardly state-of-the-art, this did at least lend the terrace an added reverberative intensity.

Two years later the East Terrace (or 'Rangers End') received a similar makeover, its roof being virtually identical to the one built at Hampden in 1967 (*see page 53*).

As a result, Celtic were able to boast more covered terracing than any British stadium other than Wembley. Yet they still had only 4,800 seats, less than half the total at both Ibrox and Hampden. An extra 3,900 seats were therefore added to the lower level of the South Stand, and to cover them, a new roof, as seen here, was built over the top of the existing stand.

In order not to obstruct views by having columns, the new roof was supported on a 'goalpost' formed by a huge, tubular steel girder, 97.6m long and 4.3m high, itself supported at either end of the seating deck by steel columns.

Completed in 1971, the finished £250,000 structure looked highly impressive. But it turned out to have two major flaws.

Firstly, its upturned profile and exposed corners offered precious little shelter. Secondly, in order for the roof to remain stable in high winds or heavy snowfall, two columns had to be fitted to the main girder. These columns were at least hinged, so that during matches they could be swung upwards, out of sight. But it was an embarrassing fault and only added to the general suspicion that Celtic lacked a clear vision for the future.

Yet Celtic were hardly alone in building problematic structures.

Seen here looming high over Dalmarnock are four of the nearly 300 tower blocks that were built across the city during the 1960s.

By 2009 all four had been demolished to make way for new housing, to be provided initially as part of the 2014 Commonwealth Games Athletes' Village.

▼ This is **Celtic Park** in the early 1990s, a period crucial in the history of both ground and club.

In the years since the image opposite was taken, Celtic had continued to invest more on terracing than on seating, a policy which ran counter to that of most other major clubs, not least Rangers, who, in response to the second Ibrox disaster in 1971, had rebuilt their own ground as an all-seater stadium from 1978–81.

This was an undoubted gamble, and yet it ensured that Celtic Park remained the largest club ground in Britain. For example, when its total was cut to 56,500, as a result of safety legislation introduced in 1975 (because of the Ibrox disaster), Celtic underook remedial work to claw this back to 67,000.

Then in 1986, £1 million was spent on a new roof over the West terrace; one that mirrored the 18 year old roof over the East terrace.

(It was from under this new roof that the picture below was taken.)

The spending continued in 1988, when to coincide with the club's centenary, a refurbishment of the South Stand resulted in a new glass fronted entrance block, extra offices, lounges and restaurants.

This left Celtic with over £3.5 million of debts, and a stadium that, for all its atmosphere and character, still lagged behind those of Britain's other leading clubs.

The crunch came in 1990, but from an unexpected quarter... Westminster.

Intent on radical action in the wake of yet another stadium disaster – at Hillsborough the year before – the government ordered that, as recommended by the Taylor Report, all senior clubs phase out their terracing by August 1994.

Celtic were not alone in reeling from this decision, but with debts mounting and a power struggle

building up in the boardroom, they now faced some stark choices.

The cheapest, quickest option would have been to reprofile the terracing and add seats. But this would have resulted in a capacity of only 34,000 seats, a large number of which would be hampered by dreadful sightlines and blocked views (not to mention the viewing distances behind each goal).

But with government and the football authorities now closely overseeing the implementation of the Taylor Report, this option was hardly viable.

Rebuilding the three terraced sides of the ground was costed at around £40m, which without a major share issue or outside investment lay beyond the means of the incumbent regime, most of whom came from families that had controlled the club for many years.

And so it was that in April 1992, almost exactly a century

after the ground's opening, a shock announcement was made.

Celtic were to team up with a development partner and leave Parkhead for a new 52,000 seat stadium to be built in Cambuslang.

It was only three miles away, but it was not the East End. And it was not Paradise.

For the next two years Glasgow pulsated with rumour and intrigue, as Celtic's partners promised all kinds of benefits. Meanwhile, to buy time before the new stadium would be ready, 5,000 seats were installed on the Jungle in 1993.

But as the months passed and still no money appeared on the table for Cambuslang, and as the fans showed their contempt by boycotting matches – one drew barely 10,000 spectators – the banks closed in.

Only a miracle could now save the Bhoys. Which of course is exactly what happened.

A Scots-born Canadian who was now a tax exile in Bermuda, Fergus McCann took over the club in March 1994 and within weeks consigned the Cambuslang plans to the bin.

Celtic Park would be rebuilt, he vowed, and this time, it would be rebuilt properly. A massively successful £12.3 million share issue helped on the money front.

But now that all-seater deadline was only weeks away.

▲ Paradise found! This was the reborn **Celtic Park** in 2009. At last, a rectangular ground for the Bhoys.

How had Celtic achieved this? Firstly they decamped to Hampden Park for season 1994–95 while Miller Construction built the North Stand (seen on the far side). Its upper tier is the only part of the stadium to require supporting pillars, at the rear of the upper deck, because for understandable reasons it was impossible to extend the stand's foundations into the Necropolis behind, and so the tier is cantilevered over Janefield Street.

Phases Two and Three, built by Barr Construction, saw the erection of the Lisbon Lions Stand (at the far end) in 1996, and the Jock Stein Stand (to the left) in 1998.

To complete the picture, two corner stands link up with the existing South Stand, which was re-roofed with translucent panels to reduce shading on the pitch.

Percy Johnson-Marshall were overall architects of the scheme. Hutter Jennings Titchmarsh acted as consulting engineers.

With a final all-seated capacity of 60,837, Celtic Park is now second in size only to Murrayfield (in Scotland), and in British club football, second only to Manchester United's Old Trafford.

But most extraordinary is how Celtic are filling their seats. Even in Jock Stein's era Celtic's average fluctuated between 25–35,000.

Since 1998 it has risen to between 53–59,000.

As the expression goes, 'Build it and they will come.'

◄ One response to the revolution that has transformed the character of football in the post-Hillsborough era has been the embrace of heritage. Cynics might say that clubs view heritage as adding value to 'the brand'. Which it does. But it is also true that most of the impetus for celebrating heritage has come from the fans themselves.

After all, chairman and directors come and go – Fergus McCann, Celtic's saviour in 1994, departed, as he promised he would, in 1999 – whereas for fans, allegiance is a life-long commitment.

Two manifestations of this take solid form outside the redbrick entrance to the South Stand.

Unveiled in 1995, the bronze statue of **Brother Walfrid** (*left*), by sculptor Kate Robinson, was funded by £30,000 worth of donations. To this the Celtic Charity Fund added a further £5,000 towards the upkeep of St Mary's Church in Calton, which played such a crucial role in the club's foundation – as a charitable organisation, it should never be forgotten – in 1888.

A second Kate Robinson statue, of **Jimmy Johnstone**, one of the Lisbon Lions, was unveiled in December 1998 (*top left*), this time funded entirely by the club.

Voted by the fans as the greatest ever Celtic player in a poll of 2002, 'Jinky' died in 2006, aged 61.

Behind these statues stands the only remnant of the pre-McCann era, the somewhat artless reception block opened in 1988. Inside this lies the original core of the 1929 South Stand, the only recognisable element of which is the stained glass panel (*above*) that once adorned the main entrance.

Meanwhile, a club museum is to be created in the former London Road School facing the forecourt.

There is a great story to tell, and a legion of fans and historians on hand to ensure that it is told well.

▲ Since the decline of Glasgow's industry, and with it a 45 per cent drop in the population since the 1960s (albeit linked also to boundary changes), the one asset regeneration agenices have been able to exploit in the **East End** has been space. Not without addressing the legacy of the past, however.

In order to rebuild Celtic Park power lines and pylons had to be realigned and hundreds of piles sunk to counteract the effects of long forgotten mineshafts.

Other parts of the East End have required major decontamination.

For years many of these areas lay grassed over and empty. But gradually they are being redeveloped. To the south east of Celtic Park (*lower right*) land has been prepared for the new indoor arena and velodrome, while to the south west, adjoining the former London Road School, the so-called 'Celtic Triangle' (*lower left*) is set to become a public plaza with commercial developments.

To the north of the Necropolis, beyond the white roofs of the Forge shopping centre (site of the Parkhead Forge), lies more open space, part of it once occupied by the Carntyne greyhound stadium.

To the east lies the former Helenvale Recreation Ground, its pitch now bare tarmac, with the green of the Parkhead Bowling Club on its southern flank (*centre right*).

Transforming this post-industrial landscape into a sustainable environment is no small task.

But for sure, sport will lie at the heart of its rebirth.

◀ A fine covering of snow blankets the Campsie Fells to the north, looking down on the cluster of Red Road tower blocks in Balornock and Barmulloch, while in the foreground, on the banks of the meandering Clyde, the thick russet vegetation of the Cuningar Loop appears to offer a softer relief from the hard edges of the city. Once the Loop was infested by rabbits, or coneys, hence its name.

But it is the green and white, the concrete and steel of Celtic Park that locates this scene most of all.

Clearly, Brother Walfrid was astute in seeing football as a powerful partner in his wider mission. In modern parlance, his creation might be heralded as a celebration of heritage and diversity.

Of course no-one denies that these same virtues have also led to polarisation.

Yet it is equally clear that today's East End needs a strong Celtic as much as Celtic needs a prosperous East End. This is still an area that suffers from amongst the highest unemployment levels and lowest life expectancies in Scotland.

In July 2014 Celtic Park will host the opening ceremony of the Commonwealth Games. By then the view we see here will be much altered.

The completion of the M74 extension, the creation of the Commonwealth Games facilities, the transformation of the Cuningar Loop into an accessible nature reserve, and above all, the re-population of the area, are measures hardly less radical than those that transformed the East End in the 19th and 20th centuries.

Those distant Campsie Fells may appear timeless and immutable.

But down in the valley, the ever-changing urban cycle keeps on turning.

Chapter Five

Pollok Park

Few individuals in Glasgow have supported sport more practically than the tenth Baronet of Pollok House, Sir John Stirling Maxwell (1866–1956). During a long life of public service he served as an MP, chaired the Forestry Commission, the Ancient Monuments Board and the Fine Art Commission for Scotland, and helped found the National Trust for Scotland. But as well as the arts, at least 13 clubs representing nine sports can point to Sir John as having played a key role in their formative years.

In this chapter we look at a sporting cluster that owes its existence to patronage, and in particular, the patronage of Sir John Stirling Maxwell, owner of the Pollok Park Estate.

Bequeathed to Glasgow City Council by his daughter Anne in 1967, this estate, now called Pollok Country Park, is best known as the location of Pollok House and the Burrell Collection. Historic Scotland ranks it as 'outstanding' on its Inventory of Gardens and Designed Landscapes, and the public appears to agree, having voted Pollok the Best Park in Britain in 2007, and in Europe the following year.

But Pollok Park has another characteristic worth celebrating: that within its 1,016 acres of parkland and woodland – the largest expanse of open space in Glasgow – lie three golf clubs, plus clubs for athletics, bowls, cricket, rugby and tennis.

To these can be added a mountain bike circuit, a riding school, a police dog and horse training unit, an orienteering centre and a network of walks which every Saturday hosts a 5km run, open to all-comers.

In addition to its art treasures and formal gardens, visitors may also enjoy a scenic stretch of the White Cart Water, spanned by an 18th century bridge, and a resident herd of Highland cattle.

And yet even though this haven lies barely four miles from the city centre, it is easy to miss, as do thousands of drivers every hour of the day, oblivious to its charms.

Partly this is owing to the fact that the M77 motorway, opened in 1997, creates a formidable barrier on its western and northern flank, while on its eastern flank the park is hidden behind estate walls, a belt of trees and a railway line.

Sir John Maxwell Stirling, the last laird of this great estate, was by all accounts a remarkable man, hailing from a remarkable family.

Over the centuries the Maxwells' great talent had been to combine business with charity, robust land management with refined scholarship, while most unusually of all, espousing radical causes and religious tolerance from an essentially conservative platform.

In that sense the family's bequest of Pollok Park to the people of Glasgow was entirely in keeping, even though their tenure of the estate spanned an astonishing 700 years. Only once was this tenure interrupted, after Sir John Maxwell was temporarily dispossessed for supporting Mary Queen of Scots at the Battle of Langside in 1568 (*see page 34*).

In more peaceful times, the eighth baronet, also Sir John Maxwell (1791–1865), divided his time between politics and philanthropy. For example he established an Industrial School for local children and championed the cause of women's education.

It was during his life that parts of the estate were first sold for housing, forming what would become the desirable suburb of Pollokshields (not to be confused with Pollokshaws, a village on the south east corner of the estate, which during the same period developed into an industrial town).

Regarding early sport on the estate, fox hunting in the area was organised by the Roberton Hunt from 1771, and after

1850 by the Lanarkshire and Renfrewshire Hunt (which still meets today, from Houston). In 1782 Renfrew historian William Semple noted the existence of a bowling green at Pollok House, and from *Fowler's Directory* we learn that a Pollokshaws Curlers' Society formed in 1808. It may well have been from this society that the Pollokshaws Bowling Club sprang in 1854, renting a green from the Maxwells just outside the park's eastern boundaries (*see page 81*).

There was also a curling pond in the park itself, on the southern bank of the White Cart Water, opposite Pollok House, where the Pollok Curling Club (whose foundation date is unknown) played until at least 1925.

But for most local people the biggest sporting draw was horse racing. First noted in the early 18th century on 'Maidland Muir' (roughly where Maidland Road is today), from at least 1754 to 1841 races were held on an impromptu course on what is now the site of the Cowglen Golf Club (*see right*).

As we read in Chapter One, these races were accompanied by races involving cocks and geese and no little savagery.

Most of the sports clubs we know today at Pollok Park were products of the later Victorian and Edwardian eras. After Sir John died childless in 1865, the estate passed to his nephew, Sir William Stirling Maxwell, whose collection of Spanish art is now one of the attractions at Pollok House.

But it was Sir William's eldest son, Sir John Stirling Maxwell, who is the hero of our piece.

Following on from the Pollok Curling Club, the second private club to form within the 'policies' of Pollok (that is, the enclosed domain, now the Country Park), »

▶ From c.1750–1883, anyone wishing to access the roads running from the south eastern edge of the Pollok Park Estate had to pay a toll at the small window seen here.

Nowadays isolated on a busy roundabout, the Category B listed **Round Toll** is one of few tangible links with the **Pollokshaws Races**.

For it was at this building that racegoers and jockeys used to gather, not to pay a toll but to have a drink, thanks to it being granted a licence during the Pollokshaws Fair.

The earliest known report of the 'Shaws Races is the advertisement featured in Chapter One, from the *Glasgow Mercury* in 1754.

No maps show the course, but we know that it was more formally laid out in about 1839 as a means of providing employment, and that it ran along what is now Kennishead Road and within the area now occupied by Cowglen Golf Club. Indeed their 14th hole is still named after the racecourse.

We also know that the best vantage point was a slope known as Green Knowe, 300 yards due west of the Round Toll, on which, according to remembrances in *The Pollokshaws News* in 1888, all 'the youth and beauty of the district assembled'. Certainly no serious men of the turf attended, most of the horses being dismissed as mere 'hacks' or 'nags'. Sometimes even cab horses were saddled up.

Perhaps because a number of Huguenot refugees had settled in the area during the 18th century, Pollokshaws became fabled for its 'queer folk'. Hence a popular Victorian ditty called **The Queer Folk i' the Shaws**, with its tale of a Glasgow lad drawn to the races.

Originally written, it is thought, by James Fisher, this version, one of several handed down, is from the Greig-Duncan folk song collection.

I thocht unto mysel ae day, I'd like to
   see a race,
For mony ither lads like me had been at
   sic a place.
Sae up I got an' wash'd mysel, put on
   my Sunday braws,
An wi' a stick into my han' I dander'd
   to the Shaws.

My mother richtly counsel'd me before
   that I gid out,
To tak guid care an my e'e wi what I
   wis aboot.
Said she, 'Ye may be trod to death
   beneath the horses' paws,
An mind my lad the sayin's true:
There's queer folk i' the Shaws'.

The races pleased me unco weel
   gosh they were gran to see.
The horses ran sae afu I thocht they
   maist did flee
When they came near the winnin post
O siccan loud huzzas
Ye wid hae thocht they'd a gaen wud
   the queer folk i the Shaws.

A bonnie lass cam up to me an ask't me
   for a gill
Quoth I, 'If that's the fashion here I
   mauna tak it ill.'
She will'd me our intill a tent an half a
   mutchin ca's
Thinks I, 'My lass I see it's true,
   there's queer folk i the Shaws.'

The whiskey made my love to bleeze
I fand in perfect bliss
So I grip't the lassie round the neck to
   tak a wee bit kiss.
When in a crack she lifts her neive
   an bangs it in my jaws
Says I, 'My dear what means a' this;
   there's queer folk i the Shaws'

A strapin chiel came up to me an took
   awa my lass
Misca'd me for a country loon, a silly
   stupid ass,
Said I, 'If I've done ony ill
   jist lat me ken the cause,'
He made his fit spin aff my hip;
   there's queer folk i the Shaws.

Aroused at last I drew my fist
   an gid him on the lug
Tho sairly I wis worried for't
   by his muckle collie dog
He bit my airms, he bit my legs
   tore a' my Sunday braws
An in the row I lost my watch;
   there's queer folk i the Shaws.

A policeman he cam up to me
   an hauled me aff to quod
They put the twines aboot my wrists
   an thump't me on the road.
They gart me pay a good pound note
   e'er I got oot their claws.
Catch me again when I'm te'en in
   by the queer folk i the Shaws.

▲ This faded photograph from c.1885 shows members of the recently created **lawn tennis** section of **Poloc Cricket Club**, posing stiffly with their rackets at **Shawholm**.

(The ancient spelling of Poloc was adopted in later years to avoid confusion with Pollok Football Club, formed in 1908, *see page 190*.)

Lawn tennis had evolved during the 1870s thanks to the invention of lawn mowers and of air-filled, vulcanised rubber balls. Sold in boxed sets, by the 1880s it had swept the world, becoming a firm favourite amongst the upper and middle classes, partly because it allowed men and women to socialise at tennis parties.

Not that all of Poloc's members approved. In 1920, as the club's centenary history notes (*see Links*), a motion was carried to prevent any

man bringing his wife, daughter or sister to the club unless he had been a member for three years.

And yet women soon made up around a third of the membership while other sports were equally embraced. In addition to tennis, over the years Poloc played host to the 3rd Lanark Archery Club, to the Renfrewshire Ladies Lacrosse team and, in the 1960s, to the Queen's Park Former Pupils' Rugby Club.

More lasting has been the club's golf section. Formed in 1889, this plays on 'Wee Poloc', a nine hole course, since reduced to six holes, laid out on the cricket pitch.

Despite **Sir John Stirling Maxwell** being so well disposed towards sport, there is little evidence that he ever participated (although he had a fine billiard room at Pollok House, which can still be seen).

But he was often to be seen out and about visiting clubs on the estate, even in his later years when confined to a wheelchair.

Here he is at Shawholm (*left*) to toss the coin before a pre-season cricket match between Poloc's A and B teams, in April 1930.

More on the cricket club and another tenant of the estate, the Clydesdale Cricket Club at Titwood, follows in Chapter Eleven.

≫ was Poloc Cricket Club. This played its first season in 1879 at Bangor Hill, on the site of the earlier Pollokshaws races.

Later that year the very same gale that put paid to the Tay Bridge in Dundee then destroyed their pavilion, only for the Estate to allocate them another field to the north of the Cart, called Shawholm, at £10 per annum.

This deal was concluded by the Trustees of the Estate, Sir John having been orphaned in 1878, while still at school at Eton.

On his coming of age in 1887 he was given a choice: to live either at his late father's preferred home at Keir, or to take up residence at Pollok, where the house had been unoccupied for ten years.

Fortunately for Glasgow's sporting interests, Sir John chose the latter, and in one of his first acts he made sure the cricket club was granted full tenancy rights (which it has retained to this day).

He would prove equally welcoming towards at least twelve other sports clubs and schools, as, over the ensuing years, the local population increased and Glasgow's boundaries crept south. (Pollokshaws, for example, was absorbed in 1912).

Sir John's espousal of sport was not entirely without self interest.

By renting out parcels of land to sports clubs he created a buffer

between his residence and the growing sprawl of Glasgow, as shown on the map opposite.

He also stipulated that a majority of the membership of his various tenant clubs should be local residents, or be feuars of the Estate. His tenant clubs were also to be strictly amateur.

In short, there were to be no Celtics or Rangers on his doorstep.

But equally Sir John remained determined that one day the entire park would be accessible to all, a process he began by opening up The Hill, in the north of the park, to the public in 1911.

In 1889 he also donated 21 acres for the layout of Maxwell Park, followed by the allocation of land next to the cricket club for the Sir John Stirling Maxwell allotments, and, in 1924, for the layout of Auldhouse Park, where two public bowling greens and six tennis courts were laid out.

He was similarly insistent that his father's art collection, and that of Sir William Burrell, bequeathed to the city in 1944, be kept together and one day displayed for the enjoyment of future generations.

As now they are.

Rare is the man who shows equal consideration for sport and the arts. But as this and later chapters on bowls, cricket and football show, such a man was Sir John Stirling Maxwell.

The map opposite shows the main sports-related sites in and around Pollok Country Park, together with Pollok House (A), the Burrell Collection Museum (B) and the Round Toll (C). Note: BC (Bowling Club); FC (Football Club); CC (Cricket Club) and RFC (Rugby Football Club).

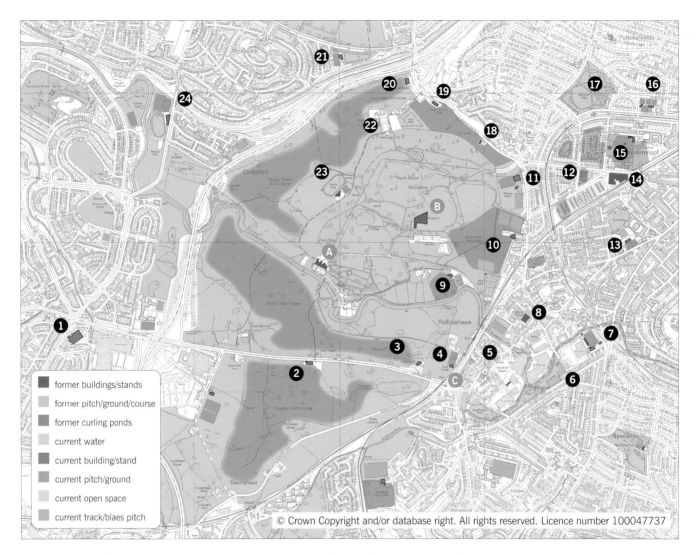

1. **Pollok Leisure Centre** (1986-)
2. **Pollokshaws Races** (1754-c.1840s), **Cowglen Golf Club** (1906-) (*see page 86*)
3. **Pollok Golf Club** (1892-)
4. **Pollokshaws BC** (1954-)
5. **Pollokshaws BC** (1854-1954)
6. **Auldhouse Park** bowling greens (c.1924-c.1970s)
7. **Newlandsfield Park, Pollok FC** (1928-) (*see page 190*)
8. **Pollokshaws Swimming Baths** (1923-1980s) (*page 213*)
9. **Shawholm, Poloc CC** (1880-) and **six hole golf course** (1889-)
10. **Netherpollok Playing Fields** (1930s-) and site of **Haggs Park, Pollok FC** (1908-28)
11. **Craigholme School pavilion** (2006-)
12. **Lilybank curling pond** (c.1860s-1910)
13. **Shawlands BC** (1862-)
14. **Crossmyloof Ice Rink** (1907-86) (*page 168*)
15. **Titwood, Clydesdale CC** (1876-) plus various hockey and bowling clubs (*page 174*)
16. **Titwood Bowling and Tennis Club** (1890-)
17. **Maxwell Park** (1890-)
18. **Bellahouston Academy pavilion** (c.1920s-)
19. **Cartha Queen's Park RFC** (club 1889, rugby 1906-)
20. **Haggs Castle Golf Club** (1910-)
21. **Mosspark BC** (1924-)
22. **Dumbreck Riding School** (1963-)
23. **Lochinch, Strathclyde Police Recreation Association** (1962-)
24. **Bellahouston Harriers** (1965-85), now **Nethercraigs Sports Complex** (2005-)

▲ Members of the **Cartha Athletic Club** gather for the opening of their new pavilion in 1906.

Backing onto Dumbreck Road, in the north eastern corner of Pollok Park, this pavilion was built next to the club's old corrugated iron pavilion (*left*), which had had to be moved northwards from its original position, by the estate entrance opposite St Andrew's Drive, when Sir John Maxwell Stirling decided to construct a new driveway leading to Pollok House in 1891.

Taking their name from White Cart Water that flows through the centre of Pollok Park, Cartha were the second club to have formed under the patronage of Sir John, in 1889, and in common with the neighbouring Poloc Cricket Club, soon took up a variety of sports.

Perhaps of greatest significance was their ladies hockey section, formed in 1902 and pictured below the year after. Until the Edwardian period few sporting outlets existed for middle and upper class women, other than tennis or archery, and not until after the First World War would working women gain the time, or the social acceptance to follow their example.

Today the hockey team, for men and women, is at Titwood (*see page 175*) – still within the former Pollok Estate– having moved in 1960. They were renamed the **Clydesdale Hockey Club** a year later. In the meantime their old club also dropped tennis and football, leaving only its rugby section, formed in 1906, to continue under the Cartha name.

▲ International rugby at the ground of **Cartha Queen's Park RFC** in the northern corner of **Pollok Park**, as Ireland face up to Argentina in an Under 21 game in 2004.

The present incarnation of Cartha dates from 1974, when its rugby section took over the club's ailing administration and expanded the original 1906 pavilion. A few years later it then merged with **Queens Park RFC** (which during the late 1960s had played at Shawholm), and between 1998 and 2000 completely rebuilt the clubhouse, as seen here.

Uninspiring, if functional, this building may be, but the goal posts on this and the club's two other pitches are definitely eye-catching.

Gifted to the club by Honorary Life Member Ramsey Arnott, who had seen similar posts used in American football on a visit to the United States, unlike conventional H-frame rugby posts, these are shaped like tuning forks.

As no other clubs in Scotland have such posts – nor any in Britain overall, it is believed – the club needed special dispensation from the Scottish Rugby Union to install them in 1984. But other than their unusual design, the only real advantage is each set of posts requires only one, rather than two sets of protective padding.

In addition to the club's four teams and youth training schemes, Cartha's original athletic tradition is maintained by sharing the facilities with the **Bellahouston Harriers**, a club formed between the wars and first based at Pollokshaws Baths.

A 'private club for gentlemen golfers', Pollok Golf Club, the first of three to be based in Pollok Park, was laid out in 1892 between the White Cart Water and the Barrhead Road. Seen above, the green of its 15th hole – the 'Bridge Hole' – occupies the site of the old village of Pollok, or Pooktoun, cleared in 1798 to ensure that views from Pollok House, completed in 1752, would not be obstructed by mere commoners. Note the bridge in the centre, also dating from the mid 18th century. On the right is the clubhouse, thoroughly modernised around its original core. However, it is the course itself which is of most interest to sports historians.

▶ In terms of its historic setting, its proximity to the city centre, and the quality and ambience of its clubhouse, **Pollok Golf Club** has much to recommend it. But it has one other quality that puts it into a class of its own in Glasgow.

For although the course was first laid out in 1892, between 1922–24 it was substantially redesigned by **Dr Alister MacKenzie**.

Captured here by the Californian photographer Julian P Graham in 1929, MacKenzie is considered by golfers and golf historians to be one of the leading designers ever.

To put this into context, there are currently three MacKenzie courses in the top 100 ranked by *Golf Digest*, one of which, the Augusta National in Georgia, laid out in 1933, is the number one.

Home to the US Masters, Augusta is the only one of the four 'major' golf championships to be staged annually at the same venue.

Another MacKenzie course, Cypress Point in California, has meanwhile been described as the 'Sistine Chapel of Golf'.

Yet MacKenzie had never intended to pursue such a career.

Born in Leeds in 1870 to Scottish parents, after graduating from Cambridge with a degree in natural sciences he went to medical school in Leeds, before serving as a 'civil surgeon' during the Second Boer War, from 1899–1902.

Only after becoming a founder member at Alwoodley in Leeds in 1907 did golf became his passion. The game itself, he said, offered considerable health benefits, and he often urged patients to take it up.

But it was course design that really fascinated him.

Alwoodley, a heathland course, was the first to benefit from his approach, followed by another Leeds course, Moortown, in 1909.

In 1914 he won a *Country Life* competition to design 'the ideal hole' for a course on Long Island, New York.

This interest in shaping the landscape extended into his service with the Royal Medical Corps during the First World War, when he accepted a drop in rank to work as a 'camoufleur', literally 'one who disguises'. The inspiration for this, he later explained, had been the Boers, whose success in the field he attributed to 'their making the best use of natural cover and the construction of artificial cover indistinguishable from nature'.

Abandoning medicine after the war, in 1920 he published a seminal book on golf architecture, so that Pollok was one of the first to be designed along the principles set out in that work.

These were that a course 'must give the average player a fair chance and at the same time, must require the utmost from the expert.

'All natural beauty should be preserved, natural hazards should be utilized and artificiality should be minimized.'

Such principles, arising, he wrote, from an 'artistic temperament' tempered by an 'education in science', put him in great demand.

In this respect he had much in common with another golfing legend, the American Bobby Jones, who had a degree in Mechanical Engineering and with whom MacKenzie worked at Augusta in the 1930s.

By then 'the course doctor', as he was known, was internationally famous. But at Pollok his final bill came to no more than £40; more expensive than James Braid, who charged another local club, Fereneze, £1 per hole (*see Chapter Eight*), but still a modest outlay for such a lasting benefit.

With such benefits comes great responsibility however. For just as important historic buildings need careful conservation, so too do examples of great golfing architecture.

Which is why, in terms of sporting heritage, the course at Pollok is no less significant than the great house which looks down on it from the other side of the river.

▲ No doubt assured by the benign presence of Pollok Golf Club, but aware too of the precarious nature of farming in the midst of an increasingly urbanised environment, Sir John Stirling Maxwell permitted two more golf clubs to form on his estate during the Edwardian years.

First, on Broompark Farm, in 1906, was **Cowglen Golf Club**, named after the nearest village.

As the name suggests, the land had long been used for grazing cattle, though more recently it had been mined for coal, and had staged the Pollokshaws Races. A curling pond and quarry also lay within its 67 acres, which the club was able to rent for £80 a year until its membership increased.

As before, Sir John insisted that two thirds of this membership should be local residents, or feuars of the Estate. The club was also warned not to allow any 'general recreation' on the course, which led to fencing being erected, much to the ire of ramblers and dog-owners.

As we learn from the club's centenary history (see Links) this did not stop the Lanarkshire and Renfrewshire Hunt clattering over the course in 1907, causing £10 worth of damage, which they refused to pay.

In common with most golf clubs the design of the clubhouse was entrusted to a member, in Cowglen's case the architect Ninian McWhannell, whom we

encountered earlier at Queen's Park FC (see page 41), where he had been a player. Clearly an all-rounder, he was also captain of Pollok Golf Club and president of the Shawlands Bowling Club.

Opened in 1907, McWhannell's clubhouse was an Arts and Crafts delight (top left). But as has so often been the case, Cowglen soon outgrew it, and extensions built since, the first as early as 1913, have all but obliterated its original character (above left).

The same might be said of the clubhouse of Pollok Park's third golf club, **Haggs Castle**, opened originally as a nine hole course in 1910, and then expanded to 18 holes in the 1920s, with the help

of leading course designer James Braid (who charged a princely ten guineas for his input).

In 1921 the club took over the Victorian Moss-Park Cottage (top) for a token £1 paid to the Maxwell Estate, but in the 1980s added an extension, as seen above.

Of the three Pollok Park courses, Haggs Castle is said to be the most challenging. In advance of the M77 works six of its holes were relaid on extra land in the 1970s, designed by Peter Allis and Dave Thomas, and thereafter it played host to several major tournaments, including the first Scottish Open in 1986 (now held at Loch Lomond).

A centenary history of the club is expected to be published in 2011.

◀ Sandwiched between Haggs Castle Golf Club and the dense woodlands on the west side of Pollok Country Park is **Lochinch**, sports ground of the **Strathclyde Police Recreation Association**.

Formed in 1938, the association obtained a lease for 13 acres of Lochinch Farm in March 1939, but were then stymied by the outbreak of war. Finally, £40,000 of funds were released in 1960 and the grounds were opened by the Lord Provost, Jean Roberts, in 1962.

Seen here is the pavilion, designed in the offices of Glasgow's first City Architect, Archibald Jury. A classic post war design, it has since been extended, thus compromising its integrity but giving the SPRA much needed space for its 15,000 members.

The grounds consist of two football and two rugby pitches, an athletics track and a bowling green.

On the opposite, eastern side of Pollok Park is another building that reflects the design ethos of its time, **Craigholme School Sports Centre**, by SMC Davis Duncan Architects, opened in 2006.

Designed to complement its woodland setting, the structure has a curved aluminium roof fixed on timber glulam beams, with Siberian larch cladding.

Sir John Stirling Maxwell, a keen arborculturalist himself, would have been intrigued by it.

▶ Half a mile east of Pollok Park in the heart of Pollokshields, and still therefore very much within the former estate of the Maxwell family, is the **Titwood Bowling and Tennis Club**, whose opening in 1890 was given due acclaim in the Glasgow society weekly, *Bailie's*.

Framed in the centre is the now familiar Honorary President, Sir John Stirling Maxwell, who was reported to have given 'a very racy and reminiscent speech dealing with sport in general and bowling and tennis in particular, referring to the social and recreative part both held in the welfare of a community.'

Note the spilling of tea into the laps of two ladies present, a scene that no doubt caused great amusement to those who scoured the page to see if their presence had been recorded, along with the minister's dog and one of the bowling team's 'skip' (or skipper).

Visiting the club today it is easy to conjure up the mood of that day, so little appears to have altered.

Certainly Sir John must have retained a soft spot for Titwood, for of all the clubs of which he became patron, it alone was granted permission to feature the Pollok crest and motto in its badge, as agreed in 1949, albeit with the words 'Under Patronage' added in order to comply with the heraldic rules laid down by the Lord Lyon King of Arms.

◀ Facing north onto a pair of greens on Glencairn Drive, the pavilion at the **Titwood Bowling Club** is one of the least altered Victorian pavilions in Glasgow, with relatively unobtrusive extensions dating from 1981 at both ends.

Accordingly it is listed Category C(S), as is the adjoining **tennis pavilion** (*below*), facing south onto Terregles Avenue. This smaller building, set at an angle and with splayed wings, was commissioned in 1913 as the tennis section grew, but not completed until 1925, to the designs of architect RJ Walker.

Five modern all-weather courts and floodlighting complete the picture, but is still one that Sir John would recognise in an instant.

Chapter Six

Govan and Bellahouston

With so many shipyards and mastmakers in the area, no sports club in Glasgow was complete without its flagpole. This is the one at Govan Bowling Club, on Vicarfield Street, where the club has been based since 1849, making it the fifth oldest bowling club in Glasgow. For years the club sat in relative isolation, with only large houses such as Fudgebank and Apsley Villa as neighbours. Since then it has seen the rise and fall of the shipyards, and now, the beginnings of an urban revival with the construction of new town houses overlooking the green.

Moving north across the M77 motorway from Pollok Park we now come to a very different sporting cluster, one whose character was largely shaped by the growth of the Clyde shipbuilding industry, and the resultant spread of Glasgow westward from the mid 19th century onwards.

Physically, Govan in the north was split from Bellahouston in the south by the construction of the M8 motorway during the 1970s. But for the purpose of this brief overview, we are considering the area as a whole.

In sporting terms this is a cluster dominated by the presence of Ibrox Stadium, home of Rangers Football Club. But as is the case with Celtic in the East End, the area's sporting heritage has numerous other sites and buildings of significance.

The story starts with the Clyde, on which so much of Glasgow's wealth has depended, offering as it did a gateway to the tobacco, cotton and sugar of the Americas.

From the mid 18th century onwards there were repeated attempts to deepen the Clyde, so

that transatlantic ships could load and unload closer to the town. But near Renfrew there remained one obstacle, a massive volcanic plug in the riverbed that in April 1854 holed the steamship SS *Glasgow* on its way to New York.

It took some 25 years to blast what became known as the Elderslie Rock into oblivion, but once it was gone, the route was now clear for Glasgow's newly emerging shipyards, steel and engineering industries to bring untold wealth to the region.

Previously in *Played in Glasgow* we have noted how much of the city's expansion took in areas of farmland, outlying towns and villages. But Govan was different.

With its roots going back to Christian settlements in the 5th or 6th centuries, and to the ancient kingdom of Strathclyde, over the centuries the parish of Govan

grew from its immediate environs around the Old Parish Church on the riverbank to take in a wide swathe of land, stretching as far as Govanhill and Polmadie in the east, and numbering over 340,000 inhabitants by the early 1900s.

Indeed the Gorbals area was originally called Little Govan.

Meanwhile the town of Govan itself, granted burgh status in 1864, had over 90,000 people by 1907, making it the seventh most populated municipality in Scotland (larger than present day Paisley). When finally it was absorbed into Glasgow in 1912, there were therefore many Govanites who felt that it should have been the other way round.

That fierce sense of identity, encapsulated by the Govan motto *Nihil Sine Labore* (nothing without work), and personified by one of its most famous sons, Sir Alex Ferguson, persists to this day.

Govan's first shipyard opened in 1839. Thereafter, a succession of great enterprises followed, each of them leaving their mark on the sporting and recreational map of the area, as seen opposite. »

Linthouse Bowling Club formed in 1909, and has a flagpole donated by the shipbuilders Alexander Stephen and Sons in 1927. The area was also represented by Linthouse Football Club, who were members of the Scottish League for five seasons before giving up the struggle to compete against Rangers and disbanding in 1900.

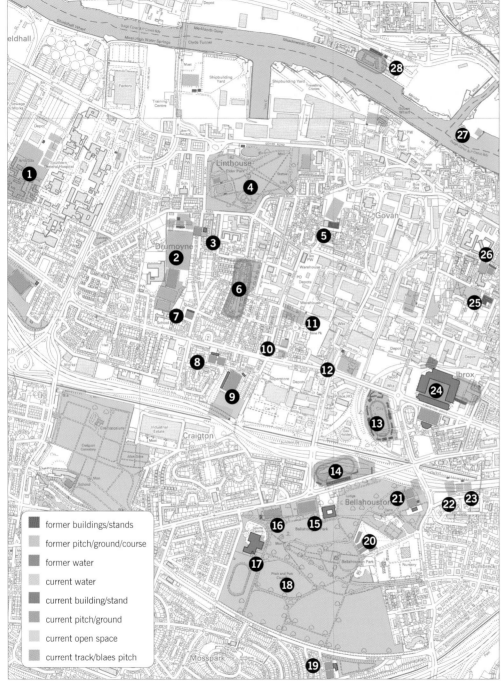

This map shows sports-related grounds and sites in the Govan and Bellahouston areas, not all of which can be identified. Note: BC (Bowling Club); FC (Football Club).

1. **Coila Park** (1922-c.1950s)
2. **Harland & Wolff sportsground**, later **Pirie Park** (c.1919-2008) now site of school
3. **Linthouse BC** (1909-)
4. **Elder Park** (1885-)
5. **Harhill Street Baths/Govan Pool** (1925-2008) now housing
6. **Govan Recreation Ground** (c.1900-14)
7. **Drumoyne BC** (1925-)
8. **Fairfield BC** (1926-)
9. **Tinto Park, Benburb FC** (1932-)
10. **Craigton public bowling greens** (1937- c.1970s)
11. **Langlands Park, Linthouse FC** (1881-1900)
12. **Moore Park, St Anthony's FC** (1929-99)
13. **Albion Stadium** (1927-60)
14. **White City Stadium** (1928-72)
15. **Palace of Art** (1938-)
16. **Bellahouston Park public bowling greens** (1916-)
17. **Bellahouston Leisure Centre** (1967-), pool (1999-), **Cycle Track** (2006-)
18. **Pitch and Putt course**, site of **9 hole golf course** (1899)
19. **Mosspark BC** (1924-)
20. **Glasgow Ski Centre** (1970s-)
21. **Bellahouston BC** (1988-)
22. **Bellahouston Tennis Club** (c.1890s-1969)
23. **Bellahouston BC** (1893-1988)
24. **Ibrox Stadium** (*see page 100*)
25. **Summertown Road Baths** (1901-82)
26. **Govan BC** (1849-)
27. **Pointhouse Inn bowling green** (mid 19th century)
28. **Meadowside, Partick Thistle FC** (1897-1908)

Legend:
- former buildings/stands
- former pitch/ground/course
- former water
- current water
- current building/stand
- current pitch/ground
- current open space
- current track/blaes pitch

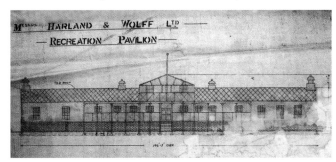

Messrs HARLAND & WOLFF Ltd — RECREATION PAVILION —

▲ Numerous Glasgow companies, such as Barclay Curle, Yarrow's and Weir's laid out sports grounds for their workers during the aftermath of the First World War. This one was **Coila Park**, the ground of the shipbuilders **Alexander Stephen**.

Founded in 1751 in the Moray Firth, and with yards in Aberdeen, Arbroath, Dundee and Kelvinhaugh, on the north side of the Clyde, the company acquired the Linthouse Estate in 1868, converting the old mansion into company offices.

Named after Stephen's favourite racing yacht and run by a workers' committee, Coila Park was laid out in 1920 on ten acres of the former Shieldhall Estate, which adjoined the Linthouse yard. Seen here is the pavilion and living quarters for the greenkeeper, whose duties were to look after four tennis courts, two bowling greens, a putting green, pitches for football and hockey, and somewhat surprisingly, a croquet lawn, perhaps a sign of the owners' tastes more than those of his staff.

Today the site is a depot for commercial vehicles, but another example of Alexander Stephen's benevolent management survives, on Cressy Street, where the Reform Club occupies what was, until the company folded in the 1970s, the Stephen Apprentices' and Boys' Club, complete with gymnasium.

Belfast-based **Harland & Wolff**, builders of the *Titanic*, arrived in 1912, buying up and merging three Govan shipyards. Their ground was laid out in 1919 on a long sliver of land in West Drumoyne, opposite the Linthouse Bowling Club.

Once complete in 1922 it had a substantial pavilion (*below*), a football pitch, two bowling greens, tennis courts and, yet again, curiously, a croquet lawn.

It was named **Pirrie Park**, after the company chairman William Pirrie (as were parks also in Belfast and Liverpool after his death two years later).

Yet once the Harland & Wolff ground was taken over by the Council in the 1960s it inexplicably became Pirie Park – a spelling since adopted by the new school built on the site and opened in 2010.

≫ Elder Park, for example, was bequeathed in 1885 by the widow of John Elder, whose company built up the giant Fairfield shipyard, across the Govan Road. In addition to bowling greens it featured a farm stocked with deer and the Elder Library.

After the First World War, two other shipbuilders, Harland and Wolff, and Alexander Stephen, laid out sports grounds within the same square mile (*see left*).

But by far the largest expanse of open space lay south, in an area of farmland once known as Meikle Govan, but since the 1830s renamed Bellahouston by its owner, Moses Steven.

Steven wished that his good fortune in business would benefit the people of Glasgow, and so after his death in 1871 his sisters set up a trust to enact that wish.

Parts of the estate were sold off for the construction of villas and fine houses, until in 1895 the remaining 176 acres were sold for £50,000 to Glasgow Corporation, to form what was then the largest public park in the city.

In social and economic terms Govan and Bellahouston were at opposite poles, on either side of the Paisley Road. And yet the park offered a green lung to working people that would be well used for sport and recreation as the new century beckoned.

◀ All over Glasgow there are examples of sports clubs forced to move on by urban developments. These images chronicle the travels of **Bellahouston Bowling Club**, and in turn, offer an insight into changing styles of pavilion design.

Founded at a coffee house on Clyde Place in 1859, the club's first green on Paisley Road (*left*) was rented from Moses Steven and bounded by Cecil Street, Clifford Street and Percy Street, at a time when the fine avenues and terraces of Kinning Park formed the outer limits of Glasgow's expansion.

In 1893 the construction of the Glasgow District Subway forced the club a few hundred yards west, to a rather quieter setting (*centre*), on the junction of Beech Avenue and Manor Road (now Urrdale Road).

Here it remained until a second relocation was enforced by the construction of the M8 in the 1970s. Amazingly however, its flagpole remained, and may still be spied (*left*), peeping out amongst the trees on the south side of the motorway's southern slip road, leading to Dumbreck Road.

The club's resting place since 1988 is also on land once owned by Moses Steven. Formerly the site of public greens, on the north eastern corner of Bellahouston Park, the club's more exposed setting (*far left*) is reflected by the architecture of its third pavilion.

▲ Photographed from the south in 1928, this view shows how much space there was between Drumoyne in the top left hand edge and **Bellahouston Park** in the foreground, and how many sports facilties there were in the area.

Using the map location numbers found on page 91 as an aid to orientation, in the bottom left, below the traffic free and tree-less Mosspark Boulevard, the corner of Mosspark Bowling Club (19) can just be seen. In the top left corner, south of Shieldhall Road (which, it will be noted, had yet to meet up with Edmiston Drive), are the greens of Drumoyne Bowling Club (7), since surrounded by housing. Below this is the original Tinto Park (9), over which the M8 now runs.

In the top right hand corner is the west terrace of Ibrox Park (24), with, below, on the right hand edge, Bellahouston Park's four public greens, on the corner of Paisley Road and Dumbreck Road.

As mentioned on page 93, this corner of the park, having been cut into by the M8, is now home to Bellahouston Bowling Club (21).

Also visible are the new White City (14) and Albion stadiums (13), north of the park, while on the south side of the park are pavilions facing eight football pitches, with the municipal golf course, opened in 1899 and apparently bunker-less at this time, to the far left.

At a time of acute economic hardship, here was a vision of the new Glasgow, a city of roads, new housing estates, fresh air and leisure opportunities.

During its boom years Glasgow gained a fine reputation for staging major international exhibitions at Kelvingrove, in 1888, 1901 and 1911. As its economy started to stutter during the inter war years, it therefore took the brave decision to repeat the exercise on the 50th anniversary of the first one.

The result was the **1938 Empire Exhibition** in **Bellahouston Park**, the largest of its kind held in Britain since the 1924 Empire Exhibition at Wembley, and an event which even today, over 70 years later, is recalled with a warm glow of nostalgia, laced with regret that its iconic centrepiece, the Art Deco Tait's Tower (of which more later) was not able to remain in situ. In fact, of the 100 or so palaces and pavilions erected over a ten month period, only one, the Palace of Art, was a permanent structure.

Seen here is a graphic view of the site from the official programme.

Two sports venues can be seen on its perimeter, thereby allowing us to compare this with the aerial view opposite, taken ten years earlier. In the bottom right hand corner is Mosspark Bowling Club, on the edge of what had been Glasgow Corporation's most ambitious inter-war housing development; a low density garden estate built to relieve overcrowding in inner city tenements.

In the top left is the White City Stadium (and not Ibrox Park as the plan's guide wrongly stated).

Ibrox Park did play a part in the proceedings, however, as we shall see overleaf.

Bottom left was the curved Palace of Industry, while to the right of the Mosspark Boulevard entrance was the Palace of Engineering, larger in area than Trafalgar Square, noted *The Times*.

In truth, local industry and engineering concerns needed all the help they could muster, which is why, at the height of the exhibition, the *Queen Elizabeth* – the largest ocean going liner ever built – was launched from the John Brown shipyard in Clydebank, on September 27 1938.

This should have been a cause for celebration. But a day later the Munich crisis reached a head, and within weeks of the exhibition's end, local shipyards and factories were already gearing themselves up to help the war effort.

How effective the exhibition had been in boosting Glasgow's reputation, or in cementing solidarity within the Empire itself, may therefore never be properly gauged, if only because of the war.

As for the public, on one hand 12.6 million paid to see its delights over its six months run. On the other, that was below the budgeted figure, partly because 1938 was the wettest summer for 35 years.

Not that that mattered. What the exhibition had shown was that Glasgow was a city still with remarkable energy and drive, and an unflinching appetite for fun.

Except that within months of its end the park had been restored to its original state so effectively that for those who had partied there, it must all have seemed like a dream.

▲ May 3 1938 and a select crowd of some 60,000 guests and exhibition season ticket holders look on as King George VI and Queen Elizabeth, the daughter of a Scottish earl, preside over the opening ceremony of the **Empire Exhibition** at **Ibrox Park**.

Battling against his stutter, the King delivered a welcoming speech heard not only in the stadium but in Bellahouston Park and around the Empire, courtesy of the BBC.

Despite the nation's economic difficulties, he said, in a voice described as 'strong and deliberate', the exhibition yet again showed that 'Scotland was not daunted, for that has never been her way'.

There followed a 21 gun salute and an RAF fly past so swift that many in the stadium saw only the shadow of the planes as they flitted across the turf.

The royal party then proceeded to Bellahouston Park, where the Queen was apparently much taken with the Ministry of Health's 'Fitter Britain' pavilion, with its uplifting slogan, 'Help Yourself to Health'.

It was a message reinforced by daily displays put on by members of the local **Women's League of Health and Beauty** (*right*), an organisation set up by Mary Bagot Stack in 1930 and with some 166,000 members by 1937.

That same year the Physical Training and Recreation Act set out wider plans to improve the nation's fitness. No-one needed reminding why. But for a moment at least, Bellahouston Park offered a glorious antidote to what lay ahead.

▲ Just as the loss of both the Crystal Palace in 1936, and of the Skylon from the Festival of Britain exhibition in 1951 are still mourned in London, so too in Glasgow is that of **Tait's Tower**, the 91m tall centrepiece of the 1938 Empire Exhibition.

Officially the 'Tower of Empire', it had been designed by the Paisley born Thomas Tait, the exhibition's chief architect, and at its summit had a viewing area for 600 people.

Most Glaswegians were desperate for it to be retained, and for years it was rumoured that it had been demolished only because it would have provided a useful marker for German bombers.

But in truth, it had only been built as a temporary structure, on a steel frame clad in asbestos panels,

a method used throughout the exhibition for speed and economy.

Even so, why, in a book on sporting heritage, should Tait's Tower be of any relevance?

For two reasons.

Firstly, what Tait and his team of talented architects, several of them Scottish, had demonstrated by the quality of their work, was just how little the British had so far been exposed to Modernist architecture, compared with other European nations and the USA, a failing which is starkly echoed on these pages. Where were the modern pavilions and grandstands of Glasgow? At Garscadden and Penilee, it is true (*see page 22*), and in engineering terms at Hughenden (*page 116*).

Otherwise, Glasgow's sports clubs, and indeed the Corporation itself, had remained – admittedly in common with most of their counterparts elsewhere in Britain – doggedly conservative when it came to new buildings.

Secondly, the tower itself may be just a memory, but there do exist at least two tangible manifestations of Tait's masterpiece.

Seen on the right is a stunning silver trophy created for the winners of a football tournament held during the exhibition, at Ibrox Park.

In this, Rangers, Celtic, Hearts and Aberdeen were matched against Everton, Sunderland, Chelsea and Brentford (then a First Division club). Celtic beat Everton 1-0 in the final in front of an 82,000 crowd at Ibrox on June 10 1938.

Measuring 60cm tall, the trophy has been on display at Celtic Park ever since, along with a smaller, simpler version awarded to one of the Celtic players, Chic Geatons. Presumably his team-mates also received one, but it is not known if any have survived.

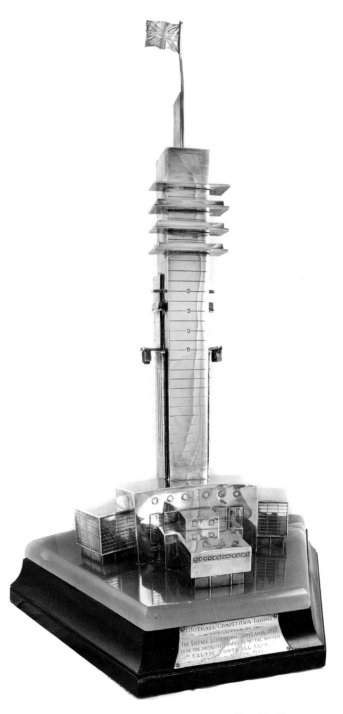

▲ It may seem ironic that the **Palace of Art**, the one permanent building to have been erected for the 1938 Empire Exhibition, and the only one to have survived in Bellahouston Park, was one of the least adventurous designs of all.

(The much bolder Palace of Engineering, it should be added, was rebuilt at Prestwick Airport, as was, reportedly, the Empire Cinema at Lochgilphead, where it is now the Empire Travel Lodge.)

Doubly ironic also that, since 1938, the Palace of Art has been used more for sport than the arts.

Designed by the Glasgow-based Launcelot Ross, in a quadrangular form around an open courtyard, during the exhibition the building's main entrance was different to how we see it today. Where now glazed screens enclose the reception area, in 1938 this area was open to the elements, with a series of bas relief sculptures on the far wall (now the back wall of the reception).

Inside were galleries displaying phases of Scottish art, including work by the Glasgow School, and such leading artists of the day as Augustus John and Laura Knight.

After 1938 it was intended for the palace to remain as a gallery, showcasing parts of the city's collection. Instead, post war restraints saw it used for community purposes from 1951 until 1968, when its galleries were converted into sports halls as an adjunct of the Bellahouston Sports Centre, on the west side of the park.

Its current incarnation as the **West of Scotland Institute of Sport** – one of six regional institutes established around the country by sportscotland, with National Lottery funding – dates from 2004.

Following a £2m refurbishment, which included the sympathetic addition of the 1930s-style glazing, the palace is now a dazzling hive of activity, offering specialised training to promising athletes in fifteen different sports, including hockey (on an adjoining artificial pitch), and judo (*right*).

A palace of art in name, therefore, but a veritable hothouse of sporting excellence, as Glasgow will witness when no doubt many of its alumni step into the breach at the 2014 Commonwealth Games.

◀ Another example of the re-use of existing features for sporting purposes lies south east of the Palace of Art, in an area of **Bellahouston Park** originally formed as an open air amphitheatre.

Initially erected by the City Council during the 1970s, and run since 1981 by an independent club, this is the **Glasgow Ski and Snowboard Centre**.

Artificial ski-slopes are a relatively new form of provision, having emerged in Britain and Italy during the 1960s. Since then there have been several leaps forward in both the technology (which arose originally from the brush making industry), and in the variety of snowsports practised. Indeed since this aerial image was taken in 2005 several improvements have taken place to the two earlier slopes, while a third has been added for free-style snowsports.

But there is one link with the past. As seen left, the ski centre is based in what was originally an open fronted bandstand, built in c.1933 to serve the amphitheatre.

Returning to the aerial view, in the lower left are, once again, the greens of Bellahouston Bowling Club, while between these and the Palace of Art (on the right) lies the Charles Rennie Mackintosh-inspired House for an Art Lover, opened in 1996 on the site of Ibroxhill House (*see page 13*).

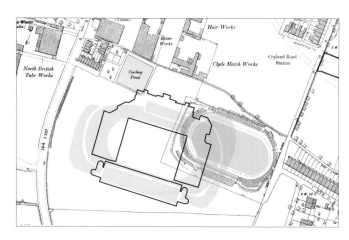

▲ By the time **Rangers Football Club** arrived at Ibrox in 1887 they were already established on the Glasgow football scene.

But why, as depicted on this Edwardian postcard, were they nicknamed the 'Light Blues' when clearly they played in royal blue?

The answer is of course that the name differentiated them from the national team, who play in a much darker, navy blue strip.

Interestingly there was a spell when Rangers changed their strip, if not their colours, to blue and white hoops. But the fans rebelled and in 1883 the traditional shirt was brought back, never to be changed again.

▶ There have in effect been three different stadiums at **Ibrox Park** since 1887. The first, seen on the base layer of this map from 1894, backed directly onto Copland Road.

Apparently it was Rangers' Honorary Secretary Walter Crichton who advocated the move to what was then beyond the western extremities of Glasgow.

As may be recalled, the club had formed in 1873 on Glasgow Green (*see page 33*). Their first enclosed ground had been at Burnbank, on the Great Western Road (*see page 173*), rented from the 1st Lanarkshire Rifle Volunteers in 1875. After one season they moved south of the Clyde to Kinning Park, to a ground on West Scotland Street, previously used by Clydesdale Cricket Club (*page 174*), and which Rangers turned into a rectangular ground holding up to 20,000. But Kinning Park was too constrained to develop so when the lease was due to expire in February 1887 – the site now lies under the M8 – Crichton looked even further west where space to expand was more freely available.

In fact the lease on the new site at Ibrox was only ten years. However the Ibrox area enjoyed good road and transport links – Ibrox station was nearby – and, best of all, there was a burgeoning population in and around Govan of mainly skilled workers at the shipyards. This being before the advent of professionalism, the club, through their contacts in the shipyards, would also be able to offer new players well paid work.

The first Ibrox Park, built by the firm of Fred Braby & Co., ('contractors for pavilions, stands, barricades and other requisites for football and cricket enclosures') opened in August 1887 and followed the standard plan of the

day, with a timber and corrugated iron corner pavilion (*below*) and mostly uncovered wooden stands and terracing built around a track.

But although deemed quite advanced at the time when a crowd variously estimated at 26–30,000 tried to squeeze in for the 1892 Cup Final, Queen's Park v. Celtic, it proved quite inadequate for the task. Three weeks later, during the first and only occasion on which it hosted an international v. England, a stand collapsed under the strain of a 21,000 crowd, causing, according to a report some years later, but oddly, not at the time, the death of two brothers.

At that point, the newly opened and much larger Celtic Park then became the city's leading venue.

And so with the lease on this first Ibrox expiring in 1899 and with Celtic Park now holding over 60,000, and Queen's Park clearly planning to replace their own ground with something larger, Rangers took out a lease on an adjacent site and resolved to start again from scratch.

As may be seen above, the footprint of the second Ibrox Park, marked in brown, overlapped the original ground and covered roughly twice its area, including the embankments behind the terraces.

The footprint of the current Ibrox Stadium, redeveloped from 1978 onwards, is outlined on top of the second Ibrox Park in blue.

Football Pavilion as erected for Rangers F.C.

ARCHIBALD LEITCH

▲ Having secured the lease on their new site and resolved to form a limited liability company to finance the move, Rangers were approached by an up-and-coming engineer **Archibald Leitch.**

Raised in the East End, where his father worked at the Parkhead Forge, Leitch was sufficiently enamoured of the Rangers to offer his services for free.

The extraordinary tale of Leitch's involvement and subsequent rise to become Britain's first ever specialist ground designer, may be read in another *Played in Britain* title, *Engineering Archie* (see Links). But the crucial detail was this.

Although his scheme provided for a large pavilion and grandstand on the south side, Rangers' lease on the site was for only ten years. Leitch therefore planned for 66,000 of the 80,000 capacity to be accommodated on wooden terracing supported by steel columns.

It was, in principle, a perfectly sensible strategy. Indeed Celtic had adopted a similar approach for the 1897 World Cycling Championships (see page 68), and the system was common in the United States (albeit for bench seating, known as 'bleachers').

But as history fatefully records, when the new stadium's capacity was first fully tested, for the visit of England on April 5 1902, the collapse of a small section of timber on the west terrace (*right*) led to the deaths of 26 fans and hundreds more injured.

The entire Glasgow and football community rallied round, raising over £9,000 for the victims.

Leitch himself endured a torrid grilling at the subsequent enquiry. But he somehow retained his reputation, and over the following decade, under his direction earth banking replaced the steel and wood terracing, as seen below in the early 1920s. Note that the barrel roof over the north terrace had originally covered the main stand of the first Ibrox, and that space behind the south stand, on the newly laid out Edmiston Drive, had by this time been cleared for the next phase of Leitch's work.

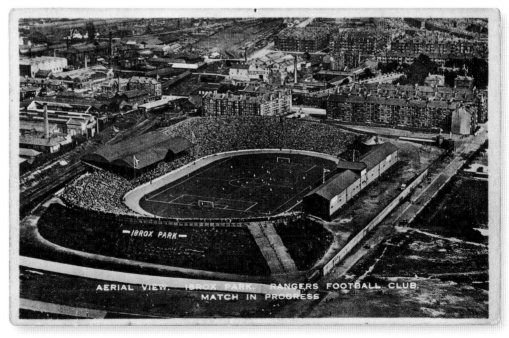

ᐱIBROX PARK

AERIAL VIEW. IBROX PARK. RANGERS FOOTBALL CLUB. MATCH IN PROGRESS

▶ By the time **Archibald Leitch** started on his next phase of work at **Ibrox Park**, in 1923, his portfolio of clients included Manchester United, Arsenal, Everton, Liverpool, both Sheffield clubs, Chelsea, Fulham, Tottenham and Aston Villa, and in Scotland, Hearts and Dundee. His firm was also about to start work on the expansion of Hampden (*see page 50*).

But although Leitch left Glasgow in 1909 and later settled in London, he was always a 'Bluenose'.

The **South Stand** at Ibrox, pictured here in an album he presented to the club shortly after its completion in 1929, may indeed be considered to be his finest work. As well it might, for at £95,000 it was then the most expensive structure ever seen at a British football ground.

Faced in Welsh red brick, it had 10,500 seats (supplied by Bennet's of Glasgow), a castellated rooftop press box, a trademark Leitch criss-cross steelwork balcony and a lower terrace for 15,496.

This, and the three other sides of terracing followed the now ubiquitous model, with concrete steppings, regulated aisles and steel barriers, patented by Leitch in the aftermath of the 1902 disaster.

The inter war years represented a golden era for Rangers.

Under the disciplinarian Bill Struth – a former stonemason and professional runner – the Light Blues won 15 League titles and the Scottish Cup on ten occasions.

Yet for all the wealth he helped generate, throughout his 34 years as manager, Struth lived in a modest flat in Copland Road. He also kept a greenhouse behind the west terrace (*right*), which, it was said, not even Celtic fans who occupied that end of Ibrox for derby matches dared to mess with.

▲ In the same way that retailers and restaurants often set up shop close to each other, so it was with greyhound tracks in **Govan and Bellahouston**. The obvious lure was affordable land and the proximity of so many industrial and shipyard workers. Even so, it seems remarkable that two such speculative ventures should have been built so close.

Shown here in the 1950s, opposite the Palace of Art was the **White City Stadium**, opened as part of a nationwide chain for greyhounds and speedway, on April 7 1928. Exactly three weeks later, on the north side of the railway, a rival company opened the greyhounds-only **Albion Stadium**.

As can be seen, this lay directly opposite **Ibrox Park** (*top right*).

Of the two tracks, the Albion was the least successful, and before it was demolished in 1960 was used by Rangers as a training ground.

White City survived until 1972, when it was cleared to make way for the M8 (More on this stadium follows on page 198.)

Also visible, above and to the left of the gas holder, is **Moore Park**, home to one of Govan's leading junior football clubs, St Anthony's ('the Ants') from 1929–91.

Today only Ibrox Park and the bowling greens in Bellahouston Park survive, while of course the distant shipyards are but a memory. There had been hope in the 1950s that orders of merchant ships might arrest the decline, but by the end of the 1990s, only one yard remained on this stretch of the river.

▶ In common with both Celtic and Queen's Park, Rangers were keen promoters of summer sports, and not only because of the income. Like his counterpart Willie Maley at Celtic, Bill Struth had been a keen athlete in his youth and was happy to maintain the tradition.

In the early years an annual favourite was the Govan Police Sports, which in 1896 started with uniformed officers competing in a two mile cycle ride. Also often seen at Ibrox were the so-called 'heavy events', staged to appeal to the area's many former Highlanders.

One obvious favourite was the 1924 Olympic hero **Eric Liddell**, himself reportedly a Rangers fan, seen here at an Ibrox meeting in the mid 1920s (*above right*).

Then during the 1938 Empire Exhibition a 50,000 crowd saw in action US pole vaulter, **Cornelius Warmerdam** (*top right*), later to break several world records.

A measure of how seriously Rangers took these meetings can be seen at the August 1935 meeting (*right*), at which a fully fledged steeplechase course was laid out, water jump and all.

After the 1960s athletics ceased at Ibrox. But in June 1980 there would be another memorable event when local lightweight **Jim Watt** outscored Howard Davis over 15 rounds (*above*), watched in the rain by 20,000 fans bellowing out 'Flower of Scotland'.

▲ Ibrox Park's weak spots were not its terracing but its giant stairways.

This is the infamous and aptly named **Stairway 13**, in the north east corner of the ground.

Two fans had already lost their lives there in September 1961 when a barrier collapsed. A further eight injuries occurred six years later, followed by 24 more in January 1969.

That should have been the signal for serious remedial work. Yet as the Old Firm derby ended on January 2 1971, the simple act of two boys bending down to pick up some items as the 80,000 crowd made its way from the ground was enough to set off a catastrophic crush in which 66 fans died and 145 were injured.

It was the worst disaster in British football history, and a wake up call not only to Rangers but the the entire football industry.

▲ In 1899 Archibald Leitch promised would-be shareholders that **Ibrox Park** would one day boast a six figure capacity, a benchmark Rangers achieved with the completion of Leitch's second phase of works in 1929.

In fact from then until the 1970s Ibrox was Britain's second largest stadium, second only to Hampden and larger even than Wembley.

Its peak, recorded only months before Leitch died, aged 73, was a crowd of 118,567 for the visit of Celtic on January 2 1939, an all-time British club record which will surely never be broken.

It is tempting, from scenes such as this, taken in October 1953 for *Picture Post* magazine, to adopt a rose-tinted view of those packed terraces. And truth be told, for

much of the time, weather willing, and for most fans, the hardier male ones at least, the experience rarely failed to transport individuals into what JB Priestley had described as 'an altogether more splendid kind of life.'

But of course it was a finely tuned balancing act, and in 1971, as in 1902, Ibrox Park found itself once again in the centre of a storm.

▶ In recent years, as the result of yet another stadium disaster, at Hillsborough in April 1989, football fans have become accustomed to seeing their beloved grounds either demolished in their entirety or at the very least transformed beyond recognition. But two decades earlier, the first football club to go through this process was Rangers.

At a national level, the most significant outcome of the 1971 Ibrox disaster was the introduction of the 1975 Safety of Sports Grounds Act. This established a system of local authority controls which, through a licensing system, sought to limit capacities to a safer level, and make clubs directly accountable for their stadium management practices.

Its effect was draconian in many instances, but it did not in itself lead to the eradication of terraces.

Rangers, however, stung by accusations of neglect and complacency, adopted a more radical plan of action.

Between August 1978 and September 1981 they cleared every inch of the north, west and east terraces, and replaced them with three all-seated stands.

Conceived partly by the Rangers manager Willie Waddell (who had seen a similar approach in Germany), but designed by the Glasgow-based Miller Partnership with Thorburn as engineers, this transformation was unlike anything any British club had ever undertaken. Not only was Ibrox physically unrecognisable – apart from Leitch's South Stand and its lower level terrace, which survived the cull – but the fans themselves found themselves having to change their mindsets completely.

The unloved running track may have gone, bringing fans closer to the touchlines than ever before.

But now the majority of them had to sit down as well.

Even worse, from a pre-1971 capacity of at least 80,000, the new Ibrox held only 44,000.

As it transpired, the £10 million cost of this redevelopment so depleted Rangers' coffers that for the next few years results, and morale, faltered so badly that attendances plummeted, to just 17,500 in 1981–82.

Seemingly bereft of atmosphere, Ibrox had become reviled, even by some of the most loyal Bluenoses.

What they did not realise then, but would do in time, was that the new Ibrox was no freak, but actually a pioneering prototype for what was yet to come.

It took boardroom takeovers in 1986 and 1988, plus a massive expenditure on the stadium before Ibrox Park felt like home again.

But throughout this difficult process the one constant remained Archibald Leitch's **South Stand**.

This status was further cemented in May 1987 when the stand became only the second at a British football ground to be listed, in its case Category B. (The first, listed at the equivalent level in England, Grade II, only three weeks earlier, was Fulham's stand at Craven Cottage, dated 1905. Its architect? Also Archibald Leitch.)

As can be seen the South Stand has since expanded upwards, with the addition of an extra tier, the 'club deck', and a new roof between 1990–94. Masterminded by architect Gareth Hutchison and engineers Blyth & Blyth, the build was immensely complex, requiring 476 piles to be sunk inside the stand's footprint, to support the extra tier without compromising the listed redbrick façade.

All this, to raise the capacity by a nett 4,000 or so seats (including extra seats added on the lower tier and in other parts of the stadium), cost £20 million.

Yet of this, £8.5 million was raised by a debenture issue that sold out in weeks, and in one section was ten times oversubscribed.

Supply and demand. The football industry was learning fast.

Watched over by John Greig (a Rangers stalwart from 1961–78), are memorial plaques to the victims of 1902, 1961 and 1971. Unveiled in 2001, the statue itself is by Andy Scott, who also crafted the famous Heavy Horse sculpture next to the M8 near Easterhouse.

Inside the Ibrox South Stand – renamed the Bill Struth Stand in September 2006 on the 50th anniversary of his death – lies a wealth of original detail; doors and leaded windows, mosaics, terrazzo flooring and marble stairs, and mahogany and oak panelling, some of which is said to have been sourced and fitted by the same craftsmen who later worked on the Queen Mary, built in the John Brown shipyard at Clydebank. In one of the several hospitality areas, called the Blue Room (*top right*), are the Senga Murray murals, depicting the history of the club (*see also page 33*).

▲ The example that Rangers set during the early 1980s in the areas of stadium design and management was, unusually in the world of football at that time, echoed by its positive embrace of heritage.

In fact long before stadium tours became commonplace elsewhere, Rangers converted the players' billiard room in the South Stand into this **Trophy Room**, on the suggestion of manager Scot Symon, who in 1959 had seen a similar room at the stadium of Real Madrid.

On the far wall is a portrait of Struth (to add to his bust in the main entrance), while the oldest piece of silverware is not related to football but is an athletics trophy awarded to one of the club's founders, Moses McNeil.

Along the corridor lies another wood panelled room, the manager's office, beautifully preserved with Struth's original desk, and a hook from which he hung a cage for his beloved canary.

Struth's influence is also seen in the dressing rooms, where still in use are pegs ordered specially by him, on which the players had to hang the bowler hats he insisted they wore, even on training days.

Always dressed immaculately himself, Struth was often to be found unwinding after matches by playing a piano in the Blue Room.

There have long been plans to create a separate museum for the club, as at Liverpool, Arsenal and Manchester United. But in a very real sense these rooms in the South Stand are the true repositories of Rangers' history.

▲ Since the sweeping changes of the early 1980s, **Ibrox Stadium** (note, no longer Ibrox Park), has continued to develop.

Viewed from the Bill Struth Stand, to the left is the Broomloan Stand, ahead is the Govan Stand, and to the right the Copland Stand, each built on the 'goalpost' system with horizontal roof trusses supported on corner columns.

Comparing this with the view on page 106 it can be seen that the open corners – disliked by all except the groundsman, who appreciated the extra ventilation – have been infilled. This measure, together with lowering the pitch, the addition of the Club Deck to the South Stand and the seating of its enclosure (*right*) have nudged the capacity up to 50,411.

Another change has seen the original multi-coloured seats replaced by more refined blue ones.

Note that the pitch perimeter track has also had a blue makeover.

▲ The changing horizons of Govan, as seen from the south in 2009.

On the distant north bank of the Clyde stands the silvery shell of Sir Norman Foster's 'Armadillo' (part of the Scottish Exhibition and Conference Centre), and on the south bank, Richard Horden's Glasgow Tower, next to the bulbous Science Centre, and the steel and glass block of BBC Scotland.

Not so easy to see from these heights are the changes being effected at street level, where new housing and light industrial units are now replacing the tenements and shipyards of old Govan.

In the midst of this evolving scene, **Ibrox Stadium** itself also stands on the cusp of change.

Were the existing structures to be tweaked further the capacity could rise to perhaps 57,000. But in 2008 it emerged that by redeveloping the stadium again, leaving only Leitch's redbrick façade in place, they could create a fourth Ibrox, holding 70,000 seats, while also redeveloping the areas immediately around the stadium.

Whether these plans will ever be carried out depends greatly on the club's ability to ride out its current financial crisis, and on the wider economy as a whole.

But whichever form Ibrox may or may not take, just as Celtic Park now finds itself at the heart of a new East End, clearly Rangers have a key role to play in the regeneration of Govan. They arrived here in 1887, just as the shipyards were putting Govan on the map. Now it is Rangers who fly the flag.

Chapter Seven

Jordanhill and Anniesland

As Glasgow's tentacles extended westward during the late 19th century, its new residents were quick to set up sports clubs on any available patch of land. During the period 1890–1930, between Hillhead (absorbed into Glasgow in 1891) and Scotstounhill (1926), 15 bowling clubs formed. Nine of these survive, including Jordanhill, which, despite its name is actually in Broomhill. Yet many of these clubs are barely noticed amidst all the other sports grounds in the Jordanhill and Anniesland area.

When seeking to understand why sporting clusters form, the answer often touches on that favourite mantra of estate agents, 'location, location, location'.

But in the case of Jordanhill and Anniesland we must add a further dimension, which is, to borrow a phrase from that noted ex-Fettes pupil, Tony Blair, 'education, education, education'.

As shown opposite, within the tongue of land bound by the Great Western Road, Anniesland Road, Southbrae Drive and Crow Road, are sports grounds relating to five educational institutions, with a further four close by.

In some cases parts or all of the grounds belong not to the schools themselves but to clubs set up by former pupils; for example the Glasgow Academicals, for alumni of Glasgow Academy. Yet they are also used by pupils, and, in some cases, such as Hillhead, by members of the general public.

For non-Glaswegians and readers educated in the state sector, this distinction between the institution, its former pupils' club, and the practices of a

standard private sports club, can be confusing, as is also the fact that certain grounds in this cluster have been used at various times by different institutions.

But complex though the area's sporting history may be, the explanation for how this cluster came about is relatively simple.

Whereas in the mid 19th century Glasgow expanded to the north, south, east and southwest, on the north west side of the city, apart from shipyards and industries springing up along the banks of the Clyde, from Whiteinch up to Yoker, there were still large areas of land ripe for development.

Here, the landscape was pockmarked by an array of small mines, claypits and brickfields. On the Jordanhill Estate, for example, five different seams of coal and ironstone were worked up towards Temple, north of Anniesland Toll.

Once these resources became exhausted, by the 1880s, however, this opened the way for the West End to extend ever further.

Much of the land, as many a housebuilder (and subsequent homeowner) was to discover,

suffered from inevitable subsidence. But for the elite schools of the West End, and by 1900 for the University, this made the area perfectly suited for the laying out of sports grounds.

As will be noted, the sporting colonisation of Jordanhill and Anniesland gained momentum after the First World War, when not only schools but a number of companies also laid out grounds, including the shipbuilders Barclay Curle (based at Whiteinch), Yarrow (at Scotstoun), and the optical firm Barr & Stroud (at Anniesland, whose ground at Netherton is now a David Lloyd club).

Since the 1970s several of these grounds have been built over, as companies have closed or moved on, and, more controversially, as educational institutions and independent clubs have sold up parcels of land to property developers, a process which continues today. Even so, the area remains remarkably well endowed and is well worth a circular walk for anyone with a penchant for grandstands and pavilions, old and new.

▲ Looking east, with the Clyde top right and the Great Western Road top left, this 2006 view shows the **Jordanhill and Anniesland** cluster of sports venues. Note: BC=Bowling Club; TC=Tennis Club, SC=Sports or Squash Club.

1. **Western TC&SC** (1924-50s)
2. **Hughenden** Hillhead SC (1924-)
3. **Kelvinside TC** Beaconsfield Rd (c.1890s-c.1969) now hospital
4. **Balgray Playing Fields, Kelvinside Academy** (1901-)
5. **Bingham's Pond** see page 159
6. **Whittinghame TC** (up to 1939)
7. **Westerlands** University of Glasgow (1912-96)

8. **Old Anniesland** Glasgow Academy (1883-c.1902), Glasgow University (1902-12) **Glasgow High School** (1919-)
9. **New Anniesland, Glasgow Academy** (c.1905-)
10. **Anniesland BC** (1977-), ex City Bakeries (1926), Drysdale Pumps (1960s), Weirs (1970s)
11. **Yarrow Recreation BC** (1945-) ex Rothley Club for Castlebank Laundry Co. (1925-45)
12. **Knightswood School** (1958-)
13. **Glasgow Academy School Ground** (1919-)
14. **Glasgow Academy, Windyedge** (1958-)
15. **Glasgow Academy Lower Windyedge** (2005-) former Laurel Bank School grounds

16. **Jordanhill School sports hall** (2005-) ex Laurel Park School (1998-)
17. ex **Laurel Park** playing fields
18. **Univ of Strathclyde, Jordanhill Campus,** former Jordanhill College (1919-92)
19. **David Stow Building** (1919-)
20. **Univ of Strathclyde** playing fields, ex Jordanhill College
21. **Jordanhill School** (1921-)
22. **Woodend BC & TC** (1909-)
23. ex **Barclay Curle sportsground**, (c.1920-68), now Burlington Gate housing, Skaterigg Drive
24. **Jordanhill BC** (1899-)

25. **Broomhill TC & TC** (1922-)
26. ex **Broomhill BC pavilion** (1879-1966) / **Whiteinch BC** (1876-1966) Central Avenue
27. **Partick Curling Club**, Victoria Park (1894-) see page 162
28. **St Thomas Aquinas School** (1958, rebuilt 2003-)
29. **Victoria Park public greens** (1908-)
30. **Whiteinch Swimming Baths** (1926-98) see page 213
31. **Victoria Park BC** (1903-)
32. **Scotstoun Leisure Centre** (1995-) and **National Badminton Centre** (2003-)
33. **Scotstoun Stadium** (c.1907, rebuilt 2008-09)

▶ This finely proportioned pavilion, one of several built in the area during the 1920s, was at **Westerlands**, the playing fields of the **University of Glasgow Athletic Club** on **Ascot Avenue**.

Designed by James Honeyman at a cost of £15,000, it was opened in May 1925, and stood east of Anniesland Station.

Westerlands was aptly named, as the university had always looked west when seeking to expand.

As noted in Chapter One, within the original university buildings on the High Street there had been an enclosed green for sport and other outdoor events (*see page 12*).

There is evidence of cricket being played by students in the 1780s, and of a club forming briefly in the 1830s. A rugby team then formed in the late 1860s, followed by a football team in 1877. Indeed the Glasgow University football club has been a regular entrant to the Scottish Cup ever since, and in 1974 progressed as far as the first round proper, before losing to Second Division Albion Rovers in a replay at Westerlands.

One graduate of the University XI from the Westerlands days was dentistry student Jim Craig, a member of Celtic's 'Lisbon Lions' in 1967.

Westerlands was one of several sports grounds used by the Athletic Club since its inception in 1881.

Following the university's move to Gilmorehill in 1870, playing fields west of the Gilbert Scott Building, off Byres Road were used.

These proved too limited for the growing numbers of students taking up sport, however, and so grounds at both Anniesland (*see page 118*) and at Bankhead, an unknown location said to be near Scotstounhill, were used during the period 1904–12.

Westerlands appears to have superceded both these grounds in 1912, but construction of its pavilion was delayed by the war. This did have one positive outcome. By the time funds had been raised, female students were now admitted to the Athletic Club, so that the new pavilion was almost certainly the first to cater for their needs (the university having first admitted women in 1903).

Various sports were played there, football, rugby and lacrosse included. But after a red blaes track costing £8,000 was inaugurated in April 1961 (replacing a reportedly uneven grass track), Westerlands became best known for athletics.

One Glasgow University athlete to shine on its track during these years was former Hillhead pupil **Menzies Campbell** – seen above right, breasting the tape at Westerlands – and later to run in the 1964 Olympics. That same year Campbell broke the British

100m record (a record he held until 1974), and was later described as 'the fastest white man on the planet'. Today he is of course better known as a prominent MP.

Westerlands was sold for housing in the 1990s and replaced by the Garscube sports complex. Also sold for housing at that time was the university's other sports ground at Garscadden (*see page 22*).

▲ Another 1920s pavilion of note is that of the **Hillhead Sports Club** at **Hughenden**, on the south side of the Great Western Road.

Hillhead is a multi-sport club, set up in 1902 by former pupils of Hillhead High School and based originally at Scotstoun (*see page 122*). Unusually the club had a ladies cricket team before a men's XI was formed.

In common with several West End schools a Hillhead High School War Memorial Trust was founded shortly after the First World War, both to honour the 180 former pupils killed in action and to raise the £16,000 needed to purchase and develop the 12½ acre ground.

Inaugurated in May 1924, Hughenden had pitches for rugby, hockey and cricket, six tennis

courts, and this pavilion, designed by W Hunter McNab, who later designed a war memorial for Hillhead School in Oakfield Avenue.

Externally faced in brick and rough cast, the pavilion's finest asset is this first floor function room, with its timber beamed roof, two war memorials on the far wall, and views over the main rugby pitch to the south.

Play in progress at Hughenden in the match between Hillhead High School F.P. and Glasgow Academicals. Hillhead's new stand, seen on the right, was filled to capacity.

▲ Such a success was the **Hillhead High School Former Pupils' Rugby Football Club**, 'the Hills' for short, that in 1934 private loans were secured for the erection of a grandstand on the south side of the rugby pitch at **Hughenden**.

In contrast to the traditional design of the pavilion built ten years earlier (*see previous page*), the resulting structure was, for its time, at the cutting edge of stand technology.

By the 1930s reinforced concrete was, it is true, already commonplace, and in the context of sport had been employed in the construction of a number of stands.

The football ground designer Archibald Leitch, for example, who had also designed Glasgow's first ever reinforced concrete building – the Sentinel Works in Jessie Street, Polmadie, in 1905 (now listed Category A) – had used it to form the base structure and seating deck of several stands, starting at Anfield, Liverpool, in 1906 (still extant, albeit much altered).

The difference with Hughenden's stand was that the application of reinforced concrete had been extended to create a cantilevered roof. That is, the roof had no supporting columns to obstruct views from the stand's single deck of nine rows and 800 seats.

In France, early forms of this type of stand (which of course is now commonplace) had appeared

at racecourses from around 1906 onwards, arriving in Britain only in 1927; first, tentatively at Epsom, but more daringly in 1929 at Northolt Racecourse in London.

Other, more modest, examples were at sports grounds in Braintree, Essex, and Finchley, London, in 1930 (the latter still extant, but again with later additions).

(*Played in Britain* will return to these stands in its forthcoming study, *Played in London*, in 2011.)

Apart from being photographed by the *Glasgow Herald*, as seen here on its opening day on September 15 1934, Hughenden's concrete stand invited no press comment at the time, not even in technical journals.

Nor were its designers especially lauded. As far as we know, this was the first and only stand ever designed by FA MacDonald, a local firm of consulting engineers who, not surprisingly, appeared to specialise in reinforced concrete.

Amongst their other works, only two others were for recreational use, both in Fife: a music pavilion at Pittencrieff Park, Dunfermline, also in 1934 (with architect John

Fraser and still in use today), and an open air swimming pool at Burntisland, opened in 1936 but closed in 1977.

At the end of the Hughenden stand's first season, the Hills were joint champions of the unofficial Scottish rugby championship, a run of success that was renewed in the 1950s, resulting in the extension of the stand with wings at both ends, apparently seamlessly, in 1956.

By this time Hughenden could claim something of a hallowed status in Glasgow rugby circles, being the breeding ground for a string of international players and hosting visits from the All Blacks, Fiji and Tonga.

As such it appeared the obvious setting for Glasgow's first foray into professional rugby in 1999, in the form of the Glasgow Warriors.

But as happened in so many other amateur rugby strongholds around Britain, the effort of turning what was essentially a small-time community ground in a middle class suburb, into a 5,000 capacity venue for professional sport, cost the host club dearly, and by the time the Warriors moved on to Partick Thistle's more advanced stadium at Firhill in 2005 (see page 189), the Hillhead High School War Memorial Trust had extended its borrowings to the limit.

Having already opened its membership to the wider public in 1969 – the first of the area's former pupils' clubs to do so – and with no other sources of funding on offer, Hillhead's response was to do what dozens, if not hundreds of other similarly sized private sports clubs around Britain have done in similar circumstances. They negotiated the sale of a strip of their main rugby pitch to a housing developer.

West of Scotland Cricket Club in Partick did the same at Hamilton

Crescent in the 1990s, selling surplus land for housing in order to pay off debts (see page 177).

Nevertheless Hillhead's plan caused great unease. Hughenden sits on the edge, though is not part of, the Glasgow West Conservation Area, and apart from the addition of floodlights for the rugby pitch (opposite), had barely developed since the 1950s. And although the development in question did not ultimately proceed, at the time of going to press a similar plan with another developer was expected to go ahead in 2011 or 2012.

Regrettably, this will mean the loss of the rugby stand, which the club argues is, in any case, surplus to its needs, now that the main rugby team, Hillhead-Jordanhill (formed by a merger in 1988), attracts too few spectators to merit such a large stand.

The club argues further that the funds generated from the housing will allow them to lay an artificial pitch on the remainder of the main rugby pitch, so that hockey can return to Hughenden after a long gap, and will fund improvements for rugby on the north side of the site, where the 'Hills' will continue to run four senior men's teams, a women's team, and various youth programmes (which in 2009 were attracting 200 children a week).

Other activities such as the tennis and cricket sections, and the use of the ground for training by the Glasgow Mid Argyll Shinty Club (formed in 1923), would also be able to continue.

No-one can pretend that the situation is ideal. But it is common, because for most clubs of Hillhead's rank – neither big enough to attract major backers, but with little recourse to public funds – land is the only asset they have left to exploit.

▲ Across the Great Western Road from Hughenden lies the **Balgray Playing Fields** of another local school, **Kelvinside Academy**.

Founded in 1878 on Kirklee Road, in common with other private schools Kelvinside soon discovered that the scholars of the day craved sport, and so in 1884 they rented an adjacent field.

But it was not enough and in 1901 they rented Balgray Farm, half a mile north.

In lieu of a pavilion the boys changed in the boat house of Bingham's Pond, directly opposite on the south side of the Great Western Road (see page 159), until the school was able to buy

and re-erect a building that had served as the press pavilion for the 1901 International Exhibition.

As at Hillhead, heavy losses amongst members of the Kelvinside Academicals club (for former pupils) during the First World War precipitated the formation of a War Memorial Trust, and in 1922 this helped fund Balgray's purchase and the 500 seat stand we see today.

By the Spring of 2010, that same stand will have received a £70,000 makeover, and be joined on its east side by a smart new pavilion costing just under £1 million designed by the Glasgow sports specialists, the Miller Partnership.

▲ Anyone coming across this creaking, though charming timber stand, dating from 1958, on the northern side of **New Anniesland**, backing onto Helensburgh Drive, might be forgiven for thinking this to be a sporting backwater. They might also ask why there is an old stand at New Anniesland, whereas the most modern stand in the area (*see opposite*), is on the adjacent ground, which is known as Old Anniesland.

Unravelling the complex history of these adjoining grounds, and of the various clubs to have played at them, is no easy task. But the story starts with **Glasgow Academy**, a school opened on Elmbank Street in the city centre in 1847.

In 1866 the Academy became the first West of Scotland school to add sport to its curriculum, having enclosed an 18 acre ground at Burnbank (*see page 173*). Its annual sports day, first held in May 1868, has been held every year since, without a single break.

From Burnbank (subsequently rented by Rangers FC for season 1875-76), the school laid out a new sports ground in North Kelvinside, before heading out further west to Anniesland in 1883.

Meanwhile, its former pupils' rugby team, the **Academicals**, or 'Accies', helped found the Scottish Rugby Union at a meeting at the school in 1873. John Arthur, whose cap is seen on page six, played a key role in this.

The Academy's next move came in 1902, when for £10,683 it puchased farmland next door. This site therefore became known as New Anniesland, while their former ground, now 'Old Anniesland', was taken over by the University.

Today the original 1908 pavilion at New Anniesland is partly hidden behind later extensions (*see page 179*), and there are no traces left of the wooden terracing and stands that hosted a 10,000 crowd, a record then for Scottish club rugby, for the visit of Heriots, from Edinburgh, in 1922. The Accies were at that time rampant, described by *The Times* 'as easily the best club in the British Isles'.

▲ While the Accies made waves at New Anniesland, after serving as one of the sports grounds used by the University, **Old Anniesland** was purchased in 1919 by yet another West End educational institution, **Glasgow High School**, once again through the medium of a war memorial trust, set up in the aftermath of the First World War.

For its new pavilion the school organised a design competition – for alumni only – won in 1924 by a young war veteran, Alexander Cullen. Opened the year after, the building was described by the competition's assessor, John Keppie, a former partner of Charles Rennie Mackintosh, as 'one of the best clubhouses in Scotland'.

Cullen went on to design two other sports buildings, at Selkirk RFC in 1926 and Motherwell FC in 1929 (neither extant).

Seen here in 2009, the Old Anniesland pavilion now finds itself adjoined by the new buildings of the Glasgow High School itself, constructed from 1976 onwards after the school had moved from its earlier headquarters in Elmbank Street. And if that location rings a bell, it is because, just as Old Anniesland had originally belonged to Glasgow Academy, so too had the buildings on Elmbank Street, before the High School took them over in 1878.

But the story becomes even more entangled when we consider the fate of the school's respective rugby teams. As the amateur game became ever harder to sustain during the late 20th century, some tough decisions had to be made.

First, in 1982, Glasgow High amalgamated with their neighbours Kelvinside to form Glasgow HK.

Then, following the sanctioning of professionalism in 1995 and the reorganisation of rugby union all over Britain, Glasgow HK merged with the Accies, to form the **Glasgow Hawks**. The W in Hawks was supposed to represent a third party to the merger, the West of Scotland club. But even though West finally opted to remain independent, the name Hawks was deemed too good to drop.

▲ The shock of the new at **Old Anniesland**, where the pavilion (*left*) has been joined by a modern high-flier. Opened in 2000, the **Jimmy Ireland Stand** was designed by the Glasgow-based Holmes Partnership and cost £1.3million.

Ireland, a former stalwart of the Glasgow High XV, a referee and one time president of the Scottish Rugby Union, had, before his death in 1998, been the last surviving member of Scotland's first Grand Slam side of 1925.

The stand that bears his name is as much an embodiment of the spirit of modern club rugby as Ireland had been in his day. With 738 seats, it incorporates a gym and various suites, not only for match days but also for use by the High School and corporate clients.

Rugby is not the only sport associated with New Anniesland.

In its early years there were three curling ponds (*see Chapter Ten*). Hockey and lacrosse internationals were staged during the 1950s, and the High School Club continues to run sections for cricket and hockey.

In June 2009 the ground also played host to the Glasgow Celtic Society's Shinty Cup Final.

▲ In an area so clearly identified with education, it is appropriate that one of its most prominent historic buildings should be one dedicated to teacher training.

This is the **David Stow Building, Jordanhill**, the last commission carried out by David Barclay of H & D Barclay architects, who, since 1875, had designed over 20 schools in Glasgow alone, including Glasgow Academy's Kelvinbridge buildings in 1877.

Completed two years after Barclay's death in 1917, the **Glasgow Provincial College for the Training of Teachers** was built in the grounds of Jordanhill House, which, since 1800, had been the seat of the Smith family. Their wealth had derived from trade with the West Indies, but amongst the family's more recent members had been Jane Smith, founder of the first school in Jordanhill in 1853, set up for the children of local miners, and James Smith, a founder member of the Royal Clyde Yacht Club and a president of the Andersonian University, forerunner of the University of Strathclyde.

David Stow, after whom the college building was later named, had himself been an enlightened pioneer of teacher training, setting up the first purpose-built college in Europe, at Dundas Vale in Cowcaddens, in 1837.

Also completed within the former Jordanhill Estate in 1921, by architects Honeyman & Keppie, and sharing the playing fields seen here with the College, was Jordanhill School, established as a 'demonstration school' for college trainees and still going strong today.

Both the school and David Stow Building are Category B listed.

However, following Jordanhill College's merger with – perhaps appropriately given the links with the Smith family – the University of Strathclyde in 1992, in 2007 it was agreed that the Faculty of Education would be relocated to a new city centre campus, and that the David Stow Building be sold for conversion into flats.

This will at least preserve the building's twin copper towers that have become so familiar to generations of students and pupils who have played on the Jordanhill pitches, while those same pitches will remain as open space, having been designated as of Special Landscape Importance in the Glasgow City Plan of 2003.

▲ Why, apart from the obvious architectural qualities of the David Stow Building, devote so much attention to **Jordanhill College** in a book on sporting heritage?

For the simple reason that a good many readers will no doubt harbour memories of being cajoled into a freezing swimming pool, or ordered to do an extra lap around the school playing fields, or worse, extra press ups on an unforgiving blaes pitch, by a graduate of Jordanhill College.

For while it is true that many a Glasgow teacher had Jordanhill as his or her alma mater – the College reached its zenith during the 1970s with some 3,500 full time students – when it came to the training of that special breed of male PE instructors, Jordanhill was *the* centre for the whole of Scotland.

This was a process that began in earnest in 1931, with the setting up within Jordanhill of the **Scottish School of Physical Education**.

Among the School's many alumni of note from the world of football are two former managers

of the Scottish national team, Craig Brown and Andy Roxburgh, who in 1994 become the Technical Director of UEFA, and Archie MacPherson, who rose to become a primary school headmaster before starting a career in broadcasting.

Seen here are two of the sports training facilities built within the Jordanhill Campus. Both were designed by Keppie, Henderson & Partners, and opened by the Queen and Prince Philip in July 1963.

The sports hall, with its elegant and airy floating roof, was built to replace the original gymnasium (which made way for the unloved Henry Wood Building, also by Keppie, Henderson & Partners, seen towering behind the David Stow Building opposite).

Neither the sports hall nor the swimming pool were destined to remain in service for long – like so many sports buildings of the 1960s having been superceded by modern trends and by the need for greater energy efficiency – and were demolished in 2003 and 2004 respectively to make

way for housing. Much of the rest of the site, the Henry Wood Building included, is scheduled to meet the same fate in the near future, leaving only the David Stow Building and the former playing fields as a reminder of a training college whose graduates, for better or worse, touched the lives of so many Scots throughout the 20th century.

▶ Just south of Jordanhill College, across the railway from Jordanhill to Clydebank, lies Glasgow's best known athletics venue, the **Scotstoun Stadium**.

Seen here in 1955, the site was originally laid out as the **Scotstoun Showgrounds** by the Glasgow Agricultural Society, some sources claim as early as 1860, when it staged the National Stallion Show.

Such showgrounds were common during the late 19th century, offering farmers and breeders a platform for parading their best livestock, and for city folk a chance to get back in touch with their rural roots. In fact monthly gatherings of the Clydesdale Horse Society continued at Scotstoun until the 1950s, and it is said that the stables there (parts of which can still be seen) offered a rich, if illicit source of manure for local gardeners and allotment holders!

Sporting activities appear to have started at Scotstoun in around 1902, when it became the first ground of the Hillhead High School's Former Pupils Club.

In March 1905 it was the start and endpoint of Scotland's National Cross Country Championships, the first of many. Watched by a crowd of 2,000 the runners completed four laps of a course which took in Anniesland. Two years later it also hosted the 5th International Cross Country Championships.

In 1914 crowds were treated to an air display by Bentfield C Hucks, 'the first English airman to fly upside down' in his Bleriot monoplane.

Then in 1915 a running track was laid, followed in the 1920s by the stand seen here, backing onto Danes Drive. (This replaced an earlier stand built on the north side, which itself backed onto the railway line, where a special halt

was provided to bring in livestock.)

Since then Scotstoun has staged many sports, but is most identified with the **Victoria Park Amateur Athletic Club**.

Formed in 1930, during the late 1940s and 1950s 'Vicky Park' was Scotland's leading athletic club, nurturing a succession of international performers. Among them were the high jumper, Alan Paterson, who represented Great Britain in the 1948 and 1952 Olympics; Andy Forbes, silver medallist in the 10,000m at the 1950 Commonwealth Games, and in the 1960s, Hugh Barrow, who broke the mile record for a 16 year old, before serving for many years as the club president.

Another favourite was the 'Balfron Bullet', Mike Hildrey, who went on to become an ace reporter for the *Glasgow Evening Times*.

In winter, club members were often to be seen after training runs soaking in the slipper baths at the nearby Whiteinch Baths while their kit dried off.

Today Vicky Park remains a leading club, with some 400 members. But their surroundings have changed considerably.

In 1996 Scotstoun's redgra track was replaced by a striking blue, eight lane 400m synthetic track, while the stand was reclad and modernised (*above*).

But as can be seen opposite, that was only the start.

Re-opened by Princess Anne in January 2010, the new **Scotstoun Stadium** is now arguably Scotland's leading athletics venue.

Designed by Glasgow City Council's in-house Civic Design team and completed at a cost of nearly £18 million (£4m of which came from sportscotland), the stadium has two new stands.

Curved around the jumping areas (*left*), the North Stand seats 1,260, covered by a tent-like, tensile roof made from PVC membrane.

Countering this, the more linear South Stand has 3,523 seats, and also houses a 100m indoor warm-up track, fitness suites, offices, hospitality lounges and all the media facilities that are nowadays required to stage regional and national meetings.

One aim is that Scotstoun will, as a result, attract athletes training in advance of the 2012 Olympics, and for it to serve in a similar role during the 2014 Commonwealth Games. But on a day to day basis it will remain the home of Victoria Park (which in 2007 merged with the City of Glasgow Athletic Club), and will also form a base for the Glasgow Warriors rugby club (who play their first team fixtures at Firhill, *see page 189*).

The stadium and its adjoining rugby pitches, however, form only the latest addition to Scotstoun.

Seen at the east end of the track, is the **Scotstoun Leisure Centre**, opened in 1995, with sports halls, gyms and a 25m swimming pool.

Alongside this are three tennis courts, four 5-a-sides pitches and one full size synthetic pitch, and the building seen on the right, the **National Badminton Centre**. This opened in 2003 and in 2007 was the venue for the World Team Badminton Championships.

Again, all these facilities were designed by the Civic Design team.

Before the stadium re-opened, Scotstoun was already the busiest of Glasgow City Council's 22 sports centres, serving 47 different clubs and used by 740,000 people in 2008.

If to that figure we add all the other adults, students and schoolchildren who, from week to week, frequent Jordanhill and Anniesland's private sports clubs and grounds, not even counting spectators it must surely approach a million people a year, a formidable concentration in an area with not one professional sports venue in its midst.

Chapter Eight

Golf

Heritage is valued highly by golfers, their clubhouses typically displaying cases full of medals, trophies, old clubs and even battered balls. This is the Duff Medal, dating from 1900, on display at Glasgow Golf Club's home at Killermont House. The motto seen here, 'Far and Sure', was that of a humble Edinburgh cobbler and champion golfer who helped the future James II beat two English noblemen at Leith in 1681. It has since been adopted by Glasgow Golf Club and several others in Scotland and the USA.

Having looked at sporting heritage in five specific areas of Glasgow in previous chapters, we begin this next section of the book – focusing on individual sports and recreations – with that most Scottish of games, golf.

Scottish in character and practice, that is, for amongst historians there continues to rage a debate over claims that golf might actually have originated in the Netherlands. Or France even.

What cannot be denied however is that the rules of golf as we know it today, and the physical characteristics of its courses, are most definitely Scottish in origin.

The first recorded reference to the game in Scotland appeared in 1457, when James II issued a ban on both 'ye futbawe and ye golf'. The success of this may be judged by the fact that it had to be repeated twice before, in 1502, its effect was compromised when James IV took up the game.

Glasgow University seemed well disposed too. In an order of 1577 that required all students to conduct themselves in Latin, to rise every morning at five and to desist from playing cards, dice and billiards, golf was exempted.

What exactly was meant at this time by the term 'golf' is not clear. There appears to have been a 'short' game in which targets such as trees or doors were used. For example, in 1589 the Glasgow Kirk Session banned it being played 'in the High or Blackfriars Yard'.

But there was also a long game played on farm land during the winter when the grass was short.

In Glasgow, Golf Hill, in what is now Dennistoun, may well have been a favoured spot, as too was Glasgow Green.

But it was in the east that the modern game truly evolved.

As noted previously, the first club formed in Edinburgh in 1744. This was followed ten years later by a second at St Andrews.

Glasgow's earliest known club then formed on Glasgow Green in 1787 (see page 28).

But as James Denholm wrote in 1804 (see Links), despite golf's popularity in Glasgow it was 'not so nearly general' as in Edinburgh, owing, he thought 'to want of a proper place'.

This 'want' held back the game in Glasgow for several decades, until from 1870 onwards, the expansion of the city's boundaries finally saw land set aside specifically for recreation.

Thus the Glasgow Golf Club was able to reform at Queen's Park in 1870, before moving to Alexandra Park four years later.

In fact so popular was this move that by 1888 the club had to limit its membership, a measure which led to the formation that year of a second club, Cathkin Braes.

From then onwards, as the following pages relate, golf took off so successfully that, according to statistics in 2008, nowhere else in Scotland, not even Fife, can claim to have such a concentration of both courses and players.

Greater Glasgow, the figures show, has 66 private clubs, 14 municipal and four commercially operated courses, all within a ten mile radius of the city centre,

As the family and friends of any golfer will attest, and as the map overleaf shows, there is no avoiding golf in Glasgow. Quite literally, the city is surrounded.

One of the best sources on early golf in Scotland is the 1721 poem *Glotta* (or 'Clyde'), written by the Belfast-born James Arbuckle whilst he was studying Divinity at Glasgow University. In this extract Arbuckle comes across golfers on Glasgow Green; their wayward strokes and curses suggesting that not that much has changed in nearly two hundred years.

◀ George Aikman's unsparing etching of **Alexandra Park**, reproduced in an 1893 book, *A Round of Links: Views of the Golf Greens of Scotland*, shows why **Glasgow Golf Club** were so keen to find a more tranquil setting (which they managed in 1895 by moving to Blackhill). Yet how many of those who could afford the four guinea entry fee, plus one guinea annual membership – higher than any other Glasgow club – derived their wealth from the industries that cast such a pall over the park?

And how many would have imagined that a century later, the Blochairn Steel Works would be but a distant memory, while the golf course lived on?

Shifting trends have also forced change on **Renfrew Golf Club** (*left*), and not only on their style of fashion. Founded in 1894, the club's original course on Haining Road, designed by James Braid, had to be relaid when the George V Dock was constructed during the 1920s. The course was then sold for housing in the early 1970s, to be replaced by their current berth on the Blythswood Estate.

Since this view of the new course was taken in 1977 the cranes at Rothesay Dock have also come down.

Thus industries come and go. But the centuries old game of golf seems never to run out of steam.

In Winter too, when hoary Frosts o'erspread,
The verdant Turf, and naked lay the Mead,
The vig'rous Youth commence the sportive War,
And arm'd with Lead, their jointed Clubs prepare
The Timber Curve to Leathern Orbs apply,
Compact, Elastic, to pervade the Sky:
These to the distant Hole direct they drive,
They claim the Stakes who thither first arrive.
Intent his Ball the eager Gamester eyes,
His Muscles strains, and various Postures tries,
Th' impelling Blow to strike with greater Force,
And shape the motive Orb's projectile Course.
If with due Strength the weighty Engine fall,
Discharg'd obliquely, and impinge the Ball,
It winding mounts a lot, and sings in Air,
And wond'ring Crowds the Gamester's Skill declare.
But when some luckless wayward Stroke descends,
Whose Force the Ball in running quickly spends,
The Foes triumph, the Club is curs'd in vain;
Spectators scoff, and ev'n Allies complain.
Thus still Success is follow'd with Applause,
But ah! how few espouse a vanquish'd Cause!

▲ Glasgow born Colin Montgomerie tees off in September 2009 to mark the rebirth of one of the city's oldest golf courses at **Ruchill Park**.

Opened in 1892 between the Forth & Clyde Canal and a railway line linking Possilpark and Maryhill Barracks, Ruchill was Glasgow's second municipal course after Alexandra Park, and was best known for its 'Miley', a mile long spine in its centre formed by two railway tunnels and two cuttings.

After years of neglect and vandalism Ruchill closed in 1997, but following sustained campaigning led by a local accountant, Alec Hunter, the course was relaid and the tunnels infilled in a £2.5m joint scheme between Glasgow City Council, sportscotland, Scottish Enterprise and the Land Fill Tax Credit Scheme.

In its new guise, designed with input from Montgomerie, Ruchill has been restyled as a Community Golf Facility, acting also as a training centre for greenkeepers and club managers. As with all six of the city's public courses, access to it is free for all under 18 year olds.

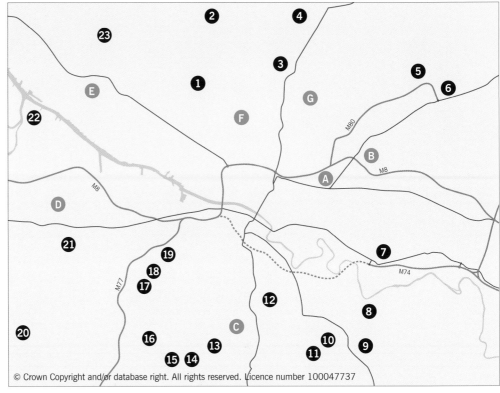

▲ This map shows the location of 30 **public and private golf courses** currently active in the immediate Glasgow area. In 1885 there were around 160 golf clubs in Britain, but only one in Glasgow. By 1910 there were 98 in the city (albeit several sharing the same courses).

The ribbon pattern observed reflects not only the urban spread of Glasgow but also the locations where affordable and, in the days before widespread car ownership, accessible land was available.

Several more clubs associated with Glasgow lie beyond this map; for example Bonnyton, nine miles south east of the city, opened in 1922, and in 1957 purchased by Jewish golfers who had been denied entry to Glasgow clubs.

Private clubs (foundation year):
1. **Glasgow Golf Club** (1787, current course 1904)
2. **Douglas Park** (1897)
3. **Bishopbriggs** (1906)
4. **Cawder** (1933)
5. **Lenzie** (1889)
6. **Crow Wood** (1925)
7. **Sandyhills** (1905)
8. **Cambuslang** (1892)
9. **Kirkhill** (1910)
10. **Blairbeth** (1910, current course 1956)
11. **Cathkin Braes** (1888)
12. **King's Park*** (1934)
13. **Williamwood** (1906, current course 1926)
14. **Cathcart Castle** (1895, current course 1925)
15. **Whitecraigs** (1905)
16. **Rouken Glen** (1926)
17. **Cowglen** (1906)
18. **Pollok** (1892)
19. **Haggs Castle** (1910)
20. **Fereneze** (1904)
21. **Ralston** (1904)
22. **Renfrew** (1900, current course 1977)
23. **Bearsden** (1891)

Public courses (opening):
A. **Alexandra Park*** (1874)
B. **Lethamhill** (c.1900)
C. **Linn Park** (1919, but 1898 as private course)
D. **Barshaw Park** (1925)
E. **Knightswood*** (c.1925)
F. **Ruchill Park** (1892–1997, re-opened 2009)
G. **Littlehill** (1923)

* nine hole course

▲ For the majority of clubs formed in the late 19th and early 20th centuries, in Glasgow as in the rest of Britain, the responsibility and financial risk of leasing, laying out and maintaining large tracts of land represented a considerable challenge, even for their middle class members. And yet such was golf's extraordinary popularity that surprisingly few clubs would fail in the attempt.

An indication of the caution shown in those early days are the clubhouses of **Ralston Golf Club** (*top left*), and **Fereneze Golf Club** (*top right*), both formed in 1904.

Ralston had started out life five years earlier as the Bellahouston Golf Club, playing on the public course at Bellahouston Park. But as this course became increasingly crowded, members resolved at a meeting at the Masonic Hall in Ibrox to form a private club.

As far as their new landlord was concerned, a golf club made for an ideal tenant. Sir Charles Cayzer of Ralston Hall (built in 1810) was a Tory MP and the owner of a profitable shipping line. He hardly needed to farm the estate, and if the golf club failed the course could easily be returned to nature.

But the club did not fail, and with a membership of 385 men, 135 ladies and 25 juniors, with 38 more on a waiting list, in 1914 Cayzer rented the club his now redundant **stable block** (*above left*), where the club has remained since.

Indeed in the interim, Ralston House was demolished in 1936, and in 1991, after the property company that owned the estate faced difficulties, the club managed to raise £465,000 to buy outright both the course and clubhouse.

A similar tale of astute management and financial control can be told at Fereneze, where the

meandering moorland course was perfectly positioned just west of Barrhead station. (Barrhead was the home of the Shanks company of sanitary ware manufacturers.)

Again, such was the golf club's success that within a few years it was able to abandon its original clubhouse and take over one of the most prominent villas overlooking the course, **Trees House** (*above*).

Built in c.1765 and with its distinctive crenellated detailing, this, along with Ralston's former stable block, is one of many listed buildings around Britain to have, in effect, been saved by golfers.

▼ Another club to have settled in the early 20th century, and in doing so to affirm absolutely its status as the senior club in the city, was **Glasgow Golf Club**, seen here at the opening of its current home, Killermont, on the banks of the River Kelvin, just north of Maryhill, in May 1904.

The club, it will be recalled – the ninth oldest in the world – had formed on Glasgow Green in 1787, reformed at Queen's Park in 1870, moved to Alexandra Park in 1874 and thence to Blackhill in 1895.

For its part, Killermont had been built in 1805 by Archibald Campbell-Colquhoun, lawyer, MP and sometime Lord Advocate, but had for some years lain vacant.

It says much about the club's membership that after prolonged negotiations they felt able to agree to an annual rent of £400, plus compensation to the farmer on the estate of £1,000; sums beyond the imagination of any other club in the city. They then spent a further £1,816 on refurbishing the house under the direction of one of their members, the noted architect John Keppie (in whose practice Charles Rennie Mackintosh was a partner).

A further coup which drew in more paying members was to hire 'Old Tom' Morris as their course architect. Killermont would be the 68th of 69 courses designed by the great man, who was by then aged 83, but who in his prime had been Open Champion four times, holding one particular record for a margin of victory that was not beaten until 2000, by Tiger Woods.

Today there are many treasures within the Killermont clubhouse (*for example see page 28*). But one of the most revered is HJ Brooks' 1898 portrait of Morris (*left*), one of only three known to exist.

The house itself is listed Category B. But golfers would argue that the club's most priceless asset is the Morris course.

▲ Three miles east of Killermont along the River Kelvin stands another historic house whose fate was to be shaped by golf.

Cawder House, built originally in 1624 by Sir Archibald Stirling, and substantially remodelled from 1813–15 by the noted Glasgow architect David Hamilton (designer of the Nelson Monument on Glasgow Green), was inherited in the 1880s by Archibald, younger brother of Sir John Stirling Maxwell, whom we encountered in Chapter Five as the owner of Pollok House and patron of three golf clubs laid out within his estate at Pollok Park.

After Archibald's death in 1931 an advertisement was placed in the local press to form a golf club at Cawder, with the result that the house and grounds were converted and re-opened in their current guise as **Cawder Golf Club** in 1933.

The dashing young society beau Max Aitken, son of Lord Beaverbrook, was named honorary captain, which no doubt helped with recruiting members.

But equally appealing was the appointment of five times British Open winner, James Braid, as course architect.

Braid was employed again when, such was the demand for membership, the club opened a second course, the Keir, to the immediate east, in 1937.

As it transpired Braid's course (one of over 200 he designed around Britain) would be plagued by subsidence, caused by old mine workings, and would need remedial work during the 1960s.

But it remains a stunning course all the same, amid beautiful countryside and a fine collection of estate buildings, including a dovecote, icehouse, lodge, stables and bridge that together with the house are listed Category A.

The club has also retained as a water hazard a boating lake created when the River Kelvin was re-routed during Hamilton's work.

But by far Cawder's most historic feature is that, running across the course, albeit hardly visible as a result of 19th and 20th century landscaping, is a section of the Antonine Wall, a turf rampart raised in 142 AD to protect the northwestern border of the Roman Empire. Excavated from the wall and displayed in the clubhouse is a legionary stone bearing a Latin inscription saying 'The 2nd Legion Augustus built this'.

So to sum up. Here we have a Category A listed clubhouse (the only one ranked so highly in Scotland), with David Hamilton's signature on it, a course by James Braid, and, by the by, a World Heritage Site running through it.

Hardly par for any course.

▶ The legendary golf architect Dr Alister MacKenzie (*see page 85*) was a firm advocate of municipal golf courses, describing them in the 1930s as one way to prevent the working classes from falling prey to the evils of Bolshevism.

Whether councillors in Glasgow agreed with that view is not known, but since laying out the city's first courses at Alexandra Park and Bellahouston Park in the late 19th century, the public greens certainly show no sign of succumbing to a red tide.

One of six such courses still operating in Glasgow is at **Linn Park**. Originally laid out by the Cathcart Castle Golf Club in 1898, the 18 hole course was taken over by the Corporation in 1919, as part of the £10,000 purchase of an 180 acre estate belonging to the Maxwell family at Pollok House.

The area east of the course was then redeveloped from 1953 onwards as the Castlemilk Estate, a bold but ultimately flawed scheme to rehouse residents from the Victorian tenements of the inner city, the Gorbals in particular.

Seen here in 1959 looking towards Drakemire Drive, the new residents of Castlemilk, ladies included, were no doubt thrilled to have such an amenity on their doorstep. Shops and schools, however, had to wait until a second phase of regeneration, starting two decades later.

Another public course, to the north of the city, is **Littlehill** (*right*).

Designed by James Braid and opened in 1923, its redbrick pavilion is seen here in 1983 as Ryder Cup stars Bernard Gallacher, from Bathgate, and Tommy Horton, show local amateurs how to get into the swing of things.

Dr MacKenzie would no doubt have heartily approved.

▲ For private clubs not in a position to take on historic buildings, as have the likes of Ralston, Fereneze, Glasgow and Cawder, the building of a clubhouse has always been the most risk-laden aspect of their existence. Hence, as we saw on page 127, most clubs start with modest ambitions.

A typical example (*above*) is that of **Bishopbriggs Golf Club**.

Founded in 1906 on the Kenmure Estate of Sir John Stirling Maxwell – the patron of so many other clubs in and around his Pollok Park Estate (*see Chapter Five*) – the club deliberately commissioned a clubhouse that could, in the event of the club's failure, be sold on the open market as a family home.

But the club did survive, and as can be seen, has added a number of extensions since.

Aesthetically, as we also saw at Cowglen and Haggs Castle (*page 86*), and will see again in the following chapter on bowling, the result of these extensions is hardly appealing. On the other hand, without them few clubs could

survive, particularly in the current climate when extra function space offers such vital additional income.

It is for this reason, combined, it is true, with the innate conservatism of most golf club committees, that architectural gems are very few and far between in golf, in Glasgow or indeed in any part of Britain.

The relatively functional and modern clubhouse of **Cambuslang Golf Club** (*right*), built in 1971, is the exception rather than the rule.

On the other hand, the vernacular domestic style to which most clubs aspire has paid off in two instances. At **Kirkhill Golf Club**, for example, the sale of the original 1910 clubhouse for residential use (*top right*), went some way towards funding a more modern replacement, immediately next door, in 2005.

Similarly, the former clubhouse of **Williamwood Golf Club**, on the corner of Eastwoodmains Road and Golf Road (*right*), was easily converted into a private school when the club had to relocate to a new course in 1932. Currently it is the office of an accountancy firm.

▲ Film star Danny Kaye was one of several celebrity golfers to call in at the Howard Street works of **John Letters & Co.**, one of the world's leading manufacturers of golf clubs, and one of around 25 Glasgow companies involved in supplying the booming golf accessory market of the 20th century.

Kaye, who also recorded a version of *I Belong to Glasgow*, stopped by in 1949. Other callers included Bob Hope, Bing Crosby and Eartha Kitt, plus a succession of leading golfers, many of whom were devotees of the Letters' best selling Golden Goose double sided putter, launched in 1946. Such was the company's dominance of the market that eight of the ten members of the 1949 Ryder Cup team, used Letters' clubs.

Set up on the north bank of the Clyde in 1918, before moving to Howard Street in 1940, and from there to the Hillington Industrial Estate in the 1950s, Letters was very much a family firm, employing all five of John's sons, his two daughters and his wife.

In an industry dominated by firms based in the east of Scotland, most run by former professional golfers, Letters was the first to harness the industrial expertise of Glasgow, most notably by perfecting the manufacture of clubs with steel shafts, as was becoming the norm in the USA, whilst more traditional rivals stuck to hickory.

By 1955 the Hillington works was making 6,000 clubs a month, half of them for export.

In the 1960s the company was bought out by Dunlop, so John Letters Jnr set up a new firm in Craigton. Like so many manufacturers, however, Dunlop included, this eventually lost out to cheaper goods from the Far East.

But at least the John Letters name lives on, the brand having been relaunched in 2005 and sold via specialist retailers in West Yorkshire. Other club makers in Glasgow from before 1939 whose names have not lived on include Donaldson's, Miller & Taylor and James Goudie of Maryhill.

Even greater than the market for clubs was that of balls...

Springvale Golf Works, Cowlairs.

▲ This 1907 postcard shows the **Springvale Golf Works** of **Hutchison Main & Co.**, Cowlairs Road, one of over 20 rubber and oil-related firms in Glasgow manufacturing golf balls during the Edwardian period.

At the time the card was issued Hutchison Main was locked into a bitter legal battle with its local rival, the St Mungo Manufacturing Co. of Broomloan Road, Govan.

Briefly, the story is this. Initially all golf balls were wooden, until in the mid 15th century the 'feathery' (made from leather casing stuffed tightly with feathers) took over. This was then superceded in the 1840s by a new wonder ball made from *gutta percha* (the sap extracted from Malaysian gum trees).

'Gutties' transformed golf. They could be mass produced and lasted longer too. (*Gutta percha* was used also to insulate telegraph cables, a process carried out by R & J Dick, whose listed Gutta Percha Works still stands on Greenhead Street.)

Meanwhile, in 1898 there came another leap forward in the form of a gutty made with a solid rubber core. Called a 'Haskell' after its inventor, and patented by a rubber company in Akron, Ohio, this ball had many advantages, one of

which, as noted by *The Scotsman*, was that it made a satisfying 'click' when struck.

Haskells were soon being copied by manufacturers all over Britain, each applying their own style of meshed pattern to the surface. But only St Mungo had a licence from Haskell, and therefore in 1904 the Americans decided to show their muscle by suing Hutchison Main for infringement of copyright.

Having failed to convince the judges on that occasion they tried again in 1906. A second appeal, in November 1907, also failed.

But in any case it was St Mungo who prevailed in the long run.

For while in 1912 Hutchison Main was taken over by the North British Rubber Company, St Mungo went on to rival Dunlop and the US giant Spalding, and by the 1930s was said to be turning out 10,000 balls a day at Govan.

Today, no trace of either the Springvale Works or of St Mungo survives, the fate also of every other British golf ball manufacturer since the 1980s. But their products are still bought and sold, that is by collectors, in what has become an astonishingly large and lucrative market in golf-related antiques.

▶ Collectors and players alike, they take heritage very seriously in golf.

By the end of 2010, 19 of the 23 private clubs shown on the map on page 126 will have been in existence for at least a century.

Each has celebrated that rite of passage with a year of celebration, and most with the publication of a centenary history.

At **Williamwood Golf Club** in 2006 they went further and built a Centenary Cairn (*right*), containing a stainless steel time capsule packed with the sort of items that today seem hardly more than ephemera, but in years to come will seem like fascinating artefacts of a lost age; a report of the 2006 AGM, a club sweater, a bag tag, the rules of golf, photographs of the course, a programme from a Burns night, a menu from their centenary dinner, and much, much more.

But how can mere objects do more than hint at what is otherwise a deeply rooted sub-culture, one that has evolved over centuries, involves millions of players (over 50,000 in the Glasgow area alone), and is played by all ages, in all weathers, to a set of rules that depends largely on trust?

For the non-golfer, a visit to any golf course offers a battery of clues to this arcane world of signs and symbols. At **Cathkin Braes**, Glasgow's second oldest club, formed in 1888, players take heed of the time and the wind direction as they tee off at the first, having already checked the barometer in the clubhouse.

The sign saying 'Preferred Lies' tells them that, this being the winter months, they can, if they so wish, move their ball a few inches or so from where it landed (where it 'lies') in order to get a better shot, or to avoid cutting up the fairway.

And at **Whitecraigs**, as they pass

by the starter's hut and eschew the temptation of a golf cart, another sign urges them to pick up from the green bin a 'pitch mark'; this, a small metal fork with which they are obliged to repair any divots or indentations their balls might cause when landing on the soft, smooth turf of the greens.

A golfer must therefore be a meteorologist, an honest citizen,

a reader of topography and a groundsman. In Glasgow he or she must also dress to withstand four seasons in a single day.

To play golf on a course that has matured over a century is to step into a unique historic landscape.

All golfers know this, yet rarely do they ever express it.

But then usually they are far too worried about their swing.

Chapter Nine

Bowls

A neat hedge, a fluttering flag, and the head of a white-shirted man engrossed in a world of his own. Wherever you are in Glasgow, you are never far from a bowling green. In 2009 there were 87 clubs in the area covered by this book, 35 of which had been in existence for at least a century – including Cathcart, seen here, formed in 1889. A further twelve are over 150 years old. No other city in Britain has such a concentration of historic bowling clubs.

To the Scots, wrote an English bowler, James Manson, in 1912, 'we owe the salvation of bowls. They stripped it of its undesirable surroundings, and made a beautiful game of it: an open air pastime without violence, second to none in its scientific and strategic possibilities.

'They gave it laws, demonstrated what constituted a perfect green and fostered the game's most valuable social feature, its democratic spirit.'

That is not to say that bowls owes its origins to Scotland.

Early forms were seemingly played in Ancient Egypt, arriving in Britain via the Romans. South of the border it was subject to its first royal ban in 1363.

In Scotland the earliest known reference is from 1496, when James IV was reported playing 'lang bowlis' at St Andrews. This, however, was probably a form of road bowling, in which the object was to throw for distance, rather than accuracy or at a target.

Yet by 1914, the dominant form of bowls in most (though not all) of England and Wales, and across all the Dominions was, as Manson put it, the 'Scotch game'.

By that he meant what we call today 'flat green' or 'lawn' bowls.

There is another form, called 'crown green' bowls, but that is confined to the north western and Midlands counties of England, the Isle of Man and parts of Wales (of which more later).

Everywhere else, here and overseas, the 'Scotch game' still dominates.

In that sense, bowls has much in common with golf, curling and football; that is, sports whose modern form and character was significantly shaped by the Scots.

Moreover, in the context of this book, although important developments also took place elsewhere in Scotland from the mid 17th to the mid 18th centuries, it was Glasgow bowlers during the 19th century who would be at the forefront of codifying and organising the game.

But what of bowls in Glasgow before then?

The first reference appears in April 1595, in a Kirk Session edict that a drum be sounded out around town to order that on Sundays there should 'be no bickering nor plays' and no 'games, golf, alley, bowls etc.'

James I of England issued a similar ban on Sunday games, bowls included, in 1617.

As was the case with golf, it is unlikely at that time that any designated areas were set aside for bowls in Scotland (although in England bowling greens, or alleys, were starting to become fashionable in the grounds of Tudor mansions).

Ordinary people simply played on any reasonably flat patch of land they could find.

But in time, as attitudes towards the playing of games relaxed – in England after the Restoration in 1660 – entrepreneurs saw in bowling a good business opportunity. In Haddington, for example, east of Edinburgh, Scotland's first public green was laid out in 1669.

Glasgow followed suit in 1695, when Mungo Cochrane gained a licence from the Town Council to lay out a green at Candleriggs. When opened, it was in a very real sense Glasgow's first ever purpose-built sports ground.

The next recorded green was laid out on Gallowgate by John Orr in c. 1750. Shown on a map of 1760, this lay between what are now Charlotte and Greendyke Streets, just south of Gallowgate.

John Struthers, a maltman of Barrowfield, took it over in 1766.

Soon after, a third green was laid out near Drygate, by the Society of Bowlers (*see right*), the town's first known association of bowlers, of which, unfortunately, very little is known.

In 1816, possibly filling a gap in the market created when the Candleriggs green was built over, there also appeared to the west of the town centre a green at Willowbank, whose significance is discussed overleaf.

South of the Clyde, meanwhile, from another map of 1817 we also know of a green at St Ninian's Croft in Hutchesontown. In addition, in a book published in 1893, Humphrey Dingley (*see Links*) reported that on the corner of Eglinton and Cavendish Streets, the Bowling Green Tavern had a green popular with cavalry officers in the 1850s.

This is of interest on two counts. Firstly, pubs with greens, though commonplace in England, were soon to become rare in Scotland. Only two others have been noted in Glasgow in the mid 19th century, at Pointhouse on the banks of the Clyde (*see page* 91), and at Bridgeton, amidst the weaving community.

None would survive, however, as, in an attempt to stem heavy drinking, gambling and general rowdyism, Glasgow's licensing authorities started clamping down on pubs offering any games at all (an attitude which led also to a »

A View of the Middle Walk in the College garden

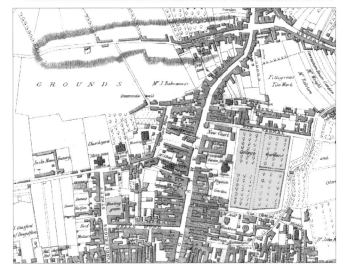

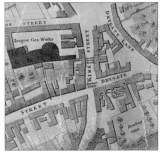

◀ The earliest known image of what appears to be bowlers in Glasgow is this 1762 engraving by Robert Paul, showing the **Middle Walk** in the University's **College Gardens**. To the north can be seen the spire of the Cathedral.

John McArthur's Map of 1778 shows where those gardens were (shaded in green), and also the location of **Mungo Cochrane's bowling green** on the east side of **Candleriggs Street**. This remained in use from 1695 until 1816, when a marketplace was built on the site (since replaced by the Merchant Square leisure complex).

The site of the College Gardens, meanwhile, is now a car park, south of Duke Street.

Changing land use is further illustrated in the two lower maps.

Bottom left is a detail from a map sold by the *Glasgow Herald* in 1807 (based on a survey by Peter Fleming). This shows the **St Crispin Place bowling green**, just to the west of an alms house on Kirk Street (now Castle Street), and east of the still extant Weaver Street.

This green had been purchased by the town's first recorded bowls club, the Society of Bowlers, who, according to James Denholm in 1804 (*see Links*) charged 10s 6d for membership, the same as the Glasgow Golf Club, which was equally reserved for the elite.

In contrast, added Denholm, use of the Candleriggs Green, then owned by Robert Crauford Esq. of Possil, cost only 'a trifle'.

Compare this with the map of the same area in 1828 (*left*) and it can be seen that the Society's green had made way for gas works, but a new green, perhaps also laid out by the Society, had been created south of Drygate.

Today the site is occupied by flats overlooking Cathedral Square.

▶ Hidden away in the changing rooms of the **Willowbank Bowling Club** on **Downside Road** is this depiction of Francis Drake, coolly playing bowls on Plymouth Hoe as the Spanish Armada approached in 1588. Rendered by the noted Glasgow stained glass artist **Norman MacDougall**, it was completed soon after the club's move to Dowanside Road in 1896.

For centuries historians have argued the authenticity of this bowls legend, particularly as the story emerged only in 1624, and not until the 1730s was Drake's involvement even mentioned.

But within Glasgow bowling circles the more contentious issue concerns not Drake but the origins of the Willowbank club itself, and more specifically, whether its claim to be the city's oldest surviving club stands up against the claims of two rivals, Wellcroft and Whitevale.

The background to this dispute, a friendly one, it should be added, is as follows.

In the early 19th century, as has been frequently mentioned, the town centre of Glasgow was huddled around the High Street and Cathedral, while to the west lay relatively unspoilt countryside.

On a part of this outlying area, called Willowbank, stood Sauchy Hall, taking its name from the word 'saugh', meaning willow tree (hence Sauchiehall Street and its famous Willow Tea Rooms).

In 1802 Sauchy Hall was bought by a gingham manufacturer called William Harley, later to become renowned for two enterprises.

Firstly came the sale of pure spring water from his estate, which he also used to create Glasgow's first subscription baths (*see Chapter 14*). Hence Bath Street.

Secondly, in 1809 he set up a pioneering dairy for the sale of unadulterated milk. So successful was this that Willowbank became a tourist attraction, prompting Harley to lay out within his grounds a bowling green and gardens, entry to which was by ticket only.

The green's probable location was on or east of where Adelaide Place Baptist Church stands, on the south side of Bath Street.

According to the Willowbank historian (*see Links*), Harley's green opened in 1816, which may be significant given that the green on Candleriggs was built over in 1816.

There is no evidence of a club ever forming at Willowbank.

But when the site was feued for building in 1831, some of the regulars, calling themselves the 'Willowbank Bowlers', combined to lay out a new green close by on Elmbank Street (on a site north of Glasgow Academy's first school buildings). This opened in

1833, and as the honours board at Dowanside Road records, the winner of the first annual medal was Gavin Walker, also in 1833.

It is on this evidence that Willowbank is able to claim that it predates Wellcroft, which formed in January 1835, and Whitevale, whose records are incomplete.

To which both rivals respond by saying Willowbank was not formally

constituted as a club until 1835.

Rather like the story of Drake, this is one historical debate that appears unlikely ever to be settled.

Nor alas, are Willowbank able to produce that original 1833 gold medal. Although they still have a printers' block depicting its design, the medal itself disappeared when its 1861 winner emigrated to America.

>> ban on darts in Glasgow pubs during the 1930s).

It was this deliberate cleaving of the link between the consumption of alcohol and bowling to which Manson was referring in 1912 when he wrote of the Scots having stripped the game 'of its undesirable surroundings'.

(Indeed by 2009 only four pub greens were known to exist in the whole of Scotland.)

Also of interest is that Dingley described the green at the Bowling Green Tavern as 'old-fashioned'.

What did he mean by this?

Most likely that the green was not flat, perhaps not even square, and therefore more akin to what we would now call a 'crown green'.

In other words, it was not only in England that the 'Scotch game' took over.

As we have noted opposite, three Glasgow clubs can date their foundation to the 1830s, or even earlier in the case of Willowbank. There was a fourth, called Albany, founded in 1833 on Stirling Road, but this wound up in 1899.

These were not the first clubs in Scotland. Kilmarnock BC was founded in 1740, while Edinburgh's Society of Bowlers drew up rules for their first Silver Jack tournament in 1771. But Glasgow's rising population meant that its first four clubs were soon joined by five more, as a result of which, instead of their members playing each other on the same green, week after week (as had been the norm for centuries), there grew a natural desire for inter-club matches.

The trouble was, each club played by slightly different rules.

So it was that in 1848 more than 200 bowlers from Glasgow, Paisley, Greenock and Falkirk met at Glasgow Town Hall to debate the possibility of setting up a National Bowling Club. Their model was the Royal Caledonian Curling Club, set up in Edinburgh in 1838. In fact many of the bowlers were themselves curlers, anxious to remain active during the warmer months.

For all the enthusiasm, the meeting failed to set up a national body. But crucially, it was agreed to appoint a committee to draw up a common set of rules, under the chairmanship of a Willowbank man, William Mitchell (*see right*).

Exactly what his final set of rules entailed, once delivered in 1849, is beyond the scope of this book, although *Played in Britain* will return to the subject in our forthcoming study, *Bowled Over* in 2012. Suffice it to say here, however, that although not perfect, Mitchell's rules transformed bowls into a national game, and remained unaltered until after his death in 1884.

Glasgow bowlers were to advance the game further in April 1888 when, at a meeting at the Religious Institution Rooms in Buchanan Street, 22 clubs agreed to form the Glasgow Bowling Association, the first body of its kind in Britain.

Seventeen of the founder clubs remain in existence.

Four years later, this time at the Waterloo Rooms in Wellington Street, the goal of a national body was finally realised with the formation of the Scottish Bowling Association.

In one respect, this diluted the influence of the Glasgow clubs. On the other hand the first president was a Partick man, the Glasgow clubs still formed the largest caucus, and Queen's Park became the host venue for the national championships, an honour it would retain until they were finally moved to Ayr in 1989.

The SBA's influence extended far beyond Scotland.

For example, in the absence of other national bodies, applications to join the SBA were received from clubs as far afield as New Zealand.

And when, in 1901, the famous cricketer and promoter of 'flat green' bowls, WG Grace, sought to establish the game in London, it was to the SBA that he turned.

Only in 1903 was an English equivalent set up, and even then its rules were based almost entirely on those from Scotland. Indeed, anticipating such a move, the SBA had cannily made sure that they had copyrighted their version.

Not only that, but over the ensuing decade, once England and Wales started playing international matches, there would be repeated complaints that most of their players were also Scottish.

Scottish domination even extended to the use of approved bowls. This was because at the SBA's first Annual Meeting, at the Central Hotel in Glasgow, in April 1893, it was agreed that the Standard Bowl for all competitions should be that of Thomas Taylor, a bowls manufacturer based, of course, in Glasgow.

As noted later, Taylors are still in business.

Today, it is true, there is a tendency to regard bowls as an old man's game, at odds with the fast pace of the modern world.

And yet there are compelling reasons why the 'Scotch game' appealed so widely and spread so far, and why of all places, Glasgow – 'the dear green place' – remains in the 21st century, a city of greens.

Time, then, to peep over that trimmed hedge to see what lies beyond.

W.W.MITCHELL.

▲ By all accounts **William W Mitchell** was a much loved man.

Born in either 1803 or 1804, he had first played bowls on the famous green at Kilmarnock.

Once qualified as a solicitor in Glasgow he became a regular at William Harley's green, later rising to senior office at the Willowbank club, and to exalted status in Scottish bowling circles.

His 1864 *Manual of Bowl Playing* is said to have been the first book ever devoted solely to the game, while his last known eulogy to bowls was an ode, penned at the age of 76 after he had just spent four hours playing at Willowbank before heading home for his Christmas dinner.

Recalling years of bowling in all weathers, he wrote:

The bools row – the bools row,
Your ain as well as mine,
O bonnily the bools row,
When summer days are fine.

O gin the wins wad stop their blaw,
O gin the sun wad shine,
O gin the snaw wad melt awa',
An' summer come again.

Ah! some no more the grass will tread
Nor ever again will play!
While others lively, look ahead,
'Thus runs the world awy.'

▲ It is a testament to the skill of the greenkeeper at **Wellcroft Bowling Club**, seen here in 1859 at **Eglinton Street**, that although lawnmowers were in production by the 1830s he stuck with his scythe.

Nor was he alone in Scotland, where greenkeeping was to evolve into such a fine art, and indeed a science, that it is reasonable to assert that as well as providing the rules for modern flat green bowling, the Scots also perfected the ground conditions that made it possible in the first place. That, and the fact that sea-washed turf from the Solway Firth was found to offer the ideal surface, not only for bowling greens but for all sports pitches (Wembley Stadium's included).

Eglinton Street was Wellcroft's second home.

The club had formed on January 30 1835 at the Wheatsheaf Inn on Clyde Terrace, a date which has led Wellcroft to claim that it, rather than Willowbank, is the oldest 'constituted' club in Glasgow.

As we noted on page 136, Willowbank beg to differ. So too do Whitevale BC, who say that although not formally registered as a club until 1836, one source has them in existence before then.

Whatever the truth – which may never be known – Wellcroft's early records are certainly the most detailed, with their original 'match book' recording the opening of their first green on Surrey Street,

'in the lands of Wellcroft', on May 30 1835. Very close to this, possibly even next to it, was the aforementioned Bowling Green Tavern, and the cavalry barracks.

Like so many early Glasgow sports grounds Surrey Street was soon subsumed by the coming of the railways, forcing Wellcroft to move to Eglinton Street in 1851.

Here, apart from the two greens seen above, the club also created a curling pond, just visible between the clubhouse (*on the right*) and the far boundary wall, and built a house for the club superintendent, at the far end of the curling pond.

If the above appears to be a refined suburban scene, what the camera does not show is the Govan

Poorhouse, overlooking the greens on the north side (that is, left of the photograph). This had moved into the former cavalry barracks in 1853. Nor does the photograph show the neighbouring gasworks, iron foundry or Port Eglinton Creosoting Works, nor the railway embankment bordering the south west side of the greens, from which this elevated image was taken.

In 1876 the construction of Eglinton Street station erased all trace of these greens and the curling pond, although it is said that the superintendent's house survived as part of that station.

Meanwhile, the vicinity of the club's first green is marked by Wellcroft Close.

▲ From the encroaching noise and grime of Eglinton Street, in 1876 **Wellcroft** moved to very different surrounds, leasing from the Council a leafy corner of **Queen's Park** (*see page 25*), where they have remained contentedly ever since.

Welcoming all who enter from Queen's Drive is this magnificent chestnut, trained over the years into a W (although the tree actually predates Wellcroft's arrival, having been planted on the day of Queen's Park's opening, in 1862).

Whether or not Wellcroft is the oldest, second oldest, or even third oldest bowling club in Glasgow, it is certainly one of the most influential, not least having won the 'Eglinton Jug' – one of the most important trophies in Scottish bowls (of which more later) – six times, including in the tournament's first year, 1857, and more recently in 2009.

Wellcroft also played a key role in the early years of inter-club competition. One of their regular outings, for example, was to take a barge down the nearby Paisley and Ardrossan Canal to play against the Priorscroft Bowling Club in Paisley.

Wellcroft's over-subscribed membership list also led to the formation of nearby Kingston BC and, further down Queen's Drive, Queen's Park BC.

But in the context of this book, there is one treasure amongst many at Wellcroft that is of particular interest.

Known as the 'coffee pot', this is a trophy, hallmarked in 1853 and depicting on one side what appears to be the pavilion at Eglinton Street (*see right, and opposite*).

Wellcroft members believe that the fluted iron columns and decorative ironwork spandrels seen on this pavilion were brought over from Eglinton Street in 1876 and incorporated into the new pavilion, where they can still be seen today (*see right and also page 1*).

If this is the case, and there seems every reason for it to be so, as pavilions were often partially re-erected from green to green, then these simple pieces of ironwork are amongst the important examples of bowling heritage in Britain today.

▲ **Partick Bowling Club's** ironwork may not be as old or ornate as that of Wellcroft, but its green, laid out in 1854, is the oldest to have remained in continuous use in the Glasgow area.

Ornamental gates are almost as common as trimmed hedges and flagpoles, one theme being to mark a centenary, as seen opposite at **Queen's Park** and **Kirkhill**.

Not all the dates tell the exact story, however.

The gate at **Whitevale** (*top right, opposite*) gives the club's foundation date as 1836, even though the club insists that it was already in existence by at least 1835. Equally, clubs often started playing a full year after they were formed, the gap being necessary to allow the new green to be readied for play. Hence in the list on this page formation dates are given.

Other club gates featured on the opposite page, below Whitevale, are **Burnside, Busby** and **Cathcart**.

Of the 87 private clubs operating in the area covered by *Played in Glasgow* in 2009, 81 were affiliated to the GBA. The others were affiliated to the Lanarkshire North or Dunbartonshire & Argyll district associations. * means GBA founder members 1888.

- 1833/35 Willowbank*, Dowanside Rd
- 1835 Wellcroft*, Queens Drive
- 1835/36 Whitevale*, Whitehill Street
- 1845 Partick*, Fortrose Street
- 1849 Govan*, Vicarfield Street
- 1849 Kingston*, McCulloch Street
- 1850 Yoker, Hawick Street
- 1854 Pollokshaws*, Pollokshaws Road
- 1857 St Rollox*, Kennyhill Square
- 1858 Bellahouston*, Dumbreck Road
- 1858 Springburn*, Broomfield Place
- 1859 St Vincent*, St Vincent Crescent
- 1861 Belvidere*, Silverdale Street
- 1861 Maryhill, Duart Street
- 1861 Rutherglen, Stonelaw Road
- 1862 Shawlands*, Pollokshaws Road
- 1866 Burnbank*, Woodlands Road
- 1866 Hutchesontown*, Rutherglen Road
- 1867 Queens Park*, Langside Road
- 1874 Cambuslang, Westcoats Road
- 1875 Busby, The Crescent
- 1877 Tollcross, Causewayside Street*
- 1888 Camphill, Langside Avenue
- 1889 Cathcart, Ashmore Road
- 1890 Titwood, Glencairn Drive
- 1893 Giffnock, Percy Drive
- 1894 Mount Vernon, Central Grove
- 1898 Thornliebank, Kennishead Road
- 1898 Newlands, Langside Drive
- 1899 Jordanhill, Randolph Road
- 1900 Chryston, Bowling Green Road
- 1900 Springboig, Springboig Avenue
- 1903 Partickhill, Partickhill Road
- 1903 Victoria Park, Dumbarton Road
- 1904 Carmyle, River Road
- 1904 Hyndland, Queensborough Gdns
- 1905 Hampden, Kingsley Avenue
- 1905 Scotstounhill, Anniesland Road
- 1905 Stepps, Lenzie Road
- 1906 Bishopbriggs, Kenmure Ave
- 1907 Shettleston, Culrain Street
- 1906 Kirkhill, Stewarton Drive
- 1909 Burnside, Burnside Road

- 1909 Clarkston, Eastwoodmains Road
- 1909 Woodend, Chamberlain Road
- 1909 Linthouse, Drumoyne Avenue
- 1909 Mount Florida, Carmunnock Road
- 1910 Baillieston, The Faulds, Baillieston
- 1910 Riddrie, Smithycroft Road
- 1913 Nitshill & Hurlet, Nitshill Road
- 1914 Cardonald, Forfar Avenue
- 1914 Foxley, Carmyle Avenue
- 1919 Weir Recreation, Albert Park
- 1920 Mearns, Ayr Road
- 1923 Stobhill Hospital, Springburn
- 1923 Whitefield, Croft Road, Cambuslang
- 1924 Hillpark, Tinto Road
- 1924 Mosspark, Mosspark Road
- 1925 Blackhill, Tay Crescent
- 1925 Drumoyne, Drumoyne Square
- 1926 Fairfield, Shieldhall Road
- 1928 Albion, Halley Street
- 1928 Kelvindale, Baronald Drive
- 1928 Kingswood, Kingsbrae Avenue
- 1930 Sandyhills, Amulree Street
- 1931 North British, Amulree Street
- 1932 Hawthorn, Spruce Street
- 1935 Whitecraigs, Ayr Road
- 1937 Garrowhill, Douglas Drive
- 1945 Yarrow Recreation, Anniesland Road
- 1947 Hillington Estate, Montrose Avenue
- 1947 Auchinairn, Auchinairn Rd, Bishopbriggs
- 1949 Barr & Stroud, Netherton Road
- 1949 Killermont, Woodvale Avenue
- 1954 Croftfoot, Thorncroft Drive
- 1961 Stamperland, Nethervale Avenue
- 1961 Corunna, St Vincent Crescent (originally GPO, formed 1906)
- 1975 Crookston, Crookston Road
- 1975 Strathclyde Police AA, Lochinch, Pollok Park
- 1977 Anniesland, Helensburgh Drive (originally City Bakeries, formed 1924)
- 1981 Castlemilk, Dougrie Road
- 1982 Templeton, Stonelaw Drive (originally Templeton Carpets, formed 1924)
- 1982 Overtoun Park, Rodger Drive (originally public green in 1912)
- 1983 Univ of Glasgow Staff, St Vincent Crescent
- 1983 Parkhead, Helenvale St (originally Glasgow Transport Dept., formed 1924)
- 1984 Darnley, Glen Moriston Road
- 1987 Balornock, Wallacewell Road

▶ A familiar sight in **Kelvingrove Park** are the bowling greens to the east of the Kelvingrove Art Gallery and Museum, seen here shortly after they were opened in 1905.

The park itself, laid out between 1852–67, had been landscaped to appeal to the growing middle class population of the West End, bolstered by the University's move west in 1870. As noted elsewhere, the park had also been the site of the international exhibitions of 1888 and 1901 (and later 1911).

The bowling greens, however, were an afterthought.

Whereas Glasgow had been at the forefront of providing public golf courses, and rented space to Wellcroft, Queen's Park and Camphill bowling clubs at Queen's Park, and Hutchesontown BC at Richmond Park, compared with other local authorities it had been slow to provide public greens.

Possibly it felt that the sheer number of private clubs already met the demand. Yet Edinburgh was similarly well endowed with private clubs and still had 13 public greens by 1902. As Parks Superintendent Duncan McLellan had discovered on a fact-finding mission to 13 other cities in 1892, Edinburgh was not alone.

Finally the Council laid out two public greens on Glasgow Green in 1903, and the response said it all. In the first two years they

were used by 19,880 and 23,462 bowlers respectively. Glasgow Green was located in a more working class area, but when the two seen here at Kelvingrove were opened, and were joined by further pairs at Queen's Park, Alexandra Park and Springburn Park, by 1906 the Council's ten new greens had totted up a total of 88,256 users.

Suitably encouraged, two more greens were added at Kelvingrove

Completed at Kelvingrove Park in 1922 to service two more greens, and six tennis courts, the Radnor Bowling and Tennis Pavilion was one of several parks pavilions designed and built around the city by Glasgow's Office of Public Works. None have fared well however, and like the boarded-up Radnor Pavilion all are expected to be phased out in the near future.

in 1907, and, as more were laid out in other parks, the total reached a peak in the 1950s of 90 public greens at 31 different locations.

Since then, the decline has been rapid, in Glasgow as in every other major city, owing to a drop in demand and rising maintenance costs, exacerbated by an increase in vandalism. As a result, by 2009 only 34 public greens remained at 12 locations.

On the plus side, overall usage remains remarkably healthy, varying in recent years (because of the weather) from 35–67,000 in the years 2008 and 2009. The greens at Knightswood and Victoria Parks were the most popular, with Kelvingrove in third place, totting up 16,000 users. Many of these, interestingly, were students, proving that bowls is by no means confined to older sectors of the community.

▲ Looking south towards the Clyde from the tower of the University in 2009, Kelvingrove Park's four original public bowling greens, known as **Kelvingrove Old**, are divided by an avenue of trees from the 1920s pair on the east side, served by the **Radnor Pavilion**.

In recent years the Kelvingrove Old greens have also been used by the Scottish Croquet Association.

No doubt in 2014 a succession of photographers will return to this wonderful vantage point to capture the most important bowling tournament ever staged in Glasgow. Because of the game's enduring popularity in countries such as Australia, New Zealand, Canada and South Africa, bowls has featured in the Commonwealth Games ever since the series started as the British Empire Games in Hamilton, Ontario, in 1930.

Temporary stands will be erected around the Kelvingrove Old greens, all of which will be renewed. The old pavilions will also be replaced.

It should be quite a sight – the 'Scotch game' coming home, 165 years after William Mitchell set the ball rolling, barely half a mile away at Willowbank.

▲ Wherever new communities sprang up in Glasgow, bowling clubs were sure to follow, one of the game's great advantages being that a green and 'bowls house' could fit comfortably within half an acre or less. Bowls houses varied according to the club's wealth, its security of tenure, and the aesthetics of its founding members.

Typical was **Kirkhill BC** (*above*), built in 1906 on Grenville Drive, before many of the surrounding villas had appeared. Its bowls house followed the standard pattern of two bay windows overlooking the greens, with an overhanging pitched roof creating a verandah.

Inside, two rooms were deemed sufficient; one as a club room, the other for changing (this being before ladies were admitted).

Also needed was a shed for the greenkeeper's tools.

A few hundred yards north, on West Coats Road, **Wellshot BC** (*top right*), started out in 1874 with a more modest brick shelter, while further south west, on Eastwoodmains Road, **Clarkston Bowling and Tennis Club** (*below right*), formed in 1909, built a delightful clubhouse in the Italian villa style. Its architectural quality may be attributed to the fact that in an emerging suburb in which no pubs were permitted (until 2006, that is), and with tennis facilities alongside, it was more likely to serve as a social centre for families as well as male bowlers.

**◀ Cambuslang Bowling
Club** exemplifies a pattern of development that will now be familiar to readers. The regret is that behind the 1979 extension stands a fine sandstone bowls house, built in 1925 in the Scottish Baronial style.

But look closer and it may be seen that this is the same green seen opposite, once the property of Wellshot BC. Indeed the neighbouring house has hardly changed at all in over a century.

The fact is that laying out the original green and building even a relatively modest bowls house had left Wellshot BC struggling under £300 of debt. Finally in 1895 the bank had had enough and a new company was set up to take over Wellshot's assets. Thus Cambuslang BC was born, in the knowledge that never again could the club afford to overstretch itself.

It is this caution that has led so many clubs to develop their facilities bit by bit, resulting in the clash of styles that we so often see today.

The same process occurred at **Clarkston** (*left*), where extensions and the addition of a porch have undoubtedly compromised the integrity of the original design.

Modern architects like to argue that 'form follows function'.

But in the world of bowling, it is function rooms that offer the real key to survival.

▲ Formed in 1898 to provide 'the means of beautiful recreation and friendly intercourse', **Newlands BC**, on **Langside Drive**, possesses a rare gem, one of only two listed bowls houses in Glasgow (the other is at Titwood, *see page 89*).

Opened in 1900 and designed by James Salmon & Son (architects also of the 1891 clubhouse at Whitevale BC), the building, now sandwiched between two later extensions, has a charming Arts and Crafts assymetry, its verandah framed by two curious pagoda-style leaded roofs and its main door set within a near circular framed porch.

Newlands was one of several south side suburbs developed following the completion of the Cathcart Circle railway in 1880. A measure of its affluence is that when the club was formed, 855 shares of £1 were taken up to go towards a total expenditure of £1,364 for the two greens, pavilion and ornamental railings.

Having two greens is a great asset for any club, allowing the ladies' and men's sections to play at the same time, but also to save wear and tear during the busiest months of the season.

▲ Of a similar vintage to Newlands, but in a very different suburban setting, is the **Hyndland Bowling Club** on **Queensborough Gardens**.

Founded in 1904, unusually the green occupies what had been a garden square in the midst of Hyndland's formal grid pattern of streets, each lined by block after block of highly desirable, four storey sandstone tenements, built between 1890 and 1914, and each with almost identical corner turrets and bay windows.

Yet in complete contrast stands a half-timbered pavilion that appears to have been transplanted from an Ayrshire village, surrounded by the most wonderful Mackintosh inspired iron railings.

The overall effect is magical, a green that manages to be both intimate and private, and yet is completely open to the gaze of passersby and local residents.

Note that each of the three games seen here in progress take place in their own 'rink', proceeding up and down the green. This is one feature of 'flat green' bowls that distinguishes it from 'crown green', in which games may take place simultaneously in any direction, even across the diagonals. Note also that both men and women are playing together, a scene unthinkable until recent years.

But for all its modernity, it still conjures up William Mitchell's words in 1864. 'Where, it may be asked, save on a bowling green, is the bitterness of sects and the violence of parties ignored and forgotten?'

▲ It is said that tougher health and safety laws have resulted in a fall in the number of working kitchens found in community halls. Not so in the bowls house, where tea cups and silver cups are equally prized, and where the quality of match day sandwiches is a serious matter.

This is the club room at **Cathcart BC**, formed in 1898 and currently with 180 well nourished members.

You can tell the importance of the match by the players' clothes.

If it is in the early stages of an SBA competition, men may wear grey trousers with their white shirts (collars obligatory). Once beyond that stage, however, the trousers, socks, even the belts must be white too. There's more scope with shoes though. They can be brown, white, grey or black.

But the most noticeable colour of all is silver, as at **Pollokshaws BC** (*top*), and **Whitevale BC** (*above*), where Mary Buchanan has been popping in for fifty years, knowing there will always be jobs to do and someone to talk to. Whitevale was once known for having doctors, lawyers and policemen amongst its membership. But did any one of them ever get out the duster?

One trophy every Glaswegian bowler would love to get his hands on is the venerable **Eglinton Jug**, awarded to the winners of an annual tournament between clubs in Glasgow and Ayrshire.

Almost certainly the oldest inter-club trophy in the world of bowls it was first contested in 1857, and is almost identical to an earlier Eglinton Jug first presented for a curling competition in 1851.

With his muttton chop whiskers and affable personality, the 13th Earl of Eglinton was an heroic figure, a one time gambler and inebriate who devoted his later years – he died in 1861, aged 49, after a round of golf at St Andrews – to the promotion of Scottish sports, not only among the monied classes but to 'the baker and the brewer, the delicate and robust'.

A regular presence on the green himself, on presenting the jug in 1857 he said that 'curling and bowling, especially among the poorer classes of our countrymen, will do more to promote their comfort and welfare and tend to their good conduct than all the beer halls and Sunday-trading bills the legislature has ever passed.'

Thus it can be said that his greatest legacy was to attach to bowling the most potent gift any sport in Victorian Britain could wish for, and that was respectability.

A blessing rest on Eglinton!
An' on his princely ha',
An' blessed be the memory
O' him that's noo awa'.

He greatly loved his fellow-men,
But saw a gap between,
An' closed it up, an' syne ilk class
Became ilk other's frien'.

William Mitchell 1864

▲ From silverware to enamelware, and the extraordinary fondness that Scotland's bowling community has for **club badges**. These, from the collection of Robert Pool, are just a few from thousands of different designs turned out since mass production of enamel badges began with the invention of the drop stamping machine in Birmingham in the 1840s.

But while collectors vie for rare examples on internet auction sites, the majority displayed in pavilions, such as at **Titwood BC** (*above*) have been donated by visiting clubs.

Less colourful are counters seen in every clubhouse, used to decide who plays who and on which rink in certain competitions. Most counters are plain wood or plastic, but those at **Hampden BC** are brass counters rescued from the North British Locomotive Company.

Hampden was founded in 1905 by former members of Polmadie BC, close to where the company's Queen's Park works were located. Many of Hampden's members worked there too. But these counters appear to have come from North British's Hyde Park works at Springburn, which closed in 1963.

VIEWS OF OUR WORKS.

Cross Cutting Lignum-Vitæ Logs

Rough Turning.

Testing

Bias.

Fitting Ivory Mounts.

Packing Finished Bowls.

Several of the processes in manufacturing BOWLING GREEN BOWLS.

▲ There are 52 nations in the World Bowls Association, but only three large scale manufacturers of actual bowls; one in Liverpool, one in Melbourne, and the oldest of them all, **Thomas Taylor** of Glasgow.

Founded originally by James Taylor in 1770 as makers of violin cases – the company is thought to be the Royal Bank of Scotland's oldest customer – in 1796 Taylor turned to the production of billiard balls, bowls (or 'woods'), and artificial limbs for wounded servicemen returning from the Napoleonic Wars.

In 1871 James' grandson Thomas (after whom the company was renamed in 1886) developed a lathe and a slate bed testing table which, for the first time, enabled bowls to be turned with a reliable degree of bias. This consistency resulted in a Taylor bowl being chosen as the 'Master Standard' by the newly formed Scottish Bowling Association in 1893, after extensive tests at the Albany Bowling Club.

On the left is an extract from Taylor's 1937 brochure, showing in the centre how bowls were tested before they left the workshops in Montrose Street.

▲ What William Mitchell did for the rules and what Scottish greenkeepers did for the playing surfaces, **Thomas Taylor** did for the bowls themselves. That is he brought a consistency to their manufacture that enabled bowlers to compete on equal terms.

Crucial to this was Taylor's ability to turn out 'woods' with a measured degree of bias.

Vital to both flat and crown green bowling, bias is the characteristic by which bowls roll in a curved projectory towards the jack. It is created by flattening one side of the bowl more than the other.

To see how this was achieved Taylors have set up in their **Bernard Street** premises – to which they moved in 1980 – a small exhibition in which is displayed one of the

company's original lathes, seen here being demonstrated by former Taylor bowls maker **John Barker**.

Until synthetic bowls came onto the market in the 1930s, all bowls were made from lignum vitae.

First imported from the island of San Domingo in the 16th century, lignum vitae ('the wood of life') is the most durable and densest wood known to man. Virtually

impervious to water, it was perfect for use in shipbuilding, for making tools, truncheons and even, during the Second World War, for the manufacture of Mosquito aircraft.

Nevertheless, as lignum vitae became harder to source various companies started to seek alternatives, the breakthrough coming in 1931 when William Hensell in Australia came up with

a 'composite' made from phenol-formaldehyde (the polymer from which Bakelite was produced).

The final death knell for lignum vitae came when tough restrictions were placed on its import, which persuaded Taylor to concentrate on 'composites' in 1968.

In truth, there is little romance in their manufacture. Much of the process is controlled by computer.

But at least there is now a choice of colour, since the rules on having only black and brown bowls were relaxed in 2001. And human touches are still required in order to finish off each bowl, to test its bias and to add the appropriate stamp and serial number so that it meets the strict requirements of the World Bowls authority.

Currently there are eleven

accredited centres in the world where bowls can be tested before being stamped, each with their own prefix letter. So if you pick up a bowl and it is stamped with the letter A, you know that it was either manufactured, or at least tested in Glasgow, where of course the whole process began.

Old woods have not disappeared altogether, however. Apparently

they are still preferred by one in ten bowlers. Indeed properly stored and looked after, a lignum vitae bowl, or 'wood', can last a lifetime, or even longer. Some clubs have woods thought to be over a century old.

Beautiful they are too, to look at and to hold, which is why for anyone interested in sporting heritage, the exhibition at Bernard Street is, quite literally, Taylor made.

Pollokshields BC's opening day on Maxwell Drive in 1865 (*top*), and the scene as it appeared in 2008. Almost certainly the green will share the same fate as that of another sporting venue on Maxwell Drive, the Pollokshields Tennis Club. Opened in 1886, its once extensive grounds are now covered by flats between Woodrow Road and Wetherby Drive.

▲ Like a Scottish version of a prairie painting by Andrew Wyeth, the boarded up windows of the **Kings Park Bowling Club** stare blindly at the billowing grass of a once fine green. At the height of the property boom in 2005, the club had succumbed, four years short of its centenary.

But it is not only in recent years that scenes like this and at Pollokshields have cast a cloud over the Glasgow bowling community. There have always been casualties.

Six years after their 'excellent' green was used by the SBA to test Taylor's bowls in 1893, Albany BC, (formed in 1833) lost out to developers. The site is now the car park of the Allen Glen Campus.

In the East End, Bridgeton BC (formed in 1851) had its green sequestered for road developments, while Polmadie was squeezed out by industry in 1905.

In more recent years, in the West End, Hillhead Bowling and Tennis Club (formed in 1849) was swallowed up by the expansion of the BBC in 1957.

Then, nine years later, the neighbouring clubs of Whiteinch (formed 1876) and Broomhill (1879) closed down to make way for the Clydeside Expressway.

Poignantly, the latter's pavilion can still be seen, boarded up and stranded between the sliproad and the back of the tenements on the west side of Broomhill Avenue.

More recently still, in 2006 the members of Farme BC, a miners' welfare club set up in 1925, found an offer from a developer too hard to resist. And in 2009 it was announced that Kingston (formed in 1849) had made a similar decision, and would disband in 2010 or 2011, making them the sixth of the 22 founding members of the GBA in 1888 to have folded.

The question is, are King's Park, Pollokshields, Farme and Kingston inevitable victims of changing demographics and unusually high property prices, or are there deeper, underlying reasons why four of Glasgow's clubs will have disappeared within the first decade or so of the 21st century?

▲ Opened in 1964 and with twelve rinks on two synthetic greens, the **West of Scotland Indoor Bowling Club** on **Rutherglen Road** is the largest of four such facilities in Glasgow. But even though they open only from September to April, in order not to clash with the outdoor season, some traditionalists fear that just as curling has become a predominantly indoor game played on artificial ice (*see Chapter Ten*), so too will bowling succumb to the warmth and predictability offered by indoor clubs.

In fact indoor bowling is hardly new. Both the Scottish and English Indoor Bowling Associations formed in the 1930s, while the Glasgow Indoor Bowling Club on Prospecthill Road, with eight rinks, has been running since 1961.

Advocates of indoor clubs argue that it is easier to introduce young people to bowling in an environment where the vagaries of the weather cannot interfere with sessions organised through schools.

Also that there is less risk of damage to the playing surface.

Certainly the indoor game has shown more willing to modernise bowling's image by turning greens into more television-friendly shades of purple, while introducing coloured bowls, jazzy uniforms and pumped up music.

For that is surely the real issue.

In a sport where the majority of players are aged over 60, and are dying off steadily, how can children of the digital age be drawn in to the game without sacrificing centuries of tradition?

▶ The game of bowls may be facing many a challenge, but that it still retains the power to bring communities together has been amply demonstrated in the northern suburb of **Balornock**, an area most associated with post war estates and the neighbouring 1960s tower blocks of Barmulloch.

In 1987 a group of regulars at the Cairn Bar on Balornock Road decided that what the area needed most was a bowling club.

Calling themselves 'the magic circle', they secured a site on Wallacewell Road, with a shed commandeered as a pavilion.

Happily the club quickly outgrew this, but instead of then setting out to build a functional, anonymous replacement – as so many bowling clubs have done – Balornock's members made a radical decision.

The result, as surely befits the city's youngest bowls club, is one of the most refreshingly modern clubhouses in Britain.

Designed by Studio KAP Architects and completed in 2005 at a cost of £250,000 – funded by a brewery, sponsors, bank loans and members' contributions – the building has caused quite a stir in Glasgow bowling circles.

In architectural circles too. In 2006 the clubhouse was one of two buildings in Scotland to win a Civic Trust award. The other was the Scottish Parliament.

However the real measure of its success is that only a few years after its opening, the club was already considering the need to extend it to cater for demand.

A familiar story, but a salutary one too. For it demonstrates that bowling and modernism are not mutually exclusive, and that those who dare can bring new life to the game, and to the communities it was always designed to serve.

◀ Modernity and continuity, the fast lane and the slow lane – on the banks of the Clyde, the 'Armadillo' and the SECC; on St Vincent Crescent, a seamless terrace of listed tenements dating from 1850, overlooking a run of four bowling greens. On the left, **Corunna BC**; in the middle, the **University of Glasgow BC**, and on the right, the two greens of **St Vincent BC**, which in 2009 became the twelfth bowling club in Glasgow to celebrate its 150th anniversary.

In a city whose population has almost halved in the last 50 years, what makes this fact, and this scene, all the more remarkable is not how many bowling clubs have disbanded, but how many have survived. As we said at the outset, whether you know it or not, wherever you are in Glasgow, you are never far from a bowling green.

Chapter Ten

Ice sports

Originally called the Drovers Inn, the Curlers Tavern on Byres Road, Hillhead, was renamed in 1849 to celebrate its role as the meeting place of the Partick Union Curling Society, formed in 1842 and restyled in 1848 as the Partick Curling Club (now Glasgow's oldest surviving club). At that time the club's curling pond lay across the road, roughly between where Great George and Cranworth Streets are now. Once there were at least 80 such ponds in Glasgow. But only one other has been commemorated, off Aikenhead Road (*below right*), west of Hampden Park.

Three forms of ice sports are 'played in Glasgow': curling, skating and ice hockey.

We bracket them together not only for the obvious reason that they all need ice, but because since the early 20th century they have depended to a large extent on an invention that we all take for granted, refrigeration, which in turn enabled the creation of an entirely new form of recreational building, the indoor ice rink.

Ice hockey we will merely touch upon because, with respect, it has never quite been the force in Glasgow that it has been elsewhere in Scotland or England (and even then its history is characterised by several periods of boom and bust).

Skating is undoubtedly the oldest of ice sports, having come to Britain, it is thought, via the Vikings. It was first described in London in the 12th century.

Scotland, it is true, has a special place in skating history, in that the world's first skating club was formed in Edinburgh in 1742. A Glasgow Skating Club followed in 1830. But again, there is not much we can say about skating in the current context because until the emergence of ice rinks – in England from 1876 onwards, and in Glasgow from 1896 (as detailed later in this chapter) – it took place on existing ponds, lakes, rivers and canals, whenever the weather made it possible.

Which brings us to curling.

Curling is, in essence, bowling on ice, although curlers might argue that bowling is actually a form of curling, but on turf.

One is a winter game, the other a spring and summer game. But they share a common set of conventions, have many terms and expressions in common, and most notably of all, in Scotland at least, share a similar ethos of companionship, combined with an antipathy towards gambling.

Even more so than bowling, however, curling is, in common with golf, a sport that may be legitimately regarded as an essentially Scottish construct. Flat green bowling, the 'Scotch game', may claim this too, but whereas there are other forms of bowling that have little to do with Scotland, there is only one code of curling.

As was engraved on the badge of one of Scotland's earliest clubs, the Duddingston Curling Society, formed in 1795: *Sic Scoti; alii non aeque felices*. Or, 'this is how the Scots enjoy themselves: the rest of mankind is not so fortunate.'

Before Duddingston, one of the earliest references to the throwing of stones in Scotland – cited by curling historian David B Smith, to whom we are indebted – is from Paisley Abbey, in 1541. Curling is also recorded at Kinross in 1668.

But the sport really came into its own after the 1780s, significantly during a period of particularly cold winters that have since been dubbed by climatologists as the 'Little Ice Age'.

In the previous chapter we noted how Scotland contributed towards four significant advances in flat green bowling; the formulation of rules and the overall governance of the game, the manufacture of standard bowls, and the perfection of playing surfaces.

However each one of these advances was predated by an almost identical series of developments in curling.

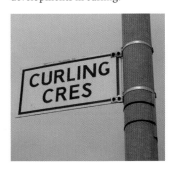

The first rules, for example, were written in 1804, and from 1838 onwards were administered from Edinburgh by the newly formed Grand Caledonian Curling Club. Renamed the Royal Caledonian Curling Club in 1843 (thanks to the patronage of Prince Albert), this was Scotland's first national association for the governance of sporting clubs.

By this time curling was already common in Glasgow. Its existence has been noted in Anderston in around 1773, while the earliest societies were formed in Pollokshaws in 1808, North Woodside in 1820, and Partick, mentioned opposite, in 1842.

Others were in Cathcart, Gorbals and Port Dundas.

In fact by 1850, according to John Burnett (see Links), roughly half of all the sports clubs in Scotland were curling clubs.

The third advance in curling concerned the stones themselves.

In the early years stones were of varying shapes and weights, often picked out from a river bed, fashioned by a stonemason and then fixed with a handle by a blacksmith. Gradually, from the late 18th century they started to become circular, until in the 1860s mechanised cutting techniques allowed perfectly circular stones to come onto the market. Just as Thomas Taylor's standard bowls transformed bowling from 1871 onwards, so too did this advance permit curlers to compete on a more equitable footing.

The third development concerned the creation of man-made curling rinks.

Two main factors have been cited as the impetus for this.

Firstly, and especially in urban areas like Glasgow, many natural ponds were either being infilled »

▲ On the few occasions in recent years during which temperatures have dropped sufficiently for Glasgow's skaters to dust down their outdoor gear, the place to gather has been **Bingham's Pond** on Great Western Road, as seen here in January 2010.

No doubt the pond has existed for many years, and may well have been used by the **Glasgow Skating Club** when they formed in 1830.

Certainly it was ideal for skating, being six and a half acres in extent and with a maximum depth of only 30 inches.

But it was Walter Bingham, a bowling green contractor, who turned it into a commercial concern in the 1880s. He tidied its edges, erected a boathouse (in which the Glasgow Skating Club rented a clubroom) and laid out a curling pond on the south west corner, as seen on the map of 1894 (right). By this time electric lighting had

been installed, allowing skaters and curlers to take maximum advantage whenever the ponds were frozen.

Bingham's family helped run the business, while Walter himself was otherwise occupied as groundsman for the Glasgow Academicals at Anniesland (see Chapter Seven).

For years Bingham's Pond was the place to skate in Glasgow, and to go boating. But as the 20th

century wore on its eastern edge was infilled – the Pond Hotel stands on this site now (above left) – while its increasingly neglected state led in 2003 to it being cleaned up and naturalised as a wildlife retreat, with extra planting and two islands raised in its centre.

Still this has left plenty of room to skate, even if such opportunities are now exceedingly rare.

J. F. KING

CURLING ON WESTBURN GREEN   THE DOVECOTE

▲ This late 19th century image shows curling on **Westburn Green**, better known since 1892 as the home of **Cambuslang Golf Course** (see page 131).

Before that, apart from curling the 30 acre expanse was used by three local football clubs, and before that it formed the grounds of Westburn House – the only surviving element of which is the octagonal 18th century dovecote seen here which, now listed Category B, is a familiar presence in the centre of the golf course.

The curling pond, however, is no more. First marked on a map of 1864, it lay between the dovecote and Clydeford Road, and was filled in by the golf club in 1947.

The scene depicts a typical Victorian 'bonspiel' (meaning a league, or alliance game), with players gathered around to check which of the stones has come closest to the intended target area, known as the 'button'.

Note the bearded onlooker in the top hat. One of the characteristics of curling often cited in stories of the game was how all classes of people were equal on the ice.

'We are brethren a', as one curling medal put it.

» or drained. Secondly, and more pertinently, from the mid 1820s onwards winter temperatures started to nudge upwards.

The Little Ice Age was not quite over, but the signs were sufficient for men of science to take matters into their own hands. Scottish men of science, that is.

The man credited with starting this process was John Cairnie, a former East India Company surgeon, who in 1833 wrote an *Essay on Curling and Artificial Pond Making*, published by the Glasgow University Press.

Cairnie's principle was simple. Instead of waiting for a large body of water to freeze, all curlers had to do was create a shallow bed with raised edges, and as temperatures fell, fill it gradually with water so that layers of ice would form.

His early attempts using clay beds proved problematic, as vegetation could penetrate the surface. Also tried were wooden planks and cast iron plates.

But inadvertently another Scot came up with the answer. His name, John Loudon MacAdam. His invention, macadamisation.

Such was the impact of Cairnie's groundwork that, despite warmer winters, the number of days on which Scottish curlers could now play was said to have quadrupled.

Maps of Glasgow during the 19th century do not always make it clear which curling ponds were natural (as at Westburn Green, *see left*) and which were created on the Cairnie principle. But David B Smith has identified at least 80 in total, and judging by the number which have regular shapes, many of these must have fallen into the latter category, or at the very least have been made shallower for curling purposes.

Certainly the three ponds of the Glasgow Academicals at New Anniesland were man-made, as were those at Bingham's Pond and Wellcroft Bowling Club.

In 1906 Matthew Gemmell noted 17 curling clubs in the Glasgow area. Among those that we can pinpoint to specific ponds were the Academicals, Lilybank, Hillhead, Partick, Pollok, Shettleston and Willow Bank.

Two appear to have been formed by curlers working in specific industries, Glasgow Timber Trade and Kelvin Dock.

But a century later, only one of those 17 clubs still has its own clubhouse and Cairnie rink, and that is the Partick Curling Club, to which we will return on the following pages.

The reason why no other outdoor facilities have survived is straightforward. As we shall also note later, in 1896 Glasgow gained its first, albeit shortlived, indoor ice rink on Sauchiehall Street. This was followed in 1907 by the Crossmyloof Ice Rink, which in two separate phases would serve as Glasgow's main focus for all ice sports until 1986. Other rinks have appeared at Kelvin Hall, in the late 1930s, at Finnieston, from 1986–97, and from 1999, at the Braehead Arena.

Outdoor ice sports are now, of course, exceedingly rare, courtesy of our warmer winters.

In 1912, Glasgow Academicals were able to curl on their tarmac rinks for 25 days, and in 1920 for 26. Yet the last time Partick's rink was used in earnest was for a brief spell during the mid 1980s.

In short, curling has survived in Glasgow only thanks to modern refrigeration techniques. Until the next Little Ice Age then, ice sports are very much confined to quarters.

▲ Not Glasgow, patently, but we include this 1979 spectacle of the **Lake of Menteith,** near Aberfoyle in Perthshire, 27 miles north of Glasgow, because it shows the last occasion on which curlers were able to gather for the most famous bonspiel of all, the **Grand Match**.

Contested between curlers from the North and South, the latter including many a Glaswegian,

such is the depth of ice required (six inches being the accepted minimum) that it has been staged only 33 times since 1847.

Tellingly, only six of those have been since the First World War.

But at least the 1979 match was one of the finest. Over 2,000 curlers saw action on a gloriously sunny day, watched by thousands of spectators (6,000 according to

one report), most of whom came well stocked with whisky, that vital accompaniment to outdoor curling.

As the *Glasgow Herald* reported, the lake's 8¼ inches of ice 'groaned and heaved under 370 tons of happy humanity'.

For the record, the North won, 3,937 shots to 3,144. But no-one really cared. That the gathering had taken place at all was enough.

As this book went to press there were high hopes that we might be able to slip in an image of the 34th Grand Match, in January 2010.

But alas it proved a false hope. Although the ice was thick enough, with the approach roads unfit to cope with the likely traffic the organisers opted not take any risks.

And so, over 30 years after the scene above, the wait goes on...

Played in Glasgow **161**

▲ This puddled patch of tarmac in a secluded corner of **Victoria Park** may not immediately catch the eye, but it is in fact the only Cairnie-style artificial curling rink known to have survived in Glasgow.

Created in 1902 by the **Partick Curling Club**, whose clubhouse is at the far end, this was originally one of two rinks. A larger one, facing the pavilion, is now part of a car park used by the Council's Land and Environmental Services division. Partick rent the site from the Council at a peppercorn rent.

As can be seen, the rink's design is simple enough, a sunken tarmac bed with concentric rings at the pavilion end (*right*) forming what is called the 'house', with the 'button' in the centre.

Such rinks are not easy to maintain, especially when there are so few opportunities to play on them. One issue is leakage, caused by cracks in the tarmac.

Since the last time an organised match took place on this rink in the 1980s, the nearest Partick have come to a repeat was in January 2010 (*top right*). Frustratingly, however, by the time club members had made all the necessary preparations, a thaw set in.

△ One further benefit of **Partick Curling Club**'s secluded location is the survival of eight original lamp posts, installed by the side of the rinks in 1911 in order to ensure that whenever there was ice, bad light would not stop play.

No doubt hoping to attract new members, the club placed notices to this effect in the *Evening Citizen*.

But then curlers have always had to seize the moment. Kilmarnock had a club which played at dawn, before the players started work, while elsewhere it was common to play by lantern light. Bingham's Pond had electric lighting as early as 1882, barely three years after incandescent bulbs were invented.

One of Partick's hardier members was 'Long' John Anderson, 6´5˝ tall, who in 1842 apparently played non-stop for 36 hours, much of that time by candlelight. Anderson was still playing at the age of 86, proof that cold air and plenty of liquid nourishment may be just what the doctor ordered.

△ Being hidden away from the public eye, on the Balshagray Avenue side of **Victoria Park**, may well have been the saving grace for **Partick Curling Club**'s charming pavilion, which dates from 1900.

For not only is the curling house unique in Glasgow, it is also one of only five historic examples known in Scotland as a whole.

As such, in late 2009 it was put forward to Historic Scotland as a candidate for listing.

Victoria Park is the club's third home. Formed as the Partick Union Curling Society in 1842, as noted earlier the club was originally based at the Drovers Inn, at a time when the Byres Road, as its name suggests, was a rural byway with barely a building on it. Partick was then an independent burgh.

In 1857 the club moved to a new pond on Peel Street (where Dyce Lane is now), just north of where a few years later the West of Scotland cricket ground was laid out (see *page 176*). For £6 they had erected a wooden pavilion, which a Mr Anderson then offered to paint with imitation bricks.

Their final move to Victoria Park, which had opened in 1887, came in 1894, courtesy of a 20 year lease at £7 per annum, negotiated with the Town Council. Next door to the site was Partick Tennis Club.

Fortunately for the curlers, if not the tennis players, their first eight years in the park coincided with a series of exceptionally cold winters, so they were quite content to curl on a conventional pond. (Down in London during the same period curlers reported enjoying around fifteen days of ice per year).

Partick were also fortunate to have wealthy patrons. The pavilion, its architect unknown, was endowed by Bailie William Kennedy, while the two artificial rinks, opened two years later in 1902, were gifted by M Hunter Kennedy (himself a prominent player) and John G Kennedy.

Ironically, the opening in 1907 of the new indoor ice rink at Crossmyloof meant that members would spend less and less time at Victoria Park as the century wore on. But on the plus side, this has resulted in the pavilion remaining virtually untouched.

A hidden gem it may be therefore, but it is a wonderfully unspoilt one too.

▶ The expression 'stepping back in time' is often used, but in the case of the **Partick Curling Club** could hardly be more apt.

When Partick members curl on the artificial ice pad at the Braehead Arena they use all the latest modern equipment. But the old stones in the clubhouse, each stored in original wooden lockers, have much in common with their 21st century counterparts. They are made from various types of granite quarried from Ailsa Craig, an island ten miles off the Ayrshire coast. This provides the beautifully speckled Common Ailsa and finer grained Blue Hone granite still favoured for their smooth surfaces.

Each stone weighs around 40lbs (18kgs), and, being virtually indestructible, will more than likely have been handed down.

In modern curling, fibreglass and graphite brushes are used to sweep the ice in front of each stone as it makes it way towards the 'house', usually accompanied by cries of 'soop her up'. In contrast, at Partick they still have a number of original corn brooms, such as would have been found in any Victorian household cupboard.

Another handcrafted accessory no longer in use in modern curling is the 'crampit' (*below*). Measuring 3-4 feet in length, this is a spiked sheet of iron which was placed on the ice to provide a steady foothold.

So few have been the occasions on which any of these vintage pieces have been used in recent decades that the Partick pavilion is almost akin to a museum of curling. Readers wishing to see it for themselves are therefore advised to take a peek when the building is opened to the public during Glasgow's annual Doors Open Day programme in September.

▲ Forming the heart of the **Patrick Curling Club** is their club room, still used for meetings and social gatherings, even if curling is nowadays confined to Braehead.

Being a winter activity, curling has always been a convivial sport. Matches were traditionally followed by that 'prince of all good dishes', beef and greens (salt beef and kale), helped down by generous servings of whisky toddy. In other words, that kettle over the fireplace was not intended for making tea.

In an adjoining room is the clubhouse 'cludgie', still with its original wooden seat.

One of the club's other historic assets is its set of minute books, in which we read of many a lively, drink-sodden dinner, often held in association with Partick's counterparts from Govan.

Thus in 1870 we read from Archibald Anderson's rather shakily enscribed minutes that at the club's AGM the President had ordered 'sum refreshment which afterwards brought out both song and sentiment and terminated a veary hapy meeting'.

▲ Dated 1726, the **Partick Bell** was used to herald announcements or rouse the villagers. Retired from service in 1779, it was presented to the **Partick Curling Club** by John Ross in April 1859, as an award to be competed for every year.

But, Ross demanded, custodians of the bell could not live further east from Partick Cross than 215 Dumbarton Road, where stood his house at Sandyford. Nor could it be in the custody of any member residing south of the Clyde.

To ensure this did not happen Ross further required two sureties of £15 each, and specified that if ever club membership dropped below eight, the bell should be handed back to the Burgh of Partick. Its use today is purely ceremonial, and decorative.

▶ Realising that circular ice rinks did not provide an ideal arena for skating or curling, the directors of the Scottish Ice Rink Company chose a more sensible design for Glasgow's first purpose-built ice rink, and indeed the first in Scotland overall.

Located close to one of the south side's largest curling ponds at Lilybank, **Crossmyloof Ice Rink** was, at the time of its opening – by Sir Charles Dundas in October 1907 – one of the most advanced in Britain.

Its ice-making equipment was powered by two gas engines, which pumped brine, cooled by an ammonia compression system, through six miles of wrought iron pipes laid on a concrete bed.

At 149 x 98 feet, the ice pad itself was large enough for six curling rinks to be in play at the same time, with viewing areas for spectators both at ground level and on an upper balcony (*below right*), where hot water radiators provided added comfort.

No doubt a few local curlers were at first sceptical about this genuinely advanced venue.

But not the Royal Caledonian Curling Club, whose 1906–07 Annual expressed the earnest hope that at last matches could now be arranged 'without any risk of interference from King Thaw,' and that as a result, 'King Frost would perhaps be taught a lesson that would make him mend his manners.'

There was however one design flaw, and that was the presence in the middle of the rink of a line of columns supporting the main roof trusses. One of these columns, as seen in the postcard view of the opening day (*top right*), was fitted with a bandstand, barely raised above head height.

RELIABLE SERIES *Real Ice* —   Skating and Curling Pavilion, Crossmyloof.

Not a problem for curling, but its presence cannot have made it easy for ice hockey players involved in Scotland's inaugural international against England played in 1909.

Nevertheless, after the technical problems suffered by the first generation of rinks, Crossmyloof represented a definite leap forward, and accordingly was visited by skaters from all over Britain. It was also a huge success as a curling venue. According to *The Times*, after only a year in operation it had around a thousand curling members, and had attracted several clubs 'from the provinces'.

A visiting team of Canadian curlers had also been impressed, while it is highly likely that a delegation from Germany paid a visit too, for in 1909 the world's largest rink opened in Berlin.

Certainly a group of curlers from Manchester tried it out, because they enlisted the Crossmyloof

manager in their campaign to build a new rink to replace the city's earlier Glaciarium, which had lasted barely a year.

They succeeded, with the result that in October 1910 the Manchester Ice Palace eclipsed anything seen before in Britain.

Two years later Edinburgh followed suit, with its first indoor rink at Haymarket.

▶ Photographed in 1950 from the corner of Dolphin and Titwood Roads, looking east, this is how **Crossmyloof Ice Rink** appeared after it had been comprehensively reconstructed in 1928–29.

In common with so many commercial sports venues, the original rink had suffered badly from falling usage once war broke out, with the result that in 1916 it remained open only thanks to a £2,000 guarantee underwritten by that great patron of Partick Curling Club, M Hunter Kennedy. But although this kept Crossmyloof open for another year or so, in early 1918 the owners accepted a bid from the giant engineering firm William Beardmore, and the building was then converted into a factory for making aero engines for the war effort.

This meant that after the war Glasgow's skaters and curlers had to travel to Edinburgh for their sport. Meanwhile plans for new rinks on Pitt Street, and in Kelvin Hall both collapsed, until once again Hunter Kennedy came to the rescue by forming a syndicate called the Scottish Ice Rink Company (1928) Ltd., to buy and reconstruct the old building at Crossmyloof.

Costing £21,500 and designed by architects Watson Salmond & Gray, the new Crossmyloof retained the original ground floor flanking walls and arched windows (as may be seen by comparing the views on this page and opposite), so that the new ice pad was the same width as the original, at 98 feet. But it was longer, at 185 feet, and crucially this time, was column free, and with more spectator accommodation, offering 1332 seats on two levels. There was also a café, termed as a 'soda fountain' on the plans.

These were heady years in the ice rink business, with at least 27 new venues opening up around Britain between 1927–39, as promoters sought to cash in on what they hoped would be a boom in ice hockey attendances. (Two other late 1920s imports, greyhound racing and speedway, prompted a similar rush of stadium construction, *see Chapter 13*).

Within a year of Crossmyloof's re-opening its operators invested further by extending the rink to 223 feet in length – perhaps in order to accommodate ice hockey more comfortably and increase the seating capacity to nearer 2,000.

Then in the mid 1930s an extra ice hall was added at the western end (on the right in the top photograph), accommodating four more curling rinks, so that curling could still take place when the main rink was in use for general skating or for ice hockey.

Crossmyloof Ice Rink in the 1970s, looking east from the junction of Titwood Road, Minard Road and Darnley Road. As many readers will be aware, after the rink closed in 1986 a Morrisons superstore was built on the site. Of 27 rinks known to have opened from 1927–39, only four survive: two in London, Kirkcaldy (opened 1937) and Murrayfield (1939).

▲ Plus fours and kilts, collars and ties on parade at **Crossmyloof** in the 1950s. For older Glaswegians, mention of Crossmyloof always elicits a response of one kind or another, some recalling it fondly as a place where couples met and fun was to be had, others shivering at the memory of how cold and draughty it became.

In truth, its final years were not bathed in such a positive light as seen here. The roofs leaked. Often the surface was awash with melting ice. One on occasion, the story goes, a Christmas tree that had been placed in the centre of the rink, but then hoisted up into the rafters, fell onto the ice in the middle of an ice hockey game (which carried on regardless).

Shades of the old bandstand.

Eventually Crossmyloof closed in February 1986, hardly mourned, partly because it was replaced by a rink at the newly opened Summit Centre in Finnieston. However this soon suffered problems of its own, partly due to subsidence, and since its rink closed in 1997, Glasgow's skaters and curlers have had to travel out to the Braehead Arena in Renfrew for the nearest indoor ice.

On this occasion at **Crossmyloof** in 1932 the Scottish ice hockey team were successful in beating the Grosvenor House Canadians (a team of Canadians based at a London ice rink). But such successes were rare, and in truth most British ice hockey teams of the 1930s were in any case dependent on Canadian imports.

In one sense this was hardly surprising, as the game had been invented in Canada in the 1860s (albeit by British settlers). It had been a Canadian champion skater, George Meagher, who had first brought the game to Glasgow in 1896, putting on an exhibition match at Hubner's Ice Palace, which cannot have been easy on its circular rink.

Nor can it have been ideal when Crossmyloof staged its first ice hockey international in 1909 – the English gaining an easy victory – with players having to avoid the columns and the bandstand.

But the revamped Crossmyloof was much better suited, and over the years played host to a succession of Glasgow teams; the Mohawks (1929–55), who became the Dynamoes until the rink closed in 1986; the amateur Mustangs, at various times between 1935 and 1951, and the Flyers in 1963–64.

Today the area's only ice hockey representatives are the Braehead Paisley Pirates, a reincarnation of the hugely successful Paisley Pirates of the 1950s, who as the name suggests, play at the **Braehead Arena**.

Opened in 1999 as part of the Braehead Shopping Centre, on the banks of the Clyde in Renfrew, the Arena's eight rink ice pad (*left*) is also now the main centre for all curling in the Glasgow area, being the home of 80 clubs in total, the Partick Curling Club included.

Chapter Eleven

Cricket

Taking guard at Stepps, where Glasgow's first suburban railway line opened in 1831. By the time this picture was taken in c.1900, the spread of railways had facilitated the formation of several district cricket leagues, each fiercely competitive and quite different in character to the more middle class cricket scene of Glasgow in the 19th century. In the background are half completed houses on Whitehill Avenue. Today Stepps is best known for its successful hockey club, formed in 1913.

Cricket, that most English of games, is not a sport normally associated with Scotland.

Yet cricket has been part of the Scottish scene since the early 19th century and was the first team sport to become established.

Undoubtedly its introduction owed much to the influx of English troops following the Jacobite rebellion of 1745. As one anonymous Glaswegian wrote of his time in Portugal with the 71st regiment during the Napoleonic Wars, around 1810, an awful lot of cricket was played during the longueurs between action.

Inevitably, Glasgow Green became the focus of cricket in Glasgow – it was first recorded there in 1826 – not only because it was one of the few open expanses of level ground in an otherwise crowded town, but because nearby, within the army barracks just to the east of the University, the soldiers used to play on the Butts, the grounds where archery had once been practised.

A 'lamentable dirge' written by Bailzie Peakodde in 1835 says much about the spirit in which the game was played on Glasgow Green. After the star player, one Bob Maxwell, had been unscrupulously detained by Squire Thomson, the impatient crowd, consisting of 'squire, commoner and whore' showered the other players with 'a cloud of dogs and cats' and tried to 'to brain them with their bats' until finally Maxwell arrived, on a stretcher.

Gambling was rife. In 1833, for example, when a Glasgow team played Perth on Glasgow Green, the *Sporting Gazette* reported the winners' stake to be £25.

In 1841 cricket's hold on Scotland would be strengthened by a War Office decree that every garrison should have a cricket ground. The arrival of English workers in Scottish mills helped too, so that by 1873, historian John Burnett has calculated, there were 200 cricket clubs in Scotland, a number exceeded only in curling.

In Glasgow, as in the rest of urban Britain, the game only spread beyond the middle classes once shorter working hours were introduced in the late 19th century. This, combined with the spread of the railways and of Glasgow itself – taking in, for example, the flat expanse of Burnbank to the west (*see opposite*) – led in 1893 to the formation of the Western District Cricket Union.

This highly competitive league, rather disdained by Edinburgh's cricketing elite, would form the basis of high level cricket in the city until the formation in 1998 of a Scottish National Cricket League.

Today, over 150 clubs are affiliated to Cricket Scotland, and the national team now plays regularly in one day tournaments.

But although still eclipsed by the likes of football, golf, bowling and curling – in the national consciousness at least – from a historical perspective the contribution made by cricket in the 19th century was fundamental.

By organising inter-club games, by securing the grounds necessary, and by setting up the frameworks under which team sports could operate, in a very practical sense it was cricketers, and cricket administrators, who laid down the foundations from which rugby and football were later able to emerge.

▲ Many readers will be familiar with this image, thought to be the earliest photograph of cricket in Glasgow. It was taken in 1871, just off the Great Western Road at **Burnbank** – described on the original print as **Woodlands Park** – during a two day encounter between local players and an All England XI, a match watched by an estimated 3–5,000 spectators. Some of them can be seen along the boundary, backing onto the tenements on Queen's Crescent.

Note that not all the players are in whites, while both umpires appear in dark suits.

Taken by an amateur photographer, Duncan Brown, the image is in the collection of the Glasgow School of Art, whose predecessor, the Government School of Design in Ingram Street, had employed Brown as a janitor.

From c.1854–78 Burnbank was one of the largest expanses of land used for sport in Glasgow, figuring in the early history of several important clubs.

Forming part of the estate of the Campbell family of Blythswood, it was described in 1866 as covering 18 acres, stretching from Queen's Crescent down to Woodlands Road, and as far west as Park Road.

The first club to play on the ground seen above was the **Caledonian Cricket Club** in 1854.

South west of this, in 1859 **Willowbank Bowling Club** (*see page 136*) opened a green on the site of what is now Willowbank Primary School (this was before the club moved to Dowanside Road in 1896). **Burnbank Bowling Club** joined them, a hundred yards south, across Woodlands Road, in 1866, where they remain today.

That same decade, backing onto Willowbank's green, on West Prince's Street the **1st Lanarkshire Rifle Volunteers** (of which Archibald Campbell of Blythswood was a founding officer in 1860) built a drill hall, using the western section of Burnbank as their drill ground.

Then in 1866 the Volunteers sub-let part of this (roughly where Montague Street now lies) to **Glasgow Academy**, for use as the school's first playing fields. In 1867 this area staged the first match in one of world rugby's longest running fixtures, the Accies v. West of Scotland.

After the Academy moved on in 1874, **Blythswood Cricket Club** took over their ground, while in 1875, a field opposite the drill hall, between what is now Dunearn Street and Woodlands Drive, was rented by **Rangers Football Club**.

Rangers stayed only one season. The ground was too small and the West End proved unpopular with their growing band of supporters.

Meanwhile, another section of Burnbank had been built over to create Arlington Street, where the **Arlington Baths Club** (*see page 204*) was opened in 1871.

The final departure was that of Caledonian CC, who gave up their lease in 1878. Queen's Park FC bought their old pavilion for £65.

And so, bit by bit the green fields of Burnbank were sold off for housing, in the case of the cricket ground above, making way for Carrington Street.

The 1840s tenements on Queen's Crescent still stand however, making it fairly easy to see where Duncan would have stood to capture this now classic scene in 1871.

▲ In 2004 **Clydesdale Cricket Club** celebrated the centenary of their ground at **Titwood** by renovating the pavilion clock tower.

The pavilion's architect in 1904 was a club member, Henry Edward Clifford, whose other commissions included four golf clubhouses, one of them at Royal Troon, in 1886.

Before moving to Titwood – to a field adjacent to the current ground – Clydesdale played on two sites at Kinning Park, both rented from the Pollok estate (*see Chapter Five*).

The first, just north of where Kinning Park Underground Station now stands, staged its opening game in September 1848, but had to be vacated once the herdsman saw the damage to his grassland.

The second, an adjoining field first used in June 1849, lay on what is now Scotland Street West.

It was at Kinning Park that Clydesdale's football section formed, reaching the first Scottish Cup Final in 1874. Ironic, then, that after they left for Titwood in 1876, Kinning Park was rented by that up-and-coming club recently based at Burnbank, Rangers FC.

▲ Founded in 1848, **Clydesdale Cricket Club** is Glasgow's oldest cricket club and the third oldest in Scotland, after Kelso (c.1820), and Grange, in Edinburgh (1832).

But its roots go back further than 1848 because it was formed at the suggestion of a Hawick man, Archie Campbell, from the merger of two earlier clubs, Wallacegrove, and Thistle (who are recorded as having played on Glasgow Green in 1832).

As noted on the left, Clydesdale started out at Kinning Park, before taking up the offer of moving to Titwood, still within the Pollok Estate, but in Pollokshields. This was an emerging suburb whose new residents would soon be spoilt for choice when it came to sport.

Just to the north, the Titwood

Bowling and Tennis Club was laid out in 1890 (*see page 88*), while on Shawmoss Road were the Lilybank curling ponds. In 1907 the area also became home to the Crossmyloof Ice Rink (*page 168*).

When Clydesdale played their first match at the Titwood Athletic Grounds, in June 1876, the site covered almost twice the size of the grounds we see today, with the cricket club occupying a pitch to the east of the ground seen above.

Backing onto Darnley Road, it was on this pitch – now occupied by Hutcheson's Grammar School – where an Australia XI were beaten by a Clydesdale Invitation team of 18 players in front of 7,000 spectators in 1880, and where four years later Queen's Park

FC played briefly while the Second Hampden was being laid out.

Queen's Park in those days used to enter the English FA Cup, and in January 1884 were drawn to play against the mighty Aston Villa.

An estimated 10,000 crowd packed into Titwood, a thousand of whom had travelled up from Birmingham by rail, on what is believed to have been the first ever 'football special'.

Queen's Park made history that day, winning 6–1, which might explain why the morning after a number of hungover Brummies were found sleeping out in the closes of Shawlands, having missed their train home.

As it happened, six years later a new station opened at Crossmyloof,

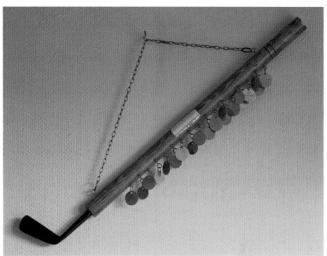

making Titwood more accessible than ever. Indeed, when in 1894 a Clydesdale player whacked a ball over the fence and it landed on a goods train, the Crossmyloof stationmaster was able to get it back, from Carlisle.

Any further risk of a recurrence ended when the cricket club moved westwards to its current ground at Titwood in 1904. Laying out a new pitch and erecting the pavilion cost £2,000, but its opening in April of that year came too late for Archie Campbell, who died shortly before.

By then Clydesdale were key members of the Western District Cricket Union, a competition that would continue until being replaced by the current Scottish National Cricket League in 1998.

Titwood itself has also undergone a major revamp in recent years.

In 1987 a bequest from a member enabled the club to form the Titwood Sports Ground Trust and purchase the site from the Pollok Estate for £29,000.

Since then the pavilion has been expanded and upgraded at great cost, but with the added benefit that in May 2007, Titwood was selected as an official venue for one day internationals.

As previous internationals against Ireland in 1986 and India in 1990 had drawn crowds of 3,500, this was a major coup for Clydesdale, especially as only one other Scottish ground, the Grange in Edinburgh, has been accorded this status.

▲ Throughout this book we have seen a number of unusual trophies, but none quirkier than this cricket stump with a golf putter attached.

The **'Clydesdale Stump'** is competed for by members of the Clydesdale Cricket Club in an annual golf tournament, with winners' names being inscribed on medallions in a somewhat humbler echo of Glasgow Golf Club's Silver Club at Killermont (*see page 28*).

But then Clydesdale, and Titwood, have always been open to other sporting interests.

Earlier we learnt how the club had a successful football section in the 1870s. To this was added a rugby section in the 1880s, a

time when it was also reported that cricket at Titwood was losing out to the new sport of lawn tennis. (**Clydesdale RFC** now play at Stonehouse, south of Glasgow).

Also at Titwood, until 1980, was a bowling green, used over the years by three works clubs, Anchorline, J & P Coats, and Wallace & Weir. The green has since been replaced in 1997 by a synthetic hockey pitch, as part of £720,000 scheme funded by the National Lottery and the Foundation for Sport and the Arts for the **Clydesdale Hockey Club**.

This club originated as the Cartha Hockey Club in 1902, before moving to Titwood in 1959.

West of Scotland, Cricket Ground   Partick

▲ Partick was still an independent burgh when this view of the **Hamilton Crescent Cricket Ground** was published in 1904, showing the tenements of Partickhill rising up in the background.

Originally used in the 1850s by two clubs, Clutha CC and Royal CC, in 1862 Hamilton Crescent was leased from Sir Archibald

Campbell (later Lord Blythswood) by **West of Scotland Cricket Club**, formed that year by a group of local businessmen led by the tobacco merchant David Carrick Buchanan (after whose family Buchanan Street was named).

Buchanan's patronage enabled West of Scotland to build a pavilion and enclose the ground with iron

fencing, thus making Hamilton Crescent the most advanced sports ground in the Glasgow area.

As such it hosted several of the most important encounters of the period; for example the visit of an All England XI in 1864, the first ever appearance of an Australian team in Scotland in 1878, and, in later years, several games involving such cricketing luminaries as WG Grace and CB Fry. After a rugby section formed in 1865 Hamilton Crescent also staged four rugby internationals, between 1873–85.

However, Hamilton Crescent's greatest claim to fame is that on a foggy afternoon on November 30 1872 it staged the world's first football international, Scotland and England playing out a 0–0 draw in front of 4,000 spectators.

With each one paying a minimum of one shilling entrance (see page 185), this generated a healthy profit of £33 for Queen's Park FC, whose amateur players had made up the entire Scottish XI.

It must also have been good business for West of Scotland, for they again rented out the ground for football for Scottish Cup Finals in both 1876 and 1877. The latter match, between Rangers and Vale of Leven, went to a replay which drew 14,000 to the ground.

Thereafter Hampden Park became Glasgow's leading football venue. But how different might football history have been had West of Scotland chosen to form its own football team and exploit what clearly was, at the time, a ground with considerable potential.

For all its amateur status, in common with Queen's Park FC the West of Scotland club made sure it maximised its gate income by installing new turnstile blocks, designed by George Beattie, in 1925. None survive, although the ornate ironwork topping this block can still be seen on the ground's boundary wall on Peel Street.

▲ Viewed in 2009, the ground of the **West of Scotland Cricket Club** has changed in several subtle ways.

Not least, since Partick was absorbed by Glasgow in 1912 Hamilton Crescent itself has been renamed Fortrose Street – seen here in the foreground, with the green of **Partick Bowling Club** (laid out in 1854) on the right.

On the left, with its prominent tower, is the 1872 Partick Burgh Hall. Beyond, the white modern flats were originally the Greenbank Leather Works (see page 185).

Least altered on the actual ground is the pavilion (right).

Opened in 1923 this still has its original decorative eaves, but has rather lost its balance since an extension was added in the 1980s. Behind is an indoor cricket school, which when opened in 1957 was the first in Scotland.

By then, the only other sport staged at the ground was hockey, the parent club having rather surprisingly terminated its rugby section's tenancy in 1945. (They now play at Milngavie.) So when the hockey players moved on in the 1970s, Hamilton Crescent became solely dependent on cricket, a risky strategy at the best of times, but one that by the early 1990s forced the now ailing West of Scotland to sell off the former rugby pitch for the flats now seen above, backing onto the former burgh hall.

Since then, happily, the club's constitution has been amended to rule out any further land sales. The ground is also more widely used, by a local school and by the footballers of St Mirren and Partick Thistle for training. This, plus ongoing efforts to raise funds have put the club on a sounder footing. But with Titwood having secured its status as Glasgow's pre-eminent cricket centre, the challenges facing West of Scotland do not get any easier.

Two more typical cricket pavilions from between the wars are those of Poloc Cricket Club at Shawholm (*see page 80*), designed by club member John Galt and opened by Sir John Stirling Maxwell in April 1930, and Kelburne Cricket Club (*right*). Formed in 1860, Kelburne moved to their current ground at Whitehaugh in 1899. As its name suggests, their Coronation Pavilion was opened in 1937.

GLASGOW ACADEMICAL CLUB
GROUNDSMAN'S HOUSE AND PAVILION

◀ We conclude this chapter at **New Anniesland**, the home of the **Glasgow Academicals**, whose 1958 timber grandstand is shown on page 118, and whose pavilion is almost certainly the oldest still in use in Glasgow cricketing circles.

The 'Accies' had rented various grounds since starting at Burnbank in 1866 (*see page 173*), but by 1902 felt it was time to settle.

A measure of their social status was that while in 1899 Rangers, a professional football club, hoped to raise £10,000 to create an 80,000 capacity stadium, the amateur Accies, with just 300 members, proposed spending £9,300 on New Anniesland.

Opened in May 1908 and designed by the Laird brothers, the club's Arts and Crafts pavilion, an adjoining groundsman's house (on the left in this image from the 1907 prospectus) and a small grandstand, together with the purchase and preparation of the ground (which included three Cairnie-style curling rinks), ended up costing over £10,680. Yet with support from the school and members' subscriptions, the Accies were able to pay it all off by 1913.

Today, after various extensions and refurbishments carried out since 1955, the core of that 1908 pavilion can still be seen, albeit in rather less rural surrounds than a century ago.

Chapter Twelve

Football

One of a network of grounds serving Glasgow's junior football scene, Petershill Park was in use for 70 years before it was left to the whims of vandals in 2005. Its replacement, opened two years later on an adjacent site, represents a radical departure from tradition, as we shall discover.

Football, it almost goes without saying, is by far the most dominant sport in Glasgow.

In terms of spectator numbers, only two British clubs, Manchester United and Arsenal, have in recent years recorded higher average gates than the Glasgow giants. In 2008-09, for example, Celtic's average of 57,761 put the club in third place. Rangers were fourth, with their average of 49,534.

But if we then analyse these figures in relation to population, it transpires that more people attend matches in the Scottish Premier League, per capita, than in any other nation in Europe.

In geographic terms, Celtic and Rangers draw their support from all over Scotland and from across the Irish Sea. It is the same in Glasgow itself, where apart from areas such as Garngad (Celtic territory) and Bridgeton (Rangers), their support spans the entire city.

However, the 'Gers and the 'Tic are by no means the alpha and omega of the Glasgow game. In this chapter, therefore, we delve below the top level to consider the city's wider football heritage,

and in particular its plethora of smaller clubs, each with their own localised areas of support, and each facing up to the challenge of survival in a rapidly changing urban and social environment.

Of course football is not just about spectating.

Compared with their fellow Scots, Glaswegians are also highly committed to playing what is so often called 'the beautiful game'.

Although comparisons are tricky, owing to how one defines the boundaries of Glasgow, Scottish Football Association records show that of 66,000 players registered nationwide, 22 per cent live in the Glasgow area. In proportion to the population as a whole, this suggests that Glaswegians are almost twice as likely to play organised football than their counterparts elsewhere.

What is more, Glaswegians have been football crazy for centuries.

Certainly an annual Shrove Tuesday ba' game was being played in Glasgow as early as the 1570s. Unruly this may have been, but it was not governed by mob rule, as some historians have

suggested. Indeed the balls, made by a local shoemaker, were paid for by the Town Council.

Anglocentric narratives of the modern game have equally glossed over the fact that the Scots were playing football on designated pitches, with goalposts and a fixed number of players per team, long before the Football Association formed in London in 1863.

Historian John Hutchinson has even discovered the existence of a football club in Edinburgh in 1824, a good 30 years before the formation of England's oldest known club.

Around the same time games were also taking place at Glasgow University. The Free Church leader Robert Smith Candlish, a student from 1818–23, was described by Lord Ardmillan as playing on the College Green 'with all the intense energy, keenness and activity' which characterised his later years.

From the 1870s we have already noted Queen's Park's contribution to the development of tactics in the early years of the Association game, and the staging of the world's first international match

The Union Jack, the Irish Tricolour and the thin dayglo line of the Strathclyde Police. This is the image of Glasgow football known to most outsiders. Yet it represents only a part of what is otherwise a wonderfully multi-layered local football culture, rich with heritage.

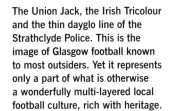

Meadowside Park, Partick.
Ground of the Partick Thistle F.C.

at Hamilton Crescent in 1872. In the 1880s it was in Glasgow where crowds of 10,000 and more first became commonplace, and where in the ensuing years three of the first purpose-built superstadiums were built between 1892-1903.

By 1906, in his report on *The Societies of Glasgow*, Matthew Gemmell noted the existence of over 50 football clubs in the city, a number that we now know to have been a gross underestimate.

Many, inevitably, have since folded; the likes of Linthouse, Cowlairs, Dennistoun Waverley and Parkhead Juniors. Yet today's total of registered clubs in

Glasgow is still at least 90, and that does not include hundreds more at grass roots level.

Gemmell also wrote in 1906, 'nothing short of royalty or a hanging in the open, draws like this game; the sixpences or shillings as the case may be are there in their thousands; strikes or dull trade affect not the gate of a big match and the stands are filled to overflowing'.

At a time when Glasgow had earned the title 'Second City of the Empire', it is no overstatement to add that it might equally have been lauded as the footballing capital of the world.

▲ **Meadowside Park** was the fourth enclosed ground **Partick Thistle** had played at since their formative years in Overnewton Park, just south of what is now Kelvingrove Park, during the late 1870s.

Opened in 1897 on the banks of the Clyde (*see page 91*), apart from the need to have a boat on standby when balls were kicked into the river, Meadowside seemed ideal. Partick Station and Partick Underground (both opened the year before) were a short walk away, and there was ferry access from Govan via Clutha Pier.

When Rangers were the visitors one day, the *Daily Record* noted

that on the Govan side of the Clyde 'the lofty gangways of the ocean liners presently in course of construction at Fairfield did duty as a grandstand, from where horny handed sons of toil found football more engrossing than business'.

But Meadowside's prime spot was also its downfall, and in 1908 the ground fell victim to what *Scottish Sport* called the 'avaricious building fiend' when the site was bought for redevelopment as Henderson's shipyard.

And so Partick Thistle went home hunting again, little realising that it would never again play in the burgh from which it took its name.

If all the world is a stage then any piece of flat ground in Glasgow was a potential football ground.

No need for stands when tenement windows or the top of a wall would do instead. No need for shirt numbers when most of the crowd knew most of the players.

And certainly no need for goalnets when there were hundreds of linesmen and boys watching every move. (Mothers and babies, it would seem, had to play a waiting game instead.)

Photographed in 1955, this is **Plantation**, an area of Glasgow laid out from the 1860s onwards on the former grounds of Plantation House. More specifically it appears to be a patch of ground between MacLellan Street and Clifford Street, now the site of Junction 22 of the M8, south west of Kinning Park Underground station.

From the players' kit, and from the number of onlookers, this was no casual kickabout. Even at this grass roots level – if grass it was, cinders was more likely – there was a high degree of local organisation.

So localised in fact that in 1886 a Govan and Plantation Junior Football Association was formed, covering no more than a couple of square miles of this corner of Glasgow at most. There was even a local cup, donated by wine merchant, Francis Lochrane, in 1885.

Not young hooligans but middle aged men in collars and ties test the thin blue line at Cathkin Park in 1961 (*right*), before Third Lanark's match v. Rangers. Virtually every attendance record in British football has been clocked up in Glasgow. And that is just the ones who were counted through the turnstiles.

▷ Before Scotland's travelling fans rebranded themselves as the jovial, kilted roustabouts of the 'Tartan Army', this was the image that most non-Scottish people had of football north of the border.

The scene was Hampden Park in May 1980, but it followed on from a pitch invasion after Scotland's victory at Wembley in 1977 (when the goalposts were broken and the turf ripped up for souvenirs).

At the time all British football was tainted by the actions of a hooligan minority. But in Scotland heavy drinking was identified as a particular added factor.

When this photograph was taken Celtic had just beaten Rangers in the Scottish Cup Final. Opinions differ as to what happened next, but a pitch invasion of celebrating Celtic supporters was answered by Rangers fans, with predictable and widely broadcast results.

The following Monday, George Younger, Secretary of State for Scotland – who as cynics were quick to point out was a member of the prominent brewing family who had sponsored the competition – set in train the legislation that would lead to a ban on alcohol at Scottish sports stadiums.

The ban was no panacea. But it certainly helped in making grounds more welcoming, and led also to England and Wales following suit in 1985.

◁ Another sign of the times was the departure in 1986 of **Clyde Football Club** from **Shawfield Greyhound Stadium,** seen here in 1956 (*and also page 199*).

Formed in 1878 in the East End (*page 59*), Clyde's gates had for years suffered not only from the dominance of Rangers and Celtic but also from the depopulation of their catchment area.

After eight years of sharing other clubs' grounds, in 1994 they finally found a home in Cumbernauld, where many a Glaswegian had also been relocated since the slum clearances of the 1960s.

Significantly, it has been fans of smaller clubs such as Clyde who have made up the bulk of the Tartan Army.

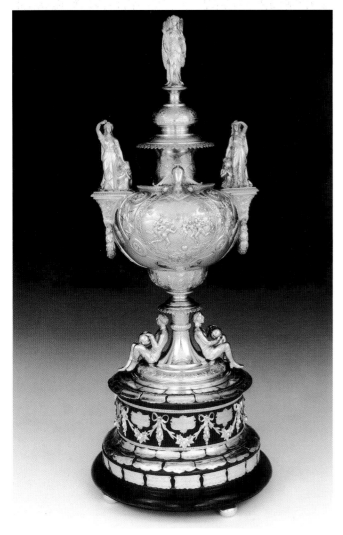

▲ Since its foundation in 1993, and its eventual opening to the public at Hampden Park in 2001, the **Scottish Football Museum** has become a repository of over 2,500 artefacts, none more richly detailed than the **Glasgow Merchants' Charity Cup**.

Dating from 1876, as its name suggests it was donated by public spirited businessmen in Glasgow, to be competed for annually by local clubs, with all match proceeds donated to charitable causes.

In its prime the competition, organised initially by Lieutenant Colonel James Merry of the Third Lanarkshire Rifle Volunteers, was keenly contested by all the major clubs in Glasgow, and overall helped raise the equivalent in current value of £11 million.

But by the time it was last awarded in 1967, set against the allure of other competitions at home and in Europe it had become an unfortunate irrelevance.

For almost three decades after that the trophy was thought to have disappeared, until your author, on behalf of the museum, discovered it gathering dust in the basement of the Scottish FA's offices.

A poignant affirmation of O'Brien's 'First Law of Football' – namely that the beauty of a trophy is always in inverse proportion to the status of the competition – the Charity Cup is now highly valued as the second oldest Association football trophy in the world.

The oldest? That is the Scottish Cup, dating from 1873, and also on display at Hampden.

▲ Just the ticket, but a priceless one all the same.

Another of the historic holdings of the **Scottish Football Museum** at Hampden, this is the only known remaining ticket from the world's first international, played at Hamilton Crescent, Partick (*see page 176*).

That it was a hot ticket we can tell from the admission fee, double or even quadruple the usual for a match at that time (sixpence becoming the norm after 1890, rising only to a shilling in 1919).

Note also that the ticket specifies Association Rules, to differentiate it from rugby football. Even then, the Scottish XI, Queen's Parkers to a man, lined up in a 6-2-2 formation and played a very different game of

passing and running compared with their more physical opponents, who lined up 8-1-1, and whose players came from areas such as Sheffield, Nottingham, Oxford and London, where quite disparate styles and even rules were still dominant.

Needless to add, the 'Scotch Professor' style would soon become the norm.

Another rare item is an image of **Andrew Watson** (*below left*), taken in 1886 when he was a member of a Scottish invitational team known as the Crusaders.

After five years of painstaking research by the Museum, it was found that Watson had been born in British Guiana in 1857, the son of a Scottish sugar planter and a local woman. Having settled and married in Glasgow (the 1881 census has him living in Afton Crescent, Govan), his career as an amateur footballer started with two minor Glasgow teams, Maxwell and Parkgrove, in the 1870s, before a seven year intermittent spell with Queen's Park from 1880–87.

Described in Douglas Lamming's *Who's Who* of Scottish players (*see Links*) as a 'fast moving defender possessed of a huge kick and

a doughty tackle', Watson was sufficiently well regarded to be made captain of the 1881 Scotland team which defeated England 6–1, and won two further caps before heading south, probably to further his career as a marine engineer.

In London he played for the Swifts in 1882, and in 1884 for the crack Corinthians, who were then, ironically, bent on challenging the supremacy of Queen's Park and the Scottish national side.

As a result of the Museum's research, it is now accepted that Watson was not only the first black footballer in Scotland but in England and in international football overall.

It appears an anonymous building on Norval Street, off Crow Road in Partick, but before it was turned into flats this was the Greenbank Leather Works, where in 1895 William Thomlinson started production of leather footballs. (His brother John opened a print works, seen just behind, in 1908.) For many years Thomlinson were one of Britain's leading ball makers, one of their best selling designs being the famous T Ball, introduced in 1921 and said to keep its shape better than all its competitors. This pristine example is also on display at the Scottish Football Museum at Hampden Park.

▶ Seemingly beached on a peninsular formed by the Port Dundas branch of the Forth and Clyde Canal, and with a timber basin as its neighbour, this was the somewhat unusual location of **Firhill**, the ground of **Partick Thistle**, as viewed from the west in the late 1950s or 1960s.

But although it lay a mile and a half from Partick Cross, and in the foreign territory of Maryhill – which like Partick had once been an independent burgh, before its absorption by Glasgow in 1891 – when Thistle arrived here in 1909 it came as a blessed relief.

After being ousted from Meadowside in 1908 (*see page 181*) the Jags, as they are known, had spent an unhappy and loss making season sharing at other grounds, Ibrox included, before the Firhill site was pointed out to them by Rangers' chairman, Sir John Ure Primrose. (He knew of the site because it had been bought for warehousing in 1907 by the Clyde Port Authority, of which he was Vice Chairman.)

Certainly there was a sizeable catchment area of local residents to the south west, where amidst the tenements on Maryhill Road stood Queen's Cross Church (in the centre of the photograph), designed by Charles Rennie Mackintosh in 1899, and now the headquarters of the Mackintosh Society.

Behind the southern goal, on Firhill Road, stood the Eglinton Chrome Tannery, which produced a soft leather that the company used to manufacture footballs. To the north and east were saw mills.

Having only one main point of access, on the ground's west side, was always likely to limit Firhill's chances of expanding, and so to an extent, by settling here, the Jags were never likely to challenge the

credentials of Glasgow's three other superbowls (which may also have been why Primrose was happy to lead them to Firhill).

Its planned opening, moreover, in August 1909, had to be called off after an inspector from the Corporation's Department of Works ruled that the terracing had not been finished to his satisfaction, a fiasco described by the *Scottish Referee* as 'unparalleled in the history of British sport'.

But Firhill did open a month later, and with Sir John's further influence, the Jags were able to buy the site in 1916 for £5,500. Not only that but by winning the Scottish Cup five years later, ironically against Rangers, they were also able to pay off this amount rather sooner than expected. Indeed the club still have the cheque they wrote out, on display in the boardroom.

And so, with Rangers, Celtic, Queen's Park, Clyde, Third Lanark and now Partick Thistle all settled at grounds of their own, after 30 years of moves and uncertainties the football map of Glasgow took on the shape it would retain for the next half century.

▶ Determined to keep up with Rangers and Celtic, both of whom were also planning new stands in the late 1920s, in 1927 Partick Thistle took the considerable gamble of spending £60,000 on ground improvements (more than Celtic would spend two years later).

Apart from expanding their banks of terracing the main expense was this new stand, with 6,000 seats and a red brick frontage with new turnstile blocks on Firhill Road.

That it appeared to be a typical Archibald Leitch stand, especially with its pedimented roof gable (*above*), was no coincidence, for it was designed by Leitch's former chief draughtsman, David Mills Duncan, who had recently set up his own firm, Duncan & Kerr. (The partnership also designed Celtic's new stand in 1929, *see page 70*.)

The Jags' reward for their ambition was to play host to an international, v. Ireland, in Feburary 1928, which drew a record crowd of 54,728 to Firhill.

Yet in the 1930s, in an attempt to bolster their finances they then experimented with staging the newly popular sport of greyhound racing, which as we will see in the following chapter, had become a major fad in Glasgow. But not, it would seem, at Firhill.

Nevertheless, further ground developments ensued in the 1950s, a period during which three League Cup final appearances,

albeit none victorious, helped the Jags finance the construction of floodlights (in 1955), and a roof over the main enclosure (*right*).

The 'Maryhill Magyars', the Jags became known at this time (after the ultra progressive Hungarian national team of the period), while it was 'Firhill for Thrills' in the local newspaper headlines.

These were heady days too for Partick's counterparts south of the river, with both Third Lanark and Clyde experiencing their own moments of glory in the 1950s and early 1960s, in the League and in Cup competitions.

But size counts in football, and as Glasgow's population and industrial base headed further into decline during the 1960s and 1970s, Firhill started to become a steadily depreciating asset in an increasingly ruthless market.

▶ **Partick Thistle** occupy a unique position in Glasgow, and in Scottish football overall. On the south side of Glasgow, Third Lanark are no more, having folded in 1967 (*see page 45*). Clyde departed for Cumbernauld in 1994 (after a difficult five year stint of sharing, as it happens, with the Jags at Firhill).

And so where once where there were six League clubs in Glasgow, now there are four, and with respect to the amateurs of Queen's Park – now ensconced in the Third Division – this leaves the Jags as the third largest club in the city.

Theirs is a role most neatly summed up in a popular ditty:

'There's a well-known Glasgow football team,
They don't play in blue, they don't play in green.'

In other words, for any Glasgow football fan who feels uneasy with the overarching dominance of the Old Firm – whether it be from antipathy towards their might or their sectarian rivalry – Firhill offers, quite literally, a middle ground.

On one hand this is an enviable position to be in, Partick constituting what the Americans would describe as the 'left field' alternative. This has made the club popular amongst Glasgow's bohemian set, amongst non Catholics and Protestants and, because of Firhill's proximity to the University, amongst students also.

On the other hand, although many a Glaswegian, when pressed, will profess to supporting the Jags, or speaks fondly of them as the noble underdogs, unfortunately not enough of them back this up by actually showing up at Firhill.

Probably the lowest point came in the late 1990s.

In common with dozens of clubs Partick had been severely stretched by the government's requirement to phase out all areas of terracing, in the aftermath of the 1989 Hillsborough disaster.

This resulted in some £2.8 million being spent on upgrading Firhill, the bulk of which went towards a new 6,263 capacity stand, named after former Jags stalwart Jackie Husband.

But with average gates of under 5,000 (Old Firm visits apart), the outlay proved too great a burden, and in 1998, with the Jags now relegated to the lower divisions, only a concerted 'Save the Jags' campaign by the fans helped stave off impending bankruptcy.

Fortunately, heroically even, since then the club has re-organised and Firhill has continued to evolve, as seen opposite.

But as is true of any corner shop with two hypermarkets on its doorstep, being Partick Thistle has never been easy, and maybe never will be. Such is their fate. But such is their destiny too.

Nowadays football kits change in design virtually every season. But rarely do clubs change colours. The Jags did however. For 60 years they wore dark blue and white, until in 1936 they borrowed some shirts from the West of Scotland Rugby Club (who played at Hamilton Crescent), and liked them so much they have played in yellow and red ever since.

▲ Viewed from the south in October 2006, the goalposts have been moved at **Firhill** to make way for Partick Thistle's latest tenants, the **Glasgow Warriors** rugby club.

Groundsharing and diversification at Firhill is hardly new. As noted earlier, in the 1930s the Jags tried to balance their books by hosting greyhound racing. In the 1980s they took in Clyde FC for five seasons. Meanwhile the Warriors, it may be recalled, Glasgow's only professional rugby union outfit, had started out at Hughenden in 1999 (*see page 117*).

Firhill today, with its all-seated capacity of 10,921 (one fifth of its peak level in the late 1920s), exemplifies many of the challenges that have faced not only the Jags but several other clubs in Glasgow.

Like Ibrox and Celtic Parks, for example, its oval shape had become an anachronism, while in common with the West of Scotland Cricket Club, surplus land has offered the prospect of survival.

Hence in 2001 the curved north terrace was cleared for the construction of a complex of student flats and hotel rooms.

In front of this, square onto the pitch, can be seen the new North Stand. Designed and built by Barr Construction in 2002-03, it holds just over 2,000 seats, and together with the Jackie Husband Stand on the right (designed by the Miller Partnership), now forms the main accommodation at Firhill.

Only on major occasions are the seats in old Main Stand (*left*) used, the building otherwise housing club offices and the changing rooms.

The future of the south, or 'City End', where the old terracing has also been cleared, has yet to be determined. But even with two sides in use, Firhill is still able to cater comfortably for both the Jags' and the Warriors' average crowds of around 3-4,000, and should Partick make it back into the top flight of football, there remains plenty of scope for further growth.

Of course that growth would partly be financed by the return of regular games against Rangers and Celtic. And therein lies the dilemma. Struggle to live with 'em, struggle to live without 'em.

In Glasgow, as in all of Scottish football, that is part of the deal.

▲ It takes a certain kind of football fan to pledge his or her allegiance to a 'junior' club, as has this hardy soul at **Lochburn Park,** home of **Maryhill Football Club,** barely a mile north west of Firhill.

The term 'junior' relates not to the age of the players, but to the clubs' status as members of the Scottish Junior Football Association. Formed in 1886, the SJFA's league structure is one level below that of the 'senior' leagues, yet remains distinct, with no promotion or relegation between the two.

In 2009 there were 164 clubs at this level, of which thirteen are based in the area covered by this book. Each has its own heritage, rooted not in the concrete and steel of grandstands and stadiums, but in neighbourhood grounds with highly localised identities.

▲ Tucked away off Pollokshaws Road and backing onto White Cart Water, this is **Newlandsfield Park,** home of **Pollok Football Club,** as shown on the map on page 81.

The best supported and recently the most successful of all junior clubs in the Glasgow area, Pollok, or 'Lok, are in many respects the community team of the South Side, especially since the demise of Third Lanark (*see pages 44-47*).

Formed in 1908 by members of the Pollokshaws Working Lads Club, they are also yet another Glasgow sports club whose early years benefitted from the patronage of Sir John Stirling Maxwell – hence their black and white colours, adopted from the Pollok heraldic shield.

'Lok first played at Haggs Park (*page 81*), until this was taken over for use as school playing fields in 1926. Two seasons at Rosebery Park (*page 63*) and Speirsbridge

followed, before in 1928 'Lok were able to lay out their current home on what was then wasteground, next door to a tramway depot (now the site of a superstore).

However in 1947 the site's owners, a firm of bleachers and dyers, gave 'Lok just six weeks to buy the ground or leave, and it was only a loan of £5,000 from the local Co-Op that saved the day.

Since then Newlandsfield Park has developed into a typical junior enclosure, with no seats and a single cover. Only in 1968 was the black ash pitch laid with turf.

In the far corner can be seen the groundsman's hut, built in the late 1940s, while behind the south goal is the social club, Lok's financial mainstay, opened in 1971.

Seeing Newlandsfield today it is hard to believe that in 1944-45 an estimated 15,000 crowd packed in for a cup tie (many of whom took up better viewing positions on the platform of the adjacent Pollokshaws East Station). By comparison, recent gates have fluctuated between 200-2,000.

But then for many that is part of the appeal. This is a no-frills ground where one can stroll in just before kick-off, drink in the bar, wander around and meet friends.

Community sport as it should be, say many. Not much glamour, for sure, but a whole lot of heart.

More characterful corrugation, just across the Glasgow border at Holm Park, on the banks of the Clyde. Yoker Athletic, formed in 1886, are the incumbents, but now share it with Clydebank FC, a club created in 2003 after its predecessors, who had played in the Scottish League since 1966, were bought out by a consortium in Airdrie. Across the road from Holm Park there stood until the 1960s the Clydebank Greyhound Stadium.

▲ There are no architectural gems at Glasgow's junior grounds, but each holds its own fascination.

Half a mile west of Ibrox, **Tinto Park**, the home of **Benburb FC** (*top left and page 91*), once held an estimated 20,000 for a cup tie in 1953. Today, even three figure gates are considered welcome.

Similarly at **Greenfield Park** in the East End (*top right and page 61*), home of **Shettleston FC** since 1933, where there are two corrugated iron terrace covers, but where the social club is often more crowded during the week than are the terraces on match days.

Perhaps the quirkiest, yet also one of Glasgow's best appointed junior grounds (with seats and floodlights) is that of **Maryhill FC** (*above*), formed in 1884.

Hemmed in between light industrial units on a plateau, and with only one access point in a corner, **Lochburn Park** was built on the site of an old quarry and once was home to the Kelvin Dock Curling Club. Unusually, the pitch is sunk so low and so tight against the perimeter wall that however their team are doing, Maryhill fans always have to look down on them.

▶ Half a century and a few hundred yards separates these two contrasting images of **Petershill Football Club**, formed in 1897 and arguably the leading junior club on the north side of Glasgow,

When **Petershill Park** opened on Southloch Street, Springburn, in August 1935, the 'Peasy', as the club is affectionately known, invited Rangers and Celtic to play the inaugural match, a smart move which attracted a 20,000 crowd.

But the Peasy were no mean draw themselves. When they reached the Scottish Junior Cup Final in 1951, for the fourth time, there was an all-time juniors record of 77,650 at Hampden Park, to see them beat Irvine Meadow.

Continuing success then financed the erection of a cover over their west terrace, in 1954 (*above*).

But it was not a lack of honours that led to Petershill Park slipping into steady decline from the 1970s onwards. Rather, the depopulation of the surrounding area and the closure of local industries left the Peasy struggling with an oversized ground in the midst of what had become one of the most deprived urban areas of Europe.

It was for this reason that in 2005 the Peasy entered into a pioneering partnership with the City Council and the Glasgow North Regeneration Agency to construct an entirely new ground and sports centre on a site to the immediate west of their pitch.

Costing £5.6 million and opened in September 2007, the new **Petershill Park Leisure Centre** (*right*) could hardly be more different than the Peasy's former home, only the retaining wall of which still remained in 2009.

For a start, there is no grass.

Instead the club now plays on one of the highest rated, FIFA accredited artificial surfaces available, a pitch used also on a daily basis by the local community. Six other synthetic five-a-side pitches now occupy the site of the Peasy's former west terrace.

Moreover, unlike the eccentric, rickety stand at the old ground, fans wishing to sit have access to a 500 seat stand incorporated within the leisure centre.

For traditionalists, the uneasy Peasies as it were, it is hard to conceive of a more radical change in surroundings. But as the modernisers counter, gates are holding up at around 3-400 (in a total capacity of 2,200), there have

been few postponements, injury levels are down, as of course are the club's maintenance costs.

Just as importantly, the club also feels that it has bolstered spirits and made it more likely that the next generation will get involved.

This may not be junior football as we have known and loved it. But it could well be a blueprint for the future.

▶ When Glasgow's sporting heritage comes to be revisited in another hundred years, what will our successors make of this quite extraordinary building on Glasgow Road in Rutherglen?

This is the social club of **Rutherglen Glencairn**, a junior football club which started life in 1896 on a ground called **Southcroft Park**, just behind the building seen here.

The scene of many subsequent triumphs, interspersed with the usual lean years, in 2006 it was the oldest surviving junior ground in the city when the Scottish Executive issued a compulsory purchase order on the site in order to clear the way for the proposed extension of the M74.

And so the 'Glens' became the latest in a long line of sports clubs to fall foul of road or rail developments, even if, as it transpired, the land on which they had been playing was found to have been contaminated (as was also the case at Rosebery Park, half a mile to the north, *see page 63*).

The social club forms one part of a two-stage, £5 million redevelopment carried out to rehouse the Glens.

On Glasgow Road, the new social club was designed by Studio KAP architects (whose pavilion for Balornock Bowling Club is featured on page 156), and although to the outside world it presents a somewhat stark, windowless brick exterior – this being an area subject to both vandalism and atmospheric pollution – its interior is surprisingly bright and finished in vibrant colour, using natural toplighting to maximum advantage.

Meanwhile, next to the social club, Australian street artist Sam Bates, whose work has cropped up all over the city in recent years, has

completed a mural depicting the highlights of the Glens' history on an adjoining wall (*above*).

As for the Glen's new ground, opened in July 2008 and named **New Southcroft Park**, this lies a few hundred yards around the corner on Toryglen Road and has a dressing room block in a robust brick style, matching that of the social club.

▲ If there is one aspect of Glasgow's sporting heritage that is certain to elicit strong reactions, it is that distinctive reddish orange substance known as **blaes** (which for the benefit of non-Scottish readers is pronounced 'blaze').

Look at any aerial view of Glasgow, for example on page 113, and it is almost impossible to miss.

Used not only for football pitches since the late 19th century, but for tennis courts, athletics tracks and school playgrounds, blaes is a crushed form of mudstone or shale. Although the type used most commonly for sporting purposes is coloured red, blaes actually derives its name from a more common form which is dark blue or, in Scottish parlance, 'blae'.

Apart from its cost effectiveness and ease of maintenance, the main advantage of blaes is that should it ever rain – as occasionally it does in Glasgow – there is less chance of the pitch turning into a quagmire.

However, as many a reader will attest all too readily, the downside is that falling over on the stuff is likely to induce scars and burns, stained clothing and the bruising of many an ego. Defenders in particular attempt slide tackles on blaes only with great caution, or in moments of acute desperation.

As long as affordable alternatives were unavailable there was little anyone could do about this.

Baptism by blaes was all part and parcel of a Glasgow childhood.

The trouble is that since a greater variety of all weather surfaces have developed, and more turf pitches have become available, Glasgow's footballers have voted with their feet, resulting in a sharp drop in bookings of Council-run blaes pitches. At the same time, new supplies of blaes have become harder to source, and substitute materials, when tried, have been found to be not so effective.

Gradual phasing out of blaes started in 1993 with the adoption of the Council's first Sport and Recreation Strategy, a strategy policymakers have followed ever since. Even so, a study conducted in 2006 found that of the 527 active pitches in the city, around 45 per cent were still blaes, of which the majority were at primary schools. Given that the replacement strategy cannot happen overnight, this means that for some years to come, the nation's would-be football stars will still have to learn to live with the scars.

That said, as, inevitably, blaes is eventually phased out across the city, it is surely to be hoped that somewhere at least one example will be preserved, if only to show future generations just how down and dirty (and gritty) sporting life could get in 20th century Glasgow.

▲ Just as the early 20th century development of indoor ice rinks put paid to the Cairnie-style curling rinks of the 19th century, could this colossal arena represent the future of football in the 21st century?

Opened in 2009 in a part of Glasgow once dominated by the Aikenhead pitheads, and built, ironically, on the site of an expanse of old blaes pitches, just east of Hampden Park (*see page 37*), the £15.7 million **Toryglen Regional Football Centre** boasts Scotland's first full-size indoor football pitch.

Overlooked by a 700 seat viewing deck, its artificial pitch is classed under FIFA regulations as Two Star, which means that

it is deemed suitable for senior competitive use. There are similar pitches at Moscow's national stadium, and at two equally famous Scottish venues, Stenhousemuir and Alloa Athletic

Outside are three more pitches of the same standard, plus thirteen seven-a-side pitches and one grass pitch, all floodlit, and all heavily booked, seven days a week.

As we have seen throughout this book, the story of sport in Glasgow is one punctuated by a series of technological advances. Toryglen is part of that continuum.

But more than that, it is one of the most astonishing sporting structures the city has ever seen.

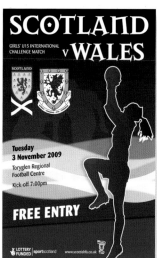

Toryglen in 2009: an indoor arena, a synthetic pitch, and two international teams of under–15 year old girls from Scotland and Wales. Never doubt, Glasgow's love affair with 'the beautiful game' shows no sign of dimming.

Chapter Thirteen

Greyhounds and speedway

Going to the dogs at Shawfield, a stadium that over the years has also staged trotting races, football, boxing, and speedway. Since 1927 no fewer than ten venues in Glasgow have staged either greyhounds or speedway racing or both, not counting tracks in nearby Yoker, Paisley and Blantyre. At its peak in 1946, greyhound racing attendances in Britain reached a staggering 34 million at over 100 tracks, compared with 35.6 million for football.

With the exception only of ice hockey, all the sports played in Glasgow thus far described could be said to have been more or less 'Made in Britain'.

Greyhounds and speedway racing, however, were imported.

The former, it is true, derived from the ancient sport of hare coursing, in which a pair of greyhounds were 'slipped' or sent chasing after a live hare.

But the trouble with coursing was that it was difficult for spectators to follow (and in the 19th century crowds of up to 75,000 used to attend the Waterloo Cup near Liverpool). To overcome this, in 1876 a trial was set up in London using a mechanical hare running along a straight track. But this was hardly better.

Instead, the solution, blindingly obvious in retrospect, emerged in California in 1912, also using a mechanical hare, but with the greyhounds circling an oval track, just like human athletes.

As detailed in *Played in Manchester* (*see* Links), Britain's first American-style greyhound track opened at Belle Vue, Manchester,

Little is known about the egg-shaped former trotting track on Janefield Street, known both as the Olympic Sports Stadium, and, after its promoter, as the Nelson Athletic Grounds. In April 1928 it staged Glasgow's first exhibition of 'dirt track' racing in front of 2,000 curious onlookers. The site is now covered by housing on Stamford Gates (*see page 61 for location*).

in July 1926. Within months two more tracks opened in London, and by the end of 1927, at least 35 more had followed nationwide, including Powderhall in Edinburgh, and Glasgow's first, at Wester Carntyne (*see opposite*).

To the horror of church leaders (though not all politicians, because of the huge tax revenues), the new tracks acted as magnets to gamblers. Unlike racecourses, such as Ayr and Hamilton, they were in the heart of big cities, and were open three or four nights a week. Even for non-gamblers the spectacle of a floodlit track proved a terrific lure.

As with any new craze, an almighty battle for custom quickly broke out. In Glasgow, as in Leeds and Liverpool, this even resulted in rival tracks opening up next door to one another. Hence after Carntyne, in April 1928 first the White City Stadium, then the Albion Stadium opened between Paisley Road West and Ibrox Park (*see pages 91, 94, and 103*).

Shawfield followed in 1932, and between 1948–54 there would also be racing at Partick

Thistle's Firhill. (There was also an unlicensed track at Mount Vernon, of which traces remain but otherwise little is known.)

All Glasgow's tracks were located in working class areas or at least close to major industrial zones. But however good business was, it could always get better, and so in 1928 dog tracks all over Britain opened up their doors to another new sport, 'dirt track' motorcycle racing.

Invented in Australia in 1923, this was first staged in Britain in February 1928 on open ground at High Beech, Essex, arriving in Glasgow the following April, first at the Nelson Athletic Grounds (*see below*), then at Celtic Park. It was also trialled at Carntyne.

But it would be on the purpose-built cinder track at White City where speedway, as it became known, would really take off.

In total, seven venues in Glasgow staged speedway at one time or another. Today, only one track remains, at the Ashfield Stadium in Possilpark. Dog racing, meanwhile, is also confined to one track, at Shawfield Stadium.

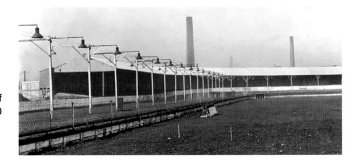

▲ Laid out on a farm and former trotting track, across the railway line from Parkhead Forge (*see page 61*), **Wester Carntyne** staged Glasgow's first greyhound race in October 1927 (nine weeks after the sport's Scottish debut in Edinburgh).

In its early years Carntyne was managed on behalf of the Scottish Greyhound Company by Jack Nixon-Browne, later to become the Tory MP for Govan and in 1959 created Lord Craigton.

This view from the east in 1932, with tenements on Myreside Street in mid-construction, shows Carntyne shortly after the management had dropped Nixon-Browne's experiment with speedway (which ran for a few meetings in 1928 and 1930 with little success, despite expenditure of £6,000 on laying out a cinder track inside the turf dog track).

More lucrative was champion welterweight Tommy Milligan's last ever fight in October 1928, which drew an estimated record Scottish crowd of 35,000. Alas for his fans, Milligan was knocked out in the first round by Welshman Frank Moody.

For years Carntyne was home to the Scottish Greyhound Derby, its 452 yard track being described as having 'long galloping straights' and 'easy bends'. From 1960-62 it was home to Bridgeton Waverley FC.

But as the surrounding industry faded, so did Carntyne, and its final race was staged in May 1972.

Since then the site has remained vacant, apart from an electricity sub-station on the former kennels area next to Carntyne Road (*top*).

▲ As speedway fans were reminded on the cover of every match programme, 'Strictly No Betting'. The riders may have all been professional, some of them earning far more than top footballers. The majority of tracks were to be found at greyhound stadiums, where bookmakers and Totalisator boards were part of the furniture. But speedway's governing body remained adamant. Their sport would never be tainted.

Before this international a flock of pigeons was released to mark the coronation. For the record, Scotland, captained by the Glasgow Tigers' Tommy Miller ('famous for his easy "armchair" style of riding') won comfortably, 70-38.

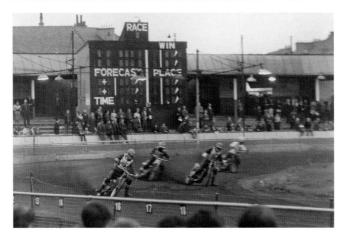

◄ The speculative nature of Britain's early greyhound and speedway stadiums meant that few, if any, ever had any structures of architectural note.

The odd Tote board here and there may have caught the eye. There were one or two moderately handsome gateways. But otherwise these were venues best experienced at night, when they came to life in a blaze of light and colour.

Moreover, many, such as **White City**, seen here in 1930 (*top*), with Bellahouston Park on the south side of Paisley Road West, were built on cheaply available gap sites alongside railway lines, far enough from housing that the barking of dogs in the kennels or the roar of bikes on speedway nights would not discomfit too many neighbours.

White City was part of a network of tracks named after the original White City Stadium, venue for the 1908 Olympic Games and adapted for greyhounds in 1927. Others were at Manchester, Newcastle, Nottingham, Cardiff and Hull.

The standard layout was for a grass dog track on the outside, 518 yards in the case of Glasgow (sand tracks were a later development), and a cinder speedway track in the centre. At Glasgow the hare's speed was controlled from a tower seen in the lower right corner of the track.

White City claimed to have 'cover for 15,000, comfort for 25,000'. But by 1967, as seen left during a Tigers v. Monarchs Scottish Cup match, it wore a distinctly dishevelled, outmoded air.

Two years later the Tigers moved to Hampden Park (*page 52*). The final greyhound race then followed in April 1972. Soon after, half the site was swallowed up by the M8, the rest being redeveloped as a police station on the corner of Helen Street.

▲ **Shawfield Stadium,** Glasgow's sole remaining greyhound track, is one of the great survivors of Scottish sporting life.

Initially laid out as a trotting track, Shawfield is first recorded as hosting a football club called Thistle in the 1870s. **Clyde FC**, previously at Barrowfield Park (*see page 59*) then took it over in 1898.

But although 'the Bully Wee' achieved great fame in the Scottish Cup, and drew a record estimated crowd of 52,000 v. Rangers in 1908 (or was it, more reliably, 48,500 v. Celtic in 1914?), their finances were rarely stable.

In 1926 therefore the chairman, an ebullient cinema owner called John 'Mac' McMahon, was keen to accept an offer of £2,000 a year from the newly formed Greyhound Racing Association (GRA) to host race meetings. Alas a clause in Clyde's lease forbad this, but 'Johnny Mac' was not to be deterred and, after seeing how greyhounds had taken off in England, he and his fellow directors formed a racing company of their own and bought the site.

The first meeting in November 1932 pulled in few punters, but by 1935 greyhounds had caught on so successfully that the football club now became the junior partner.

One trick Johnny Mac employed to boost interest was to arrange for lots of smart cars to be parked outside on race nights, thereby attracting more wealthy punters.

Certainly trainers loved Shawfield's 473 yard track, which

one annual described as 'the fastest and easiest course in Britain', after it became the first British venue to have banking on its bends (a great boon as flat tracks were said to have induced a malady amongst dogs known as 'track leg').

It was also amongst the first venues to install a Totalisator board and photo-finish equipment, and, as noted on page 21, held the record for a boxing match in Scotland when 40,000 saw Benny Lynch beat Peter Kane in 1937.

But, like White City, by the 1970s Shawfield appeared to be on its last legs. In 1971 the GRA bought it, but they too struggled to make it pay, and in 1984 Glasgow's sole surviving dog track was put up for sale.

Clyde played their last game there in April 1986 – they later moved to Cumbernauld – but then the GRA's plans to sell up to a supermarket fell through, and so racing resumed under new owners, only this time with bikes as well.

Clyde's newest tenants? The much travelled **Glasgow Tigers,**

once of White City, whose Shawfield debut drew an 8,000 crowd.

Speedway lasted until 1998, after which Shawfield reverted to greyhounds only, on three nights a week. Excellent value too, at only £5 or £6 for ground entry.

The question today is how long can Shawfield carry on racing?

As can be seen on the 2005 aerial view above, it sits within the

Clyde Gateway regeneration area, close to where the M74 extension will run. Shawfield also now finds itself entirely within South Lanarkshire, the boundary with Glasgow having moved to the other side of Shawfield Drive in 1996.

Thus in more ways than one Shawfield sits on the edge; a great survivor afloat in a sea of urban and social change.

◀ As in ice hockey, the American style names adopted by Britain's speedway clubs reflect the fact that this was an imported sport aspiring to a modern, racy image.

However also in common with ice hockey, perennial cash crises since the very early days have seen Britain's speedway clubs form and reform under different promoters, and swap venues, towns and cities with confusing regularity.

Since 1946 the **Glasgow Tigers**, the city's only remaining club, have raced at White City, first from 1946–54, followed by ten years in abeyance. They then reformed at White City in 1964 before the demolition of the stadium to make way for the M8 forced them to relocate to Hampden Park from 1969–72 (*see page 52*).

There then followed 15 seasons outside Glasgow, at Coatbridge (1973–77), at two venues in Blantyre (1977–86), and at Workington in Cumbria in 1987.

Returning to Glasgow the following year the Tigers raced at Shawfield from 1988–98, and have, since 1999, been based at Ashfield Stadium (*right*).

Preceding the Tigers at Ashfield from 1949–53 were the **Glasgow Giants**, formed by promoters Norrie Isbister and Johnnie Hoskins.

Hoskins arrived from Australia in 1928 and in a lifetime dedicated to speedway seemed to have a hand in almost every franchise going (of which there have been many).

Ever the showman, he made the Giants stand out by equipping each rider not in standard black leathers but in individualised red, blue, white and hooped leathers.

His equally flamboyant son Ian promoted the Tigers at White City, his party piece being to have the riders burn his hat in front of the fans after every match.

▲ Dirt track action at **Ashfield Stadium** in 2009, as the **Glasgow Tigers** (in the red and white) face the Scunthorpe Scorpions.

After the Second World War, the Giants regularly commanded crowds of 10–20,000 at Ashfield, whereas today's gates are more usually around 500–1,000.

One thing that never changes, however, is the race format. Two riders from each team complete four laps around the track, on bikes that can accelerate faster than a Formula One car (from 0-60mph in 3.5 seconds), and yet which have only one gear, one footrest, no rear suspension and, just to add to the thrill, no brakes.

Throttling and sliding round the bends are the essence of success. And of course speed. A typical race lasts less than a minute. Bravery helps too, for this is a dangerous game, which is one reason why it caught on in the first place.

But for many racegoers the overwhelming sensations are of the thunderous noise of the 500cc single cylinder engines, accompanied by the pervading smell of grease, cinders, oil and methanol, laced with burning rubber.

An acquired taste perhaps, but for its devotees, well worth a bit of spare change to keep the Tigers' tanks topped up for action (*below*).

▲ The Tigers call it **Ashfield Stadium**, but to regulars of **Ashfield Football Club** it is **Saracen Park**.

Opened in 1937, it was named after the giant Saracen Foundry that, until the 1960s, dominated the surrounding district of Possilpark and from which much of the decorative ironwork seen in Glasgow originally derived (*see page 139 for one likely example*).

Giants promoter Ian Hoskins apparently spotted the ground's potential when passing by on a train from Edinburgh in 1948.

Speedway has a quite different ethos from football. The Giants' leather clad heroes, several of them Australian, sported exotic names like Ken 'the White Ghost' Le Breton, Merv Harding and Gruff Garland.

But while the Giants folded in 1953, followed by the Tigers in 1954, Ashfield FC soldiered on, as they had done since forming in 1886, and as they continued to do until the reborn Tigers came knocking on their door in 1999.

Some historians argue that imported sports – the likes of speedway, ice hockey and basketball – only ever enjoy fleeting highs when the times are right and the promoters are willing.

But at Saracen Park, with its crooked terracing and patched up stand there appears to be a genuine, earthy sort of symbiosis at work.

Here we have two great old Glasgow sporting names; off the beaten track as it were, co-habiting in a corner of the city that few visitors ever have cause to visit.

In speedway too, lies a sport that once seemed so ultra-modern, yet now appears steeped in heritage.

Chapter Fourteen

Swimming

No aspect of sporting heritage is liable to get people more heated than a threat to an historic swimming pool. Or any public pool for that matter. Second only to walking, swimming is Scotland's favourite form of physical activity amongst adults, while amongst children it ranks third after football and cycling. Yet when Glasgow's first indoor swimming pool was opened in the early 19th century, it was the private hot and cold baths, rather than the plunge pools for swimming, that were the main attraction. Hence the existence of Bath Street, rather than Pool Street, in the city centre.

On June 21 1831 an order was issued by the Parliamentary Trustees of the River Clyde and the Harbour of Glasgow, as follows:

'Whereas frequent complaints have been made, of late, by respectable Inhabitants of this City, and by Strangers, of the practice, which has for some time prevailed, of numbers of young Men assembling on the Banks of the River, immediately below the Harbour, for the purpose of bathing, and of their exposing their persons on the banks of the River, and in the wake of Steamboats, in breach of public decency, and to the great annoyance of respectable Individuals, walking on the banks of the River, or travelling in the numerous Steam Vessels, which now ply on the Clyde...

'And whereas the said indecent practice is not warranted by law, and cannot be justified on the grounds of health or cleanliness, there being ample space and accommodation for bathing for such purposes, in the less frequented parts of the Clyde, or Kelvin, The Magistrates and Council of Glasgow, and other

Parliamentary Trustees for the enlargement of the Harbour at the Broomielaw, and the improvement of the navigation of the Clyde... hereby Enact and Ordain that no Persons whatever shall in future bathe in the river Clyde, from the Bridges of Glasgow downward to the junction of the Kelvin with the Clyde, after Six o'Clock in the morning, under a Penalty not exceeding £5 for each offence.'

We noted earlier how for ice skaters and curlers a combination of warmer winters and the evolution of ice rinks transposed their activities from outdoors to indoors, from the natural world to one that was man-made.

Glasgow's swimmers went through a similar process, if for rather different reasons.

As chronicled by historian Peter Bilsborough (see Links), until pollution and increased river traffic dictated otherwise from around 1850 onwards, there were several favoured swimming spots along the Clyde; the most popular being Fleshers' Haugh at Glasgow Green (where the banks sloped down to form a beach-like area),

and a deeper spot further down stream known as Dominie's Hole. Also popular was a stretch on the Gorbals side where the emission of hot water from a cotton mill offered obvious benefits.

It was the sheer number of men and boys swimming, and drowning in the Clyde, that led to the formation of the Glasgow Humane Society in 1790.

William Harley was the first entrepreneur in the city to offer indoor baths, at Willowbank in 1804. He offered individual hot and cold baths, and for swimming a small plunge pool, measuring 57' x 30'. This was followed in 1839 by the Glasgow Public Baths Company opening premises on 106 West Nile Street, again with a small plunge pool. (The building still stands, but was substantially remodelled as offices in 1898.)

Both these early establishments were of a type known in Britain as 'subscription baths', and were aimed purely at the middle and upper classes. Following outbreaks of cholera during the 1830s, however, there began moves both in Liverpool and

Readers interested in more detail on the history and development of indoor swimming pools in Britain are referred to an earlier publication in the Played in Britain *series,* Great Lengths *(see Links).*

London to establish similar baths, but at prices more affordable to working class urban dwellers.

The result was the 1846 Baths and Wash Houses Act. This gave local authorities the power to borrow money to erect baths (for personal washing) and wash houses (for clothes and linen).

No mention of swimming at all.

Yet once these new facilities started opening, most of them extremely basic, it was soon realised that their most popular features were the plunge pools (which had actually been provided to offer the cheapest possible form of communal bath).

So, as new baths were built, the plunge pools grew larger, until by the time the legislation was eventually adopted in Scotland in the 1870s, the die was cast.

Scotland's first publicly funded swimming baths were in Dundee, opened in 1873.

But in the meantime the private sector took the initiative, opening Scotland's first substantial indoor pool, measuring 80' x 32', on Storie Street, Paisley, in 1868. It was funded by J & P Coats, whose works provided the hot water.

Three years later a group of Glasgow businessmen in the West End decided to build their own baths. Only their creation, the Arlington Baths Club, was for gentlemen members only, not for the general public.

Such was its success that over the next two decades a further four private baths clubs formed in Glasgow, at Hillhead, Govanhill, Pollokshields and Dennistoun.

Remarkably, as we shall report, two are still operating today.

As for Glasgow Town Council, it took its first action in 1877, creating an open air swimming pool in Alexandra Park. Nearly 18,000 swimmers paid to use it during its first summer season, and it is believed to have remained in use until the First World War.

But the real leap forward came in August 1878 with the opening of the city's first public baths and wash house, at Greenhead, on the north side of Glasgow Green.

This conformed to what was by then the norm in Britain, with two swimming pools, a section for 'slipper' baths and spray showers (for personal washing), and a laundry, or 'steamie' as it would become known in Scotland.

After Greenhead ten more public baths were built before 1918.

Figures from 1913-14 show just how popular they were. In a city with a population of 785,000 (as of the 1911 census), the Baths Department recorded a total of 850,557 admissions for swimming (12 per cent of them female), and nearly 350,000 for bathing (of which 20 per cent were female).

As at all Britain's public baths, Friday nights were the busiest for bathing, and Saturday nights for swimming, largely because that was when the water was at its dirtiest, so admission prices were at their lowest. (The water was then emptied overnight and the pool scrubbed down before refilling on Sunday, a practice which survived until continual circulation and filtration systems were perfected in the late 1920s).

Health and recreation benefits apart, one of the biggest drivers of usage at Glasgow pools was sport.

By 1914, 109 swimming clubs had formed in the city, each of which participated in regular competitions, annual galas, and in games of water polo, a game that was born in Scotland and honed in pools in both Glasgow and Paisley in the late 1870s.

Another aquatic distinction held by Glasgow is that in 1892 the world's first ever accredited ladies' race was staged at the Townhead Baths, on Collins Street. Taking place over 200 yards, it was won by a Miss E Dobbie in a time of four minutes, 25 seconds.

After the First World War four more pools were built, but then, mirroring the pattern seen in most British cities, there would be no further developments before Glasgow's first post war pool opened at Drumchapel in 1966.

Since then a steady programme of closures has left just a handful of pre-1939 public baths standing, of which only one, at North Woodside, has an operational pool.

On the other hand, usage at the city's eleven other modern pools far outstrips the levels of yesteryear.

Culture and Sport Glasgow, the body set up to manage the city's leisure centres, reported that in the year 2008-09, 1.3 million visits to pools had been recorded, and that was in the public sector alone.

A plaque on the corner of West Nile Street and Bath Street (where else) commemorates Glasgow's first public baths, set up in 1804 by the mercurial William Harley, a gingham manufacturer who sold clean water and pure milk to the public from his Willowbank estate, where he also laid out a bowling green. The handbill below dates from 1829, the year of Harley's death, and has James Monteath in charge of the baths.

▲ One of the forgotten pioneers of Glasgow sport, **William Wilson** (1844–1912), was the author of the first modern manuals on swimming, diving and life-saving, and the man who effectively invented the game of **water polo**.

Originally the bathsmaster at the Arlington Baths Club (*see right*), in 1877 Wilson was asked by the Bon Accord swimming club in Aberdeen if he could suggest a contest that might amuse spectators inbetween races at swimming galas.

In response Wilson devised what he called 'aquatic football', a game demonstrated in 1878 at the opening of the **Victoria Baths Club**, Butterbiggins Road, to where Wilson had moved from Arlington.

Within months the game had been renamed water polo (for reasons never clearly understood). In October 1879 goalposts were introduced, and in 1885 it was formally recognised by the Amateur Swimming Association in London. By 1900 it was an Olympic sport.

Water polo was more than just a game however. For public baths all over Britain it provided a steady source of income as crowds flocked to see matches at the height of its popularity between the 1880s and 1939.

▲ With only a brass plate on the door to reveal its identity, the **Arlington Baths Club** on Arlington Street, a cul-de-sac in the Charing Cross area, could hardly be more discreet. Yet here stands the oldest private baths club in Britain, and possibly even the world.

When opened in August 1871, seven years before the city's first public baths, Arlington lay on the edge of Glasgow's expansion westwards, with the sports grounds of Burnbank to its immediate north and west (*see page 173*).

Moreover, as noted earlier, this was not just another subscription baths where anyone with sufficient funds could swim. This was a members-only gentleman's club.

At first Arlington offered only a swimming 'pond' (as pools are

often called in Scotland) and a suite of private baths. These were, and still are housed in that part of the club – originally a single storey block flanked by two pedimented gables – which lies at the far end of Arlington Street (as seen above).

To this was added in 1875 a Turkish Room, at the rear of the south end, to which a single storey extension with a third gable was added in 1893, to house a reading room and billiard room. (This extension can be distinguished by the higher level of its eaves.)

Added soon after was the current two storey entrance hall, with its three arched openings.

Finally, in 1902, upper storeys to both the south and north of the entrance block were built, to achieve the continuous two storey terrace we see today.

So successful was Arlington – by 1875 membership topped 600 – that two further clubs followed in 1878, the Western at Hillhead (*see page 206*) and the Victoria on Butterbiggins Road, followed

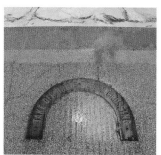

in 1883 by Pollokshields and Dennistoun (*page 207*).

For any private enterprise, in any age, to maintain a swimming pool is no small matter, which is why so few private clubs survived once public baths became available. But to have survived into the 21st century, as Arlington and Western have managed – and to have done so whilst occupying historic buildings – represents even more of an achievement.

But if entry to this scrubbed but clubbable haven inevitably comes at a price, at Arlington this has at times gone way beyond the payment of annual fees.

Indeed by 1987 Arlington had reached a crisis point.

The Glasgow Development Agency offered £184,000 for repairs, but only if the members matched that pound for pound.

This was insufficient, however, and after remedial work eventually started in 1993 a further crisis was only averted when Historic Scotland, who had listed the building Category B in 1986, also pledged £130,000.

Yet still the building needed more, so in 1996 the club had to apply for another £561,000 from the Heritage Lottery Fund, a sum awarded only on condition that the facilities be open to the public (albeit partially, at set times), and that the constitution be amended so that if the club was ever wound up the proceeds would go to the National Trust of Scotland.

By 2004 most of the work had been done, albeit at a cost of £1.2m, and today the club is back on an even keel, with a new gym and a membership of over 750.

There are clubs all over Glasgow, burdened, like Arlington, both by the stigma of elitism and by the responsibility of maintaining an historic building. That they survive is, of course, for the prime benefit of their members.

But they are indubitably part of Britain's wider sporting heritage too.

In Arlington's case, the club is also, along with Western, one of the only pools left in Britain where swimmers can still swing on rings and trapezes suspended above the water – a feature once common to most Victorian pools.

To see them in use, type in Arlington Baths on the YouTube website.

Arlington's Turkish Room has barely changed since 1875, and nor have the rules, which require no raised voices, and all boots to be removed before entering the pool area. One rule that has been relaxed however is that regulation 'pants' (or costumes) – blue for men, red for women – are no longer compulsory.

▲ Described as either Spanish or Venetian Gothic, the Cranworth Street entrance of the **Western Baths Club, Hillhead**, is virtually unaltered since it opened in April 1878. But as we learn from William Mann's history of the club (see Links), its stately exterior masks an often troubled history.

Indeed the club started out life heavily in debt, having raised only half the £20,000 needed to complete the building, designed by two Hillhead residents, William Clarke and George Bell. After the collapse of a local bank in 1879 it then needed a £6,000 loan to stay afloat, before sinking altogether in 1884, literally, when subsidence caused the pond to leak.

For the next two years the club stood boarded up, until 'sporting Glaswegians' were persuaded to launch a £10,000 rescue.

Thereafter Western's fortunes improved, and by 1887 there were 657 members, including 86 women, all enjoying the amenities of a typical Victorian club; musical evenings, billiards and whist,

combined with swimming, water polo and the restorative joys of the Turkish bath. Apparently on Sundays it was common to see men turning up in dressing gowns, ready for their morning dip.

By coincidence it was on another Sunday morning that the Western's world was to change forever. On July 31 1977, the roof over the pond fell in.

No-one was hurt, but after years of rising costs and chronic under investment the club was faced with a complete overhaul, not only of its fabric, at a cost of over £1 million, but also of its Victorian values.

Dropped were the sort of policies that were once an all too familiar blot on the Glasgow sporting scene, such as quotas for Catholics and Jews and the denial of full rights for female members. Equally radical was the securing of a drinks licence, the construction of a gym and sports hall, and most shocking of all, the introduction of mixed bathing.

As a consequence, the Western now has over 2,300 members and a waiting list.

▲ Measuring 90' x 30', the pond at the **Western Baths Club** was, until the opening of Aberdeen's Esplanade Baths in 1898, the largest in Scotland.

Today, its defining characteristic is not its size, but its church-like appearance and almost reverential ambience, a quality that Western's bathsmasters have always striven hard to maintain.

Note that, as at Arlington, there are still rings and a trapeze overhanging the water, and that the filigree cast iron roof trusses each have the letters W and B picked out in their roundels. Also noteworthy are the recessed corner steps.

Otherwise, only the modern cubicles at the far end are reminders of the major revamp that took place following the crash of '77.

◀ There are numerous period details to savour in the sumptuous interior of the **Western Baths Club**; a grand central hallway and staircase, mosaic flooring, intricate plasterwork and carved masonry, stained glass and a panelled billiard room. But even if none of these existed, the building's Category B listing could still be justified on the basis of the pool hall alone.

Rarest of all its original details is the **diving stage** (or 'dail' as these features are sometimes called in Scotland). Since increased concerns over health and safety, diving boards *per se* have become rare enough. But this late Victorian cast iron structure is believed to be the sole surviving example of a type that was once ubiquitous in Britain's swimming pools, public and private.

Almost as rare, and becoming rarer every year, are the **spittoons**, incorporated within the hand rail.

Note how, underneath the spittoon, the tiled wall of the pond appears to be sloping inwards. This is not an optical illusion. The pond's sides do indeed curve inwards towards the floor, yet another design facet believed to be unique (and presumably intended to make the cleaning of the pond easier in the days before filtration).

Also worth noting are various distance markers set into the pond's marble edges, showing judges and trainers where 50, 100 and 200 yard races should finish (the pool being 30 yards in length).

Finally, along the western side of the pond can be seen a line of original poolside cubicles, with the viewing gallery above. For never let it be forgotten, swimming pools are also sporting arenas, and there have been competitive meetings and water polo matches at the Western since at least the 1890s.

▲ Only the figure of Neptune flanked by mermaids, carved in the pediment above the window on the right, hints at the original use of what is now the **Craigpark Masters Snooker Club**. For when opened in 1883 this French Renaissance building formed the entrance block to the **Dennistoun Baths Club**, one of five private baths clubs opened in Glasgow between 1871-83.

Details of the club are sketchy. Its architect is unknown. Its pond measured 73' x 35' (which by 1883 had become the standard). Members of the baths' swimming club also appear in competition records as late as 1966.

No trace of the actual pool can be seen today. Instead, after the baths club closed in c.1983 the structure at the rear was demolished. Thus pool hall made way for snooker hall

Its proprietor recalls that it took three attempts to infill the pond with concrete before the floor was strong enough to bear the weight of the club's 28 full size tables.

But it was well worth it because Craigpark is now arguably the finest snooker hall in Scotland, which means also that the rather fine former baths entrance block, now Category B listed, is also in safe hands.

▶ Opened facing onto Glasgow Green in August 1878, on the site of Glasgow's original 19th century wash house, the **Greenhead Baths and Wash House** housed Glasgow's first public swimming pools (*for location see page 60*).

City Architect John Carrick oversaw its design, employing the Italian Renaissance style that was not only his favourite but was also often used by Victorian architects, who considered their baths, quite justifiably, to be direct descendants of their Roman predecessors.

There were two pools; the men's measuring 75' x 40', and the ladies' 40' x 20'. (That there was a separate ladies' pool at all was in itself something of an advance on earlier baths.) Also within the complex were 34 private 'slipper baths' and a modern steamie or laundry with 40 stalls.

Carrick's department would be responsible for further baths at North Woodside (*see opposite*) in 1882, Cranstonhill (1883), Townhead (1884) and Gorbals (1885), before his successor AB McDonald embarked upon a further programme of works, starting with **Kay Street Baths**, in Springburn (*right*), opened in April 1898.

This was followed a month later by Maryhill (*see page 212*), Govan (1901), and both Whitevale and Kinning Park (1902).

In short, ten baths in 24 years, and that excludes twelve other baths and wash houses built without pools (one of which still stands on Tollcross Road, Parkhead).

Greenhead, the first, closed in 1960 and was demolished in 1961 to make way for an extension to the Templeton Carpet Factory.

Kay Street followed in 1981, but in this instance the site was redeveloped with the Springburn Leisure Centre (*page 215*).

◄ Only a brief stroll from the city centre yet set in a proverbial 'world apart' in the midst of a council estate on the north side of the M8, the **North Woodside Leisure Centre** in **Braid Square** is Scotland's oldest operational public baths.

But while the neo-classical exterior is readily identifiable as John Carrick's 1882 original, as is the roof structure and the balconies of the main pool (*below left*), all else has been substantially altered as the result of a £1.6m revamp carried out by one of Carrick's successors, City Architect Christopher Purslow, in 1991.

Hence there is now a fitness suite in the former ladies' pool and a gym in the former steamie.

As to the main pool, purists may quibble at the level of intervention; the UPVC window frames, the reshaping of the pool to create the feel of a spa, the various fountains and off-the-shelf statuettes.

But this is a reinterpretation of a Victorian baths, not an attempt at faithful preservation. Nor can it be denied that even in its prime, North Woodside was exceptionally basic, and would have seemed outdated even by the 1920s.

That it survived the culling of Victorian baths in the 1970s and 1980s is therefore remarkable in itself. And if the new decor is not to everyone's taste, its 120,000 annual users may well beg to differ.

▲ While most Victorians came to agree that swimming was beneficial to children, the question arose of where was best to meet that need.

Often the staff at public baths complained that they were unable to supervise large groups of excitable juveniles. There are even reports of the police having to be called to restore order.

But worse, as may be imagined before efficient water filtration became commonplace from the 1920s onwards, the invasion of a pool by a horde of children whose personal hygiene, habits and behaviour were questionable, did not go down well with either the staff or adult swimmers.

Some local authorities got round this by building 'penny baths' for boys. But others, following on from the lead of Liverpool in the 1880s, decided to build swimming pools

within school grounds. Along with Bradford, Nottingham and Leeds, Glasgow was one such authority.

Above is the pool and gym of the **Springboig Industrial School**, established in 1905 as a special school for hard core truants.

Today the site is occupied by Springboig St John's School, which in 2006 filled in the pool and turned the space into a multi-gym.

Employers were also quick to see the benefits of swimming, resulting in the formation of numerous works-based swimming clubs. These girls, posing at Kay Street Baths in c.1920, worked at Hoey's, a large general store on Springburn Road. The number of females swimming at public pools in Glasgow tripled between 1900 and 1914.

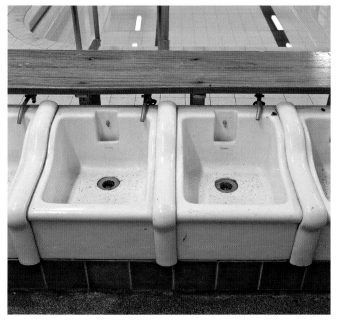

▲ A familiar sight to anyone passing up and down Byres Road is this, the former swimming pool of **Church Street Primary School**, opposite the Western Infirmary.

Opened in 1903 and closed in 1997 (although the adjoining school closed much earlier in 1976), this was one of eight school pools built between 1885 and 1904 by the **Govan School Board** (a body with strong Socialist leanings and whose jurisdiction extended beyond Govan into both Glasgow and Partick).

Only in Liverpool was this figure exceeded.

Of the eight school pools, apart from the two operational ones mentioned on the left, three others are, like Church Street, awaiting either redevelopment or demolition.

They are at the former Bellahouston Academy on Clifford Street, opened in 1885 (just south east of Ibrox); Balshagray Public School on Broomhill Avenue, Partick, opened in 1904, and Greenfield Primary School on Nimmo Drive, opened in 1901 and where, it is said, virtually every child in Govan learnt to swim, Alex Ferguson included.

Since Greenfield closed in late 2009 and was taken over by the Govan Workspace Ltd., the fate of its pool has yet to be decided.

One other operational school pool, but dating from c.1930, is at St Cuthbert's Primary School, on Auckland Street, Possilpark.

▲ Concealed within the depths of **St Bride's Primary School** on Craigie Street, Govanhill, is one of two Victorian school pools still in operation in Glasgow.

Much used it is too. Being of shallow depth, only 19m long and extremely private, it is in daily use by pupils of St Bride's and of other local schools, by ethnic minority groups who prefer single sex sessions, and by after school clubs.

St Bride's was designed by John Gordon and Thomas Baird.

The other functioning Victorian school pool is at Lorne Street, Kinning Park, designed by Hugh and David Barclay, who were themselves swimmers at the Western Baths Club.

Both St Bride's and Lorne Street were opened in 1894, and both are now Category B listed.

▲ Following its closure in 1985 **Maryhill Public Baths** on **Burnhouse Street** stood derelict for over 20 years (*top*), a fate shared by many historic baths in Britain.

Usually, those fortunate enough to be rescued have ended up being converted to non-sporting uses, for example as pubs, theatres, places of worship, retail outlets or flats (as at Whiteinch, *see opposite*).

Maryhill, however, has, in 2010, come back to life as a sports centre, thanks to a £7.5 million refit by Glasgow City Council's Development & Regeneration Services department.

Firstly, a new 25m pool has been built on the northern section of the site (backing onto the 1878 Maryhill Burgh Hall, itself also subject to a restoration project).

Secondly, the baths' external walls, dating from 1898, have been cleaned up and restored, and thirdly, the former pool hall (*above*) has been gutted, its roof structure and its glazed brick walls restored, and the pool tank and service ducts excavated to a reduced depth in order to provide the required height for the area to be used as a dry sports hall.

So specialised are today's modern leisure centres in both their design and building services that it is hard to imagine any of them ever being adapted for non-leisure or non-sporting uses. But with their robust load bearing walls and often high levels of thermal efficiency, historic baths are different.

As at Dennistoun (*see page 207*), one of the most common outcomes is for the pool shed at the rear to be cleared and for the entrance block to be converted.

This is what has also happened at the former **Whiteinch Baths** on Medwyn Street (*above*). Opened in 1923 but superceded in 1995 by the Scotstoun Leisure Centre (*page 113*), the former entrance block has recently been converted into flats by developers Dundas.

Also dating from 1923, and designed along with Whiteinch by Glasgow's Office of Public Works under Thomas Nisbet, the fate of the former **Pollokshaws Baths** (*above right*) is much less certain.

Viewed here from Christian Street, its pool hall stands in the foreground, while beyond on Ashtree Road are the former slipper baths and a steamie. After these facilities were closed in the 1980s the baths served as a gym. But it has lain vacant since 2007.

Just off Gallowgate an uncertain future also threatens the Category

B listed **Whitevale Baths** (*right, and page 60*).

Opened in 1902 and overlooked since 1968 by the two tallest tower blocks in Glasgow, Whitevale was for many years the busiest baths in Glasgow; its two pools, 42 slipper baths and Turkish baths being used by over 150,000 people a year. (Only the South Side Baths in the Gorbals approached this level).

Its main pool could hold up to 770 spectators for galas and water polo matches, while its 66-stall steamie was also Glasgow's busiest, with some 200 users a day.

After its closure in 1986 the small pool was converted into a tenants hall, but this had to be closed in 2004 because of asbestos contamination (a problem common at baths modernised in the mid 20th century).

Like Pollokshaws, Whitevale has remained unused since.

◀ Finally, of all the historic baths in Glasgow, none has been the focus of more controversy than **Govanhill Baths** on **Calder Street**.

Opened in 1917 and now listed Category B, as many readers will be aware, Govanhill was the scene of an epic 140 day occupation by campaigners protesting against Glasgow City Council's decision to close the baths in 2001. That this occupation was then followed by an eight month picket outside the building marks out the South Side Against Closure group (SSAC) as amongst the doughtiest of any British baths campaigners on record (although in 1979 a sit-in at Fulham Baths in west London lasted over a year).

Since 2001 the Govanhill campaign has scarcely abated.

Street parties have been held, a campaign headquarters and fund raising shop set up. In 2005 a Govanhill Baths Community Trust (GBCT) was set up, one of its first acts being to commission Buro Happold engineers to report on the building's structural integrity (which was found to be essentially sound).

Eventually the campaigners' persistence paid off when in 2006 the Council agreed that the GBCT would be given a 99 year lease to operate the building, if it could present a viable business plan.

A further hurdle was crossed in 2008 when the two sides finally joined forces to establish a project team, tasked with formulating a brief for the baths' future.

Drawn up by Nord Architects, these plans envisage what is described as a Wellbeing and Sporting Complex – health provision being given such prominence because Govanhill is an area of great deprivation, in a constituency where in recent years life expectancy has actually fallen.

Thus the two main pools will be restored for swimming, while converting the third into a hydrotherapy pool.

Other areas of the building will be converted into a gym, an asthma clinic, a café with roof garden, and a crèche, with the rear section, where the steamie stood, making way for social housing.

One measure of public interest in the Govanhill scheme has been its popularity during Glasgow's Doors Open Days. When re-opened in October 2008 for the first time in over seven years, over a thousand people queued for entry. A year later that figure had doubled.

But then the Govanhill campaign was always more than an attempt to save an historic building and to restore local access to swimming. For by harnessing the energies of local people and putting them in the firing line against the might of the authorities, the GBCT has galvanised Govanhill as a whole, to the extent that the Trust has also set up a Centre for Community Practice to offer training and advice to other groups who feel they have been neglected by central and local government procedures.

Nevertheless, there is still a mountain to climb on Calder Street.

Having been granted planning permission for the scheme in July 2009, the Trust now has to raise £12.5 million, no easy task in the prevailing economic climate.

As has been shown elsewhere, there really is no quick fix. Fulham's drawn out battle ended in failure. In Manchester the Victoria Baths Trust is still working hard 17 years after its baths closed. On the other hand, as noted earlier, Maryhill's campaign took over 20 years before its ends were achieved.

Swimmers, it would seem, really are prepared to go that extra length.

◀ While North Woodside and, hopefully one day, Govanhill, offer the prospect of swimming in an historic pool – as enjoyed by members at Arlington and Western – elsewhere in Glasgow the pace of construction has been even more prolific than that of the Victorian and Edwardian period.

Starting with Greenhead's closure in 1960, 14 of the city's 15 pre-1939 baths were closed over a 40 year period. Mainly this was owing to their deteriorating fabric or to demographic shifts.

But it was also driven by the nationwide trend towards leisure pools, and to pools of the approved metric lengths of 25m or 50m.

Since Glasgow's first post war pool opened at Drumchapel in 1966, 22 leisure centres have been built or refurbished, twelve of which include pools. Moreover, in contrast to other cities around Britain, every one of these was designed by the Council's in-house architects.

Shown here is the **Springburn Leisure Centre** (*top*), opened in 1995 and refurbished in 2003.

Tollcross Park Leisure Centre (*centre*), opened in 1996, has the city's only 50m pool, hence its selection as a venue for the 2014 Commonwealth Games. Tollcross is also the base of the leading local club, the City of Glasgow Swim Team, formed in 1993.

Bellahouston Leisure Centre (*left*), opened in 1968, revamped in 2001, is the most popular, with 207,000 visits in 2008-09.

Apart from these and Drumchapel, other pools are at Castlemilk (1969, refurbished 2009), Easterhouse (1972, refurbished 2006), Whitehill (1978), Scotstoun (1995), Pollok (1986), Gorbals and Holyrood (both 2000), and of course Maryhill (2010).

Chapter Fifteen

Doocots

Designed for the keeping and breeding of pigeons – both for their flesh and for their dung – dovecotes or doocots (pronounced 'dookits'), have long been a feature of the Scottish landscape. The oldest known example, in Mertoun, dates from 1576. This category A listed doocot is 18th century, and has been re-erected on Hamilton Road, just east of Mount Vernon station. But what, you may ask, however old or fine they may be, have doocots got to do with sport?

We conclude our survey of Glasgow's sporting heritage with a building type whose inclusion requires us to broaden somewhat our definition of what is meant by the word 'sport'.

For in this chapter our focus is the modern, urban doocot.

Not the handsome, historic doocots that, as seen left, can be spotted all over Scotland, on several golf courses included, such as at Cawder and Cambuslang (*see page 160*). Instead, these doocots are basic, homemade pigeon lofts.

No doubt many a reader will have passed by some of these rudimentary structures without even registering their existence. Or if they have noticed, dismissed them as no more than tall sheds.

Yet each is purpose built for a very specific form of competition.

But first, their inhabitants.

The rock pigeon, or dove (*Columba Livia*) is the world's oldest domesticated bird.

In Britain, the rearing of pigeons for food, or as targets for hunting, or for the carrying of messages, is thought to have begun with the Normans.

Pigeon racing as we know it today, meanwhile, also has its roots across the Channel, in mid 19th century Belgium. It spread to England by the 1880s, and led to the formation of the Scottish Homing Union in 1907. In 2009 the Union had over 3,000 members.

But racing pigeons are not the only pigeons bred for competition.

Another breed is known as the Horseman. First cited in 1693, this was a bird bred originally for its ability to catch other pigeons, a sort of avian kidnapper.

Yet another breed is the Pouter, which appears to the layman to have a distinctive, puffed up chest, and is also distinguished by its heightened promiscuity.

Cross breed these two lively characters, as generations of pigeon fanciers have done since at least the early 18th century, and you get the wonderfully titled Horseman Thief Pouter.

Or, as it is better known in Glasgow, the 'big doo'.

Big doos do not race. Nor are they bred for their looks, although some are impressive nevertheless.

Rather, the role of the big doo is purely to try to lure a fellow doo over to its owner's doocot, so that it can be captured.

In other words, Glasgow's doocots form the focus of an elaborate, timeworn, city-wide ritual of seduction and abduction.

And what of the doo men themselves (and they are all men)?

Like the birds they rear, they too are a special breed. Invariably working class, often tutored in the subtle arts of pigeon handling by their fathers or an older brother, they are a tight-knit community.

They have no formal set up. No trophies, no written rules, no officials. Each is an independent operator within an informal network of pals and rivals.

There is a tendency for those who operate within the highly regulated sport of pigeon racing to look down on the doo men.

But what no-one can deny is that they come from a long tradition that takes in the whole Central Belt, with Glasgow as its epicentre.

One estimate is that there are at least a thousand doocots across the city.

▲ Wherever a patch of land is cleared, such as here at **Craigend** in **Easterhouse,** there is always a chance that doocots will appear.

Easterhouse was developed to rehouse Glaswegians uprooted by slum clearances in the Gorbals and East End in the 1950s and '60s.

From a peak of around 60,000 inhabitants in the 1970s it now has under 30,000 which, ironically, has led to much of that post war housing itself to be demolished.

This area was originally the site of a school. Apparently within a fortnight of it being cleared the first doocot had gone up. Five can be seen in this photograph, taken in 2009. Overall there was said to be nine in the immediate vicinity.

This clustering is intentional because, unlike racing pigeons, which fly for hundreds or even thousands of miles, doos tend to stay within confined areas, known as 'the square', usually measuring up to one or two square miles at most. There is therefore no point in building an isolated doocot.

Apart from Easterhouse, similar clusters can be seen in other post war Glasgow schemes, the likes of Castlemilk and Pollok. Indeed rather like bowling greens, once one is aware of their existence, doocot spotting can become a game in itself; the main difference being that the majority are on exposed areas of public land.

In theory each doocot is designed to be easily moved at a moment's notice. But with so much land available, some have survived for thirty years or more.

▲ Not all doocots are on public ground. Many are barely visible in back gardens, or on window ledges, balconies or roof tops.

Not all are out in the 'schemes' either. For example these two well established lofts are in the East End, close to Duke Street (*above*) and Glamis Road (*right*).

Each is square in plan and is around 4m tall, with a robust timber frame clad in an assortment of re-used galvanised or corrugated metal sheeting.

Matte black or green seem to be the favoured colours, and although no doocot is specifically marked, the identity of its owner will be more than likely known to most people in the locality.

On the Duke Street example, to prevent unwarranted entry either by vermin or by rivals (this being a highly competitive world in which disputes, thefts and even arson have been known), the single entry point (for humans at least) is located at mid-level, allowing access only by ladder. A further opening just below roof level is there to let in light for when the doo man calls by, as he must on a regular basis, to feed his charges and clean out the 'roof crate', the space where the pens for the 'working' birds are housed.

Usually the highest and darkest nest box in the loft is occupied by one of the cocks.

But cock or hen, the only way out for the birds to fly is via the letterbox-sized opening in the roof, and it is up there where the main action takes place.

◄ The key components of a doocot are its 'landing board' and 'hood'.

Essentially what happens, or is supposed to happen, is this.

A cock and hen will be paired up, allowed to bond and breed, and generally 'homed' in the doocot.

The pair is then separated for a period, to build up what doo men call their 'guts' (or sex drive), before one of them is allowed to fly off in search of a new mate.

Having consummated his or her desire, a good doo will then fly straight back to its doocot and call for its new acquaintance to follow.

This might not work at all. Or the other doo might go only as far the rooftop, in which case the 'working' bird' has to work that bit harder to entice it onto the landing board.

If successful, the doo man then pulls on a wire to swing the hood up and over the landing board, and as seen here at Craigend, the capture is complete.

A doo man's delight!

The trapped bird will then either be swapped for another doo from outside 'the square', or sold, perhaps at one of the impromptu Sunday night 'doo shops' held at a pigeon supplies store on Westmuir Street in the Parkhead area.

A cock may fetch £5–10, a hen maybe £15–25. But no-one is in this for the money, and the proceeds more often than not go towards the next bag of seed.

Far more important is the process; the rearing and nurture of the birds, the assessment of each one's character and worth, the maintenance of the loft, the watching, the waiting.

This is a long game, a game of patience. But it is also one that offers the doo man that precious commodity; a quiet, intimate and lofty haven from the follies of mankind on the ground below.

Chapter Sixteen

Conclusions

First awarded in 1873, the Scottish Cup – the oldest Association football trophy in the world – is one of many historic artefacts held by the Scottish Football Museum. Since opening at Hampden Park in 2001 the Museum has numbered amongst the top three per cent of visitor attractions in Scotland. But while other sports might struggle to attain similar levels of interest, they have much to learn from the work carried out at the Museum.

As Glasgow prepares to host the most important international event in its sporting history – the 2014 Commonwealth Games – we hope that this book will offer a reminder, not only to ourselves but also to the wider world of just how much Glasgow has contributed to the development of global sport.

But *Played in Glasgow* should not be viewed as an end in itself, and for this reason we conclude with a few practical suggestions on how various agencies in Glasgow may wish to build upon this study.

Doors Open Days

Firstly, we recommend that the city's many historic sports clubs follow the example of Partick Curling Club by allowing the public entry to their premises during Doors Open Days.

Not only do many of these clubs have a fascinating story to tell, but they can also help promote their own sports to a new audience.

Many clubs have already done this in London. The Govanhill Baths Community Trust can also vouch for the benefits to be accrued from opening their doors.

Learning from football

Glasgow is fortunate to have as a focal point the Scottish Football Museum at Hampden Park, whose exhibitions, research work and outreach programmes have already demonstrated how interest in sporting heritage can help build a wider understanding of local and national history.

For example, by setting up the Scottish Football Heritage Network in 2007 – a forum for representatives of senior clubs to help them preserve and celebrate their own football heritage – the Museum has laid down a template that could usefully be mirrored by other sports in the city.

Bowls and rugby, sports that between them have a wealth of records, documentation and historic artefacts, would in particular benefit from this sort of co-ordinated approach, backed up by professional advice.

Another significant programme in which the Museum has been involved has been the use of archive football photographs in a pilot scheme designed to help sufferers of dementia, run

in conjunction with local health services.

This too is an area in which sporting heritage can be of value if treated with sensitivity.

Commemorations

There are several sports-related sites that merit consideration for some form of commemoration, such as a plaque.

These include the site in Govan where Britain's first black footballer, Andrew Watson, is recorded as living in 1881 (*page 185*); the site of the Victoria Baths Club on Butterbiggins Road, where William Wilson devised the rules of water polo (*page 204*), and the site of the Willowbank bowling green on Elmbank Street, where William Mitchell, the man who drew up the first recognised rules of modern bowls, was a member (*pages 136–37*).

These are sites of great significance in the overall context of international sport, and in the case of Willowbank, offer a direct link with the 2014 Commonwealth Games, in which bowls will be one of the key sports.

Historic sports buildings

Buildings for sport are of course already eligible for protection under the current system of listing.

In 2009 there were 27 listed buildings in Glasgow either purpose-built for sporting use or, as with the Glasgow Climbing Centre (*see right*), subsequently adapted for sport.

Arising from the research conducted for this book, further candidates for consideration include the main pavilion of the Queen's Park Bowling and Tennis Club (*page 38-39*), Clincart Farm (*page 57*), the Glasgow High School War Memorial Pavilion at Old Anniesland (*page 118*), the pavilion and adjoining tarmac curling rink of Partick Curling Club (*page 162–65*), and the Firhill Street façade of the main stand at Partick Thistle FC (*page 188*).

Readers may have their own suggestions, which should be forwarded to Historic Scotland.

Buildings at risk

As of 2009 there were six sports related buildings on the Scottish Civic Trust's Buildings at Risk Register, five of which are featured in *Played in Glasgow* (the sixth is the former 1934 gymnasium of Possil School on Balmore Road).

A welcome removal from that list in 2010 will be the restored Maryhill Baths (*page 212*), hopefully to be joined in the near future by Govanhill Baths (*page 214*), and the West Boathouse (*page 32*).

The one factor that links these three buildings is that trusts have been set up to help steer their future. This leave two former baths that appear to need all the friends they can muster; Whitevale Baths (*page 213*), a fine building whose potential we hope will soon be recognised by a sympathetic

developer, and the former Pollokshaws Baths (*also page 213*) which is not on the Buildings at Risk Register but whose future must also be a cause for concern.

Hopefully the examples of both North Woodside (*page 209*) and Maryhill offer some hope that these two buildings' recreational heritage might yet be honoured in one form or another.

Collections and archives

Glasgow has good cause to thank a number of dedicated collectors for their efforts to gather up and preserve a wealth of sporting artefacts and ephemera, and, in most cases to share their collection with the public via the internet.

It is vital that wherever possible these holdings are entrusted to the public realm.

Similarly, sports clubs should be encouraged to entrust their historical records to museums or university archives for safe keeping and for the benefit of historians.

Further research

Much has already been written in academic circles on the Scottish contribution to the evolution of Association football, and the central role in this played by Glasgow clubs and individuals.

However there remains much to do in countering anglocentric narratives on football history, and therefore it is to be hoped that current research initiatives in this area, being conducted through the Scottish Football Museum and by individual historians, will be given the encouragement and resources they need to present their findings to the wider public.

Our brief study of the world of Glasgow doocots also suggests that here is another field worthy of further research, particularly in the

recording of oral testimonies of the doo men themselves.

For its part, *Played in Britain* is already committed to continuing its research into early bowls in Glasgow and the contribution of both William Mitchell and Thomas Taylor to the modern game.

Education and events

Patently 2014 offers tremendous opportunities for broadening knowledge and appreciation of sporting heritage.

Initiatives might include conferences on Glasgow sport, the creation of materials targeted at local schools and the general public, such as via guided walks and lectures, and the involvement of the city's media base in terms of web creation, film making, photography and art.

Clearly, as we hope *Played in Glasgow* has demonstrated, there is still much to learn, and above all, much to celebrate.

From the corner of Paisley Road West and Merrick Gardens, Ibrox Church, completed in 1868, looks pretty much like any Victorian gothic church. But step inside and this is what now fills the nave, Scotland's largest indoor climbing centre. We have already noted how several historic buildings have been converted into golf clubs. Ibrox Church, converted in 1994, demonstrates the potential of other redundant buildings around Glasgow for possible sporting and recreational use.

Links

Where no publisher listed assume self-published by organisation or author

Where no publication date listed assume published on final date within title, ie. 1860–1960 means published 1960

Abbreviations:
UP University Press
BSSH British Society of Sports Historians
ACSH Association of Cricket Statisticians and Historians

Sporting history

Burnett J *Sporting Scotland, Scotland's Past in Action* National Museums of Scotland (1995)
Burnett J Riot, *Revelry and Rout: Sport in Lowland Scotland before 1860* Tuckwell Press (2000)
Chambers W & R *Information for the People* Chambers (1842)
Collins T & Vamplew W *Mud Sweat and Beers A Cultural History of Sport and Alcohol* Berg (2002)
Durie A J *Sport and Leisure in Victorian Scotland* Dalesman Books (1988)
Jarvie G & Burnett J (eds) *Sport, Scotland and the Scots* Tuckwell Press (2000)

Glasgow general

Glasgow Necropolis Heritage Trail Glasgow City Council (nd)
Borthwick A *Yarrow and Company Limited: 1865-1977*
Daiches D *Glasgow* Andre Deutsch (1977)
Eyre-Todd G *Who's Who in Glasgow 1909* Gowans & Grey (1909)
Mahon AJ *A History of Kinning Park* & *District, Glasgow* (2003)
Massie A *Glasgow, Portraits of a City* Barrie & Jenkins (1989)
McLellan D *Glasgow Public Parks* John Smith (1894)
Merchant City Glasgow, The Obscure History Merchant City Townscape Heritage Initiative *(2005)*
Moss MS & Hume JR (eds) *Glasgow as It Was* Hendon (1975)
Moss MS & Hume JR *Shipbuilders to the world: 125 years of Harland and Wolff 1861-1986* Blackstar Press (1986)
Pearson L *Tile Gazeteer: a guide to British tile and architectural ceramics locations* Richard Dennis (2005)
Smart A *Villages of Glasgow North of the Clyde* John Donald (2002)
Smart A *Villages of Glasgow South of the Clyde* John Donald (2002)
Williamson E, Riches A, Higgs M *The Buildings of Scotland: Glasgow* Yale UP (2005)
http://bestlaidschemes.com
www.csglasgow.org
www.glasgowarchitecture.co.uk
www.glasgow.gov.uk
www.glasgowguide.co.uk
www.glasgowhistory.co.uk
www.glasgowmerchantcity.net
www.glasgowusermanual.com

www.glesga.ukpals.com
www.hiddenglasgow.com
www.theglasgowstory.com

Chapter 1. Played in Glasgow

Corporation of the City of Glasgow Handbook on the Municipal Enterprises (1904)
Glasgow Delineated Wardlaw & Cunninghame (1826)
Isaac Merritt Singer West Dunbartonshire Council (nd)
Adams G *Gallowgate Infantry Barracks* (2005)
Billcliffe R *Charles Rennie Mackintosh* John Murray (1986)
Bilsborough P *The Development of Sport in Glasgow* University of Stirling, unpublished thesis (1983)
Bilsborough P *Sport for boys in Glasgow 1866-1914* Physical Education Review 11 (1988)
Chapman R *The Picture of Glasgow* (1812)
Cleland J *The Rise and Progress of the City of Glasgow* J Smith (1840)
Denholm J *The History of the City of Glasgow and its Suburbs* A Magoun (1804)
Hamilton W *Descriptions of the Sheriffdoms of Lanark and Renfrew* (1710)
Hunter M *100 Years of Tennis in the West of Scotland 1904-2004* West of Scotland LTA (2004)
Murray B The Old Firm, Sectarianism, Sport and Scoiety in Scotland John Donald (1984)
Murray D *Memoirs of the Old College of Glasgow* Jackson Wylie & Co. (1827)
Myers F *History of Springburn* (1997)
Senex *Glasgow Past and Present* D Robertson (1856)
Smith JG & Mitchell JO *The Old Country Houses of the Old Glasgow Gentry* James Maclehose & Sons (1878)
Taylor A *Played at the Pub* English Heritage (2009)
www.bennylynch.co.uk
www.clarioncc.com
www.clydesdaleharriers.co.uk
www.clydewaterfrontheritage.com
www.renfrewshireleisure.com
www.scottishcroquet.org.uk
www.shettlestonharriers.org.uk

Chapter 2. Glasgow Green

Clyde Heritage Guide from Glasgow Green to Dumbarton Clyde Waterfront Heritage (2009)

Glasgow Green, Gateways to the Green; Glasgow Green, Greenery; Glasgow Green, History & Renewal Glasgow City Council (2006)
Souvenir Programme Jubilee Regatta on the Clyde Clydesdale Amateur Rowing Club (1907)
Colville J *Glasgow Golf Club 1787–1907* John Smith (1907)
Gemmell M *The Societies of Glasgow* (1906)
Macdonald H *Rambles Around Glasgow* J Cameron (1860)
www.clydearc.org.uk
www.clydesdalearc.org.uk
www.clydewaterfront.com
www.glasgowhumanesociety.com
www.glasgowrowingclub.org
www.glasgowubc.com

Chapter 3. Queen's Park
Bell B *Still Seeing Red A History of Third Lanark AC* Glasgow City Libraries and Archives (1996)
Galbraith R *The Hampden Story* Mainstream (1993)
Inglis S *The Football Grounds of Britain* Collins Willow (1996)
Laird R *Third Lanark Athletic Club* NPI Media (1999)
Robertson FHC *The Men With Educated Feet* Queen's Park FC (1992)
Robertson F & Ross D *The First 100 years of Hampden* First Press Publishing (2003)
Robinson R *History of the Queen's Park Football Club 1867-1917* Hay Nisbet & Co (1920)
www.queensparkfc.co.uk
www.queensparkbowlingclub.co.uk

Chapter 4. East End
Greig T *The Bully Wee - Clyde Centenary Brochure* (1977)
MacBride E, O'Connor M with Sheridan G *An Alphabet of the Celts* ACL and Polar Publishing (1994)
Walker J *History of Glasgow Corporation Transport* (2006)
www.celticfc.net
www.clydefc.co.uk
www.kerrydalestreet.com
www.semple.biz

Chapter 5. Pollok Park
National Trust for Scotland Guide to Properties (2007)
Opening of Lochinch Sports Field City of Glasgow Police Athletic Association (1962)
Poloc Cricket Club Centenary 1878-1978
Browning RHK *Haggs Castle Golf Club* GW May (1937)
Doak T, Scott J & Haddock M *The Life and Work of Dr. Alister MacKenzie* Wiley (2001)
Ferguson R *Pollok House* National Trust for Scotland (2004)
McCallum A *Pollokshaws, Village and Burgh, 1600-1912* Alexander Gardner (1925)

Morris C *A History of the Cowglen Golf Club 1906-2006* (2007)
Ogilvie SM *Pollokshields Panorama* (1990)
www.alistermackenzie.co.uk
www.carthaqp.org
www.clydesdalehockey.org.uk
www.cowglengolfclub.co.uk
www.friendsofmaxwellpark.co.uk
www.haggscastlegolfclub.com
www.julianpgraham.com
www.parkrun.org.uk
www.pollokgolf.com
www.titwoodbowlingclub.co.uk

Chapter 6. Govan & Bellahouston
A Shipbuilding History 1750-1932 Alexander Stephen & Sons
Bellahouston Park Heritage Trail Glasgow City Council
Allan J *The Story of the Rangers* 1873-1923 (1923)
Inglis S *Engineering Archie, Archibald Leitch football ground designer* English Heritage (2005)
Kenna R *Scotland in the Thirties* Richard Drew (1987)
McKean C *The Scottish Thirties* Scottish Academic Press (1987)
Ralston G *Rangers 1872: The Gallant Pioneers* Breedon Publishing (2009)
http://govan.eveningtimes.co.uk/area/shipbuilding-in-govan.html
www.bella.webnode.com
www.clydewaterfrontheritage.com
www.empireexhibition1938.co.uk
www.garscubeharriers.co.uk
www.gracesguide.co.uk
www.pearceinstitute.org.uk
www.rangers.co.uk
www.sunnygovan.com

Chapter 7. Jordanhill & Anniesland
Glasgow Academical Club Centenary Volume 1866-1966 Blackie (1966)
Campbell W *A Short History of Jordanhill* unpublished Strathclyde University Archives (1931)
Cowie W *Jordanhill, the history of a district* unpublished nd Strathclyde University Archives J/Est/1/1
http://www.strath.ac.uk/archives/cat/jhill/cowie1.html
Low DM *Kelvinside Academy 1878-1928* William Hodge (1928)
MacLennan HD *Shinty's Place and Space in World Sport* The Sports Historian, No. 18, 1 BSSH (1998)
MacLennan HD *Shinty in Glasgow* Aberdeen University unpublished PhD (1998)
MacLeod I *The Glasgow Academy* The Glasgow Academicals' War Memorial Trust (1997)

General websites
www.historic-scotland.gov.uk
www.british-history.ac.uk
www.britishpathe.com
www.buildingsatrisk.org.uk
www.citystrolls.com
www.electricscotland.com
www.geo.ed.ac.uk
www.oxforddnb.com
www.scotcities.com
www.scottisharchitecture.com
www.scottishcivictrust.org.uk
www.scotland.org
www.scran.ac.uk
www.sisport.com
www.urbanrealm.co.uk
www.wikipedia.org.uk

Newspapers & journals
Glasgow Evening News; Glasgow Evening Times; Glasgow Herald; North British Daily Mail; The Observer; Scottish Athletic Journal; Scottish Referee; Scottish Sport; Scottish Umpire; The Scotsman; The Times Online Digital Archive 1785-1985

Simpson & Brown Architects *Jordanhill Campus Glasgow Conservation Audit* Strathclyde University (2007)
www.ghkrfc.com
www.glasgowhawks.com
www.glasgowhigh.co.uk
www.hawkssoar.everythingrugby.com
www.kilmeny.vispa.com/scotstoun.htm
www.theglasgowacademy.org.uk
www.wsmclean.com

Chapter 8. Golf

Golf Courses as Designed Landscapes of Historic Interest European Institute of Golf Course Architects / English Heritage (2007)
Crampsey RA *History of Cathkin Braes Golf Club 1888-1988* (1988)
Cunningham J & Wylie J *Cartha 1889-1905 A Retrospect* Inglis Kerr (1905)
Gilroy M *Windyhill Golf Club Centenary 1908-2008* (2008)
McGhee N *Killermont The Home of Glasgow Golf Club* (2003)
Peter McGowan Associates *Survey of Historic Gardens and Designed Landscapes in East Dunbartonshire* East Dunbartonshire Council (2006)
www.bonnytongolfclub.com
www.britishgolfmuseum.co.uk
www.cambuslanggolf.org
www.cathcartcastle.com
www.cathkinbraesgolfclub.co.uk
www.cawdergolfclub.co.uk
www.crowwood-golfclub.co.uk
www.douglasparkgolfclub.co.uk
www.ferenezegolfclub.co.uk
www.glasgowgolfclub.com
www.johnletters.com
www.kirkhillgolfclub.org.uk
www.ralstongolfclub.com
www.renfrewgolfclub.net
www.roukenglengolf.co.uk
www.sandyhillsgolfclub.co.uk
www.thebishopbriggsgolfclub.com
www.whitecraigsgolfclub.com
www.williamwoodgc.co.uk

Chapter 9. Bowls

150th Anniversary of Ayrshire v Glasgow for the Eglinton Trophy (1987)
Hampden Bowling Club 1905-2005
Kelvingrove Park Heritage Trail Glasgow City Council
Kirkhill Bowling Club, A Centenary History 1906-2006
Scottish Bowling Association Handbook (various)
Dingley HJ *Touchers and Rubs on Ye Anciente Royale Game of Bowles* Thomas Taylor and David Bryce & Son (1893)

McKellar RJ *Willowbank 150* (1985)
Mitchell W *The Manual of Bowl Playing* William Macrone (1864)
www.cambuslangbc.btinternet.co.uk
www.clarkstonbtc.org.uk
www.glasgowbowling.co.uk
www.hyndl.demon.co.uk/hyndland/all/c7bowlgr.htm
www.kilwinning.org/sport/bowling.htm
www.scottish-bowling.co.uk
www.taylorbowls.com
www.welly.4t.com

Chapter 10. Ice Sports

Cairnie J *Essay on Curling and Artificial Pond Making* WR McPhun (1833)
Cran JD, MacKinnon Snr L, Kinloch G *Partick Curling Club A History of the Club 1842–1995*
Cyclos *The Art of Skating With Plain Directions of the Most Difficult and Elegant Movements* Thomas Murray (1852)
Kerr J *History of Curling - Scotland's Ain Game* David Douglas (1890)
Roach J *Puffins Return to Scottish Island Famous for Curling Stones* National Geographic News (27.10.2004)
Smith DB *Curling, an illustrated history* John Donald (1981)
Smith DB *Curling Places of Scotland* David Smith (2008)
Weir RS *Curling: The Roaring Game* Golf Illustrated nd
http://curlinghistory.blogspot.com
www.ambaile.org.uk
www.curlingbasics.com
www.icehockeyuk.co.uk
www.partickcurlingclub.co.uk
www.royalcaledoniancurlingclub.org
www.scottishcinemas.org.uk
www.sihss.se

Chapter 11. Cricket

Poloc Cricket Club Centenary 1878-1978 (1978)
Bone DD *Fifty Year Reminiscences of Scottish Cricket* Aird & Coghill (1898)
Courtney S *As Centuries Blend, 106 years of Clydesdale Cricket Club* John Miller (1954)
McLeish D *International Cricket Grounds of Scotland* ACSH (2005)
Potter D *Encyclopaedia of Scottish Cricket* Empire (1999)
Stuart CD *West of Scotland Football Club 1865-1965* Hodge & Co. (1965)
www.clydesdalecricket.org.uk
www.poloc.com
www.wdcu-cricket.net
www.westofscotlandcricketclub.co.uk

Chapter 12. Football

The Book of Football Amalgamated Press (1906)

Anderson I *Caledonia Dreaming* Sam's Publishing Corp (2001)

Heany J *Junior Football* unpublished ms (1996)

Hutchinson J *The Football Industry* Richard Drew (1982)

Inglis S *The Football Grounds of Great Britain* Collins Willow (1987)

Kay J *The Archive, the Press and Victorian Football: The Case of the Glasgow Charity Cup* Sport in History, Vol 29, Issue 4 BSSH (2009)

Lamming D *A Scottish Soccer Internationalists' Who's Who, 1872-1986* Hutton Press (1987)

McGlone D & McLure B *The Juniors 100 Years* Mainstream (1987)

Potter D & Jones PH *The Encyclopaedia of Scottish Football* nd

Smailes G *The Breedon Book of Scottish Football Records* Breedon Books (1995)

Stephen D *Glasgow Charity Cup* unpublished ms (2001)

Twydell D *Rejected FC of Scotland Vol 2: Glasgow & District* Yore Publications (1993)

Vamplew W *Sports Crowd Disorder in Britain 1870-1914* Journal of Sport History Vol 7, No 1 (1980)

Vamplew W The Glasgow Charity Cup 1876-1966 *Revista de História de Esporte* (2008)

Williams G *The Code War* Yore Publications (1994)

Wright I *Rutherglen Glencairn 1896-1996*

Younger G *Secretary of State for Scotland Statement on the Hampden Riot* Hansard (May 12 1980)

www.11v11.co.uk

www.arthurlie.com

www.clydebankfc.co.uk

www.footballcentral.org

www.historicalkits.co.uk

www.petershillpark.org.uk

www.pollokfc.co.uk

www.ptearlyyears.net

www.ptfc.net

www.rsssf.com

www.scottishfootballmuseum.org.uk

www.themainstand.com

www.thirdlanarkac.co.uk

Chapter 13. Greyhounds & Speedway

Greyhound Racing Encyclopedia Fleet Publishing (1948)

Bamford R & Jarvis J *Homes of British Speedway* Tempus (2006)

Genders R *The Encylopedia of Greyhound Racing* Pelham Books (1981)

Genders R & NGRC *The Encylopedia of Greyhound Racing* Pelham Books (1990)

Henry J & Moultray I *Speedway in Scotland* Tempus (2001)

Inglis S *Played in Manchester* English Heritage (2004)

www.glasgowspeedway.co.uk

www.shawfieldgreyhounds.com

Chapter 14. Swimming

Bilsborough P *100 Years of Scottish Swimming* SASA (1988)

Campbell A *Report on Public Baths and Wash-houses* Carnegie United Kingdom Trust (1918)

Campbell D *Scottish Baths 1868–1914 and their Conservation* Heriot-Watt University thesis (1993)

Gordon I & Inglis S *Great Lengths, the historic indoor swimming pools of Britain* English Heritage (2009)

Mann WM *The Baths, the story of the Western Baths, Hillhead from 1876-1990* Western Baths Club

McLeod N *Tales of the Arlington* Hyndland Press (1997)

Sinclair A & Henry W *The Badminton Library - Swimming* Longman Green & Co (1916)

www.arlingtonbaths.co.uk

www.govanhillbaths.com

www.thewesternbaths.co.uk

Chapter 15. Doocots

Buxbaum T *Scottish Doocots* Shire Publications (1987)

D'olier J *Horseman – The Thief Pouter* Winckley Press (2002)

www.cichlidlovers.com/birds_horseman_dookits.htm

http://glasgowsdoos.webs.com

www.horsemanpouters.co.uk

www.horsemanthiefpouters.com

www.mccannhistoricbuildings.co.uk/truthaboutdovecotes

www.pigeoncote.com

www.shuonline.co.uk

Chapter 16. Conclusions

www.doorsopendays.org.uk

www.glasgowclimbingcentre.com

www.historic-scotland.gov.uk

Credits

Photographs and images

Please note that where more than one photograph appears on a page, each photograph is identified by a letter, starting with 'a' in the top left hand corner of the page, or at the top, and continuing thereafter in a *clockwise* direction.

©Royal Commission on the Ancient and Historical Monuments of Scotland

99a, 108c; ©RCAHMS Aerofilms Collections: 43a, 50a, 63, 94, 197

Stuart Wallace photographs

inside cover, back flap, 1, 4, 6, 9, 21b, 22a, 23a, 31b, 32a, 36b, 38, 39, 42ab, 57a, 74, 75abc, 77, 89abc, 93c, 97b, 98ab, 107ab, 108a, 110a, 111, 112, 118b, 120, 123a, 129, 131a, 134, 136ab, 139ab, 141ace, 142b, 143, 146, 147, 148ab, 149, 150c, 152, 153abcd, 154bc, 155, 156ab, 174ab, 175, 177ab, 178a, 179b, 180b, 188ab, 190ac, 191bcd, 192c, 195a, 200c, 201a, 207b, 211ac, 213bc, 215ac, 216, 217, 219a, 228

Photographers

Ian Adam: 200b; Julian P Graham / Loon Hill Studios: 85; Hugh Hornby: 157b; Keith Hunter / Archial Architects: 87b; Keith Hunter / Studio KAP Architects: 193a; Simon Inglis: back cover bcd, 8, 26, 36ac, 49b, 65ab, 123b, 127cd, 131bcd, 133abcd, 140, 141bdf, 145ab, 148c, 150b, 158ab, 162ac, 163ab, 164abc, 165abc, 178b, 180a, 199a, 201b, 202, 203a, 204bc, 205abc, 206ab, 207acde, 209ab, 211b, 212a, 214ab, 218ab, 219bcde; Duncan Lamont: 116b; Brian Morgan: 86d; Ged O'Brien: back cover a, 44b, 47c, 90ab, 93b, 117, 139c, 185c, 191a, 194c; Robert Perry: 194a

Archives and agencies

T&R Annan & Sons Ltd: 15a, 138, 142a; Clydebank Library: 16b; ©Culture and Sport Glasgow (Museums): 16a, 29ab, 64ab, 122a, 182a; Getty Images: 104d, 105a; The Glasgow School of Art Archives and Collections: 173; Guthrie Aerial Photography: 113, 199c; Herald & Evening Times, Glasgow: 2, 21a, 45a, 51a, 68b, 72b, 76, 80b, 96b, 97a, 104b, 116a, 122b, 130a, 161, 169ab, 170, 171a, 182b, 186, 187ac, 194b, 196a, 198c, 199b; ©Illustrated London News Ltd / Mary Evans: 12a, 30, 95; ImacImages Photography: 118a, 119; Steven McKenna Photography: 99b; The Mitchell Library: front cover, 11, 13, 15b, 18ab, 20ab, 21c, 43b, 62abc, 70ab, 82b, 92ab, 93ad, 101ab, 130b, 132b, 137, 151a, 154a, 167, 176b, 187b, 196b, 198b, 208ab, 210b; Press Association Images: 33, 104c, 108b, 110b, 189; The Scottish Football Museum: 40b, 41a, 48a, 49a, 50b, 52b, 53a, 56, 59a, 66-7, 184ab, 185ade; The Scottish Football Museum / Bob Laird: 44a, 45ab; The Scottish Football Museum / Colin McPherson: 220; Scottish Studios and Engravers Ltd (Strathclyde University Archives JCE/7/16/6): 121ab; Scottish Studios and Engravers Ltd (Strathclyde University Archives JCE/12/14/10): 121c; SNS Group: 72a; DC Thomson: 96a; University of Glasgow Archive Services: 19b, 78, 114a

Licensor www.scran.ac.uk

©East Dunbartonshire Council: 172; ©East Renfrewshire Council: 14, 127b; ©Glasgow City Archives: 210c; ©Glasgow City Libraries, Information and Learning: 12b; ©Glasgow University Library: 203b; ©National Library of Scotland: 59b, 125a, 135d, 159b; ©Newsquest (Herald & Times): 35, 103, 125b, 132a; ©RCAHMS B/31777/cn: 53b; ©RCAHMS B/55447: 73; ©RCAHMS SC791542: 79; ©RCAHMS B/41184/cn: 106a; ©RCAHMS B/41180/cn: 106b; ©RCAHMS B/4191/cn: 109; ©RCAHMS SC612819: 185b; ©RCAHMS GW/3649: 17; ©The Scotsman Publications Ltd: 51b, 71, 104a, 105b, 114b, 183ab, 192b; ©Scottish Life Archive: 34; ©University of Glasgow: 135a; ©University of Strathclyde: 135bc, 166

Donated photographs

The publishers wish to thank the following individuals and organisations: Peter Bilsborough: 68a; Cambuslang Bowls Club: 144b; Cambuslang Golf Club: 160; Cartha Queen's Park RFC: 83; Don Clements Photography: 22b; Clydesdale Cricket Club: 82a; Peter Colvin: 52c, 198ad, 200ad; Culture & Sport Glasgow: 215b; Allan Donaldson: 159a, 171b; Dundas Estates & Development: 213a; Clino d'Eletto: 48c, 69, 101c, 181; East Renfrewshire Council Library and Information Services: 144c; Mike Floate: 192a; William Frame: 19a; Glasgow Academicals / Geo-Graphics Design: 179a; Glasgow City Council: 23c; Glasgow City Marketing Bureau: 27, 157a; Glasgow Golf Club: front flap, 128ab; Glasgow Golf Club / Alan Donaldson: 28ab, 124; Glasgow University Boat Club: 32b; Dr Ian Gordon: 204a; Haggs Castle Golf Club: 86c; Historic Scotland / David Henrie: 115, 212bc; Steve Hosey / DRS Graphics: 126; ©George King / www.pikodesign.com: 221; Kirkhill Bowls Club: 144a; Steve Lindridge / Ideal Images: 7; Kathryn MacLeod: 190b; Paul MacNamara: 100a; Jack Murray: 41b, 44c, 48b, 58, 176a; Ewen Nicolson: 46, 47ab; Pollok Golf Club / Hawkeye Photography: 84ab;

Robert Pool: 10a, 23b, 54, 150a, 210a; Queen's Park FC / Ian Cairns: 55, 57b; Jean Rafferty: 40a; Ralston Golf Club/ John Mclaughlin: 127a; Rangers FC: 102ab; Scottish Football Association: 195b; Gordon Simpson: 31a; David B Smith: 168ab; Ron Smith: 162b; Summerlee Museum of Industrial Life: 52a; Stuart Taylor: 193b ; Thomas Taylor: 151b; Titwood Bowling & Tennis Club: 88; Bert Walker: 87a

Printed sources

The Book of Football Amalgamated Press (1906): 40c; *Poloc Cricket Club Centenary 1878-1978*: 80a; *Scottish Football Annual 1891–92*: 100c; Browning RHK *Haggs Castle Golf Club* GW May (1937): 86b; Morris C *A History of the Cowglen Golf Club 1906–2006*: 86a

Acknowledgements

Glasgow is a city I fell in love with the moment I first saw it in 1986. Though the list of those who have helped with this book can never be complete, the following are due special mention.

Firstly, my eternal thanks for the support of my beloved Diane, who now gets me back after four years.

John Dunlop was also a great help, spending many a long day driving me around the city.

On behalf of myself and the *Played in Britain* team, special thanks go to Stuart Wallace for his tireless efforts in the field; Dr Irene O'Brien and her staff at the Mitchell Library; Malcolm Cooper, Ranald MacInnes, Patrick Connor, Richard Strachan, James Steel, David Mitchell and Jennifer Johnston-Watt of Historic Scotland; Richard McBrearty of the Scottish Football Museum for his wisdom and patience; postcard collector Jack Murray; Jim Ryan of the Glasgow Bowling Association and Ian Urquhart and his colleagues at Thomas Taylor Bowls.

For their invaluable knowledge we are indebted to David B Smith, Hugh Hornby, Dr Ian Gordon, Dr Hugh Dan MacLellan and that great champion of Glasgow sport, Bill Mann.

From Culture and Sport Glasgow we received great support from Karen Cunningham, Gordon Anderson, Gordon Boag, Suzanne Rough, John Egan, Ewan Anderson, Lynn Colvin, Brian McHenery and Kevin Giddings, and at Glasgow City Council from Kerr Robertson, Jim McCreaddie, Stephen Hosey, Mike Fraser, Willie Graham and Joe Nelson.

Thanks are also due to Karen McCall (sportscotland), Jim McNeish (Glasgow Herald & Times), Keith Young (Poloc CC), Gordon Simpson (Clydesdale ARC), Alan Irons (Cartha Queens Park), Mike O'Reilly (SRU Library, Murrayfield), John Thomson (West of Scotland CC), Hugh Barrow (Glasgow Hawks), Peter Schill (Partick Curling Club), Douglas Dunlop and Mike Stanger (Clydesdale CC), Bernie Mitchell (Hillhead Sports Club), Andrew Johnson (Govanhill Baths Community Trust), Stuart Murray (Wellcroft Bowling Club), Peter Colvin, Myra Hunter, Ernest Johnson, Craig Morris, Stuart Boyd and Jamie Wire.

Played in Manchester
Simon Inglis (2004)

Played in Birmingham
Steve Beauchampé and
Simon Inglis (2006)

Played in Liverpool
Ray Physick (2007)

Engineering Archie
Simon Inglis (2005)

Liquid Assets
Janet Smith (2005)

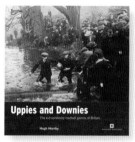

Uppies and Downies
Hugh Hornby (2008)

Great Lengths
Dr Ian Gordon and Simon Inglis
(2009)

Played at the Pub
Arthur Taylor (2009)

Played in Tyne and Wear
Lynn Pearson (2010)

Future titles

The British Olympics – Britain's Olympic heritage 1612–2012 Martin Polley (2011)
Played in London – charting the heritage of the capital at play Simon Inglis (2011)
Bowled Over – the bowling greens of Britain Hugh Hornby (2012)
For more information **www.playedinbritain.co.uk**

▲ Sporting heritage is as much an affair of the heart and soul as it is about historic buildings or fine architecture.

Glasgow Perthshire Junior Football Club started out in the 1880s as a cricket team formed by Perthshire men who had come to the big city in search of work and security. Only occasionally have 'the Shire' made the headlines, and only occasionally do their gates at **Keppoch Park** – their home since 1933, backing onto the former Possilpark tram and bus depot on Hawthorn Street – rise above 100. It was only in 1980 that Shire were even able to lay turf on what had been, until then, a cinders pitch.

There are no stands or terraces, and like so many junior grounds, bowling greens, tennis clubs and the like dotted around Glasgow, nothing that might cause the casual passerby to take a second look.

And yet without the dedication of an unsung body of volunteers and enthusiasts, scenes like this would not be possible.

Without them, Glasgow would be much the poorer. More than that, some would argue that it would not be Glasgow at all.